DISCRIMINATION AND DENIAL:
SYSTEMIC RACISM IN ONTARIO'S LEGAL AND
CRIMINAL JUSTICE SYSTEM, 1892–1961

Many people believe that race relations in Canada are characterized by tolerance and compassion, and their complacent attitude has largely gone unchallenged, owing to an absence of racially based, systematic, and empirical data. In this study, Clayton Mosher combines extensive qualitative and quantitative data in new ways, and examines the antecedents of systemic racism in Canada's legal and criminal justice systems. He focuses on the experiences of Asians and Blacks in the province of Ontario for the 1892–1961 period and presents evidence of racism in Canada's immigration policies, as well as in its society through poor access to housing and property, employment, and services. His analysis demonstrates that Canadian law has been used to control and disadvantage Asians and Blacks through both direct action and interpretation, and through silence and complicity.

Mosher finds the explanation of criminal justice outcomes for minority groups in the interrelationships between the criminal justice system and other social institutions. He follows how differential police attention accorded minorities resulted in their experiencing higher rates of arrest, particularly for drug and public-order crimes, and how minorities' treatment in the criminal courts was negatively affected by the views held by court officials. Discrimination was rationalized in the popular media through stereotypical images of Asians and Blacks that defined them as threats to White victims.

Mosher relates his findings to a current trend in reporting by Canadian media that racializes crime, and to the overrepresentation of minority groups in Ontario's criminal justice system as documented in the report of the Commission on Systemic Racism in Ontario.

CLAYTON JAMES MOSHER is Assistant Professor in the Department of Sociology at Washington State University.

CLAYTON JAMES MOSHER

Discrimination and Denial: Systemic Racism in Ontario's Legal and Criminal Justice Systems, 1892–1961

UNIVERSITY OF TORONTO PRESS
Toronto Buffalo London

© University of Toronto Press Incorporated 1998
Toronto Buffalo London
Printed in Canada

ISBN 0-8020-0787-2 (cloth)
ISBN 0-8020-7149-X (paper)

Printed on acid-free paper

Canadian Cataloguing in Publication Data

Mosher, Clayton James
  Discrimination and denial : systemic racism in Ontario's
  legal and criminal justice systems, 1892–1961

  Includes bibliographical references and index.
  ISBN 0-8020-0787-2 (bound)   ISBN 0-8020-7149-X (pbk.)

  1. Discrimination in criminal justice administration –
  Ontario – History.   2. Race discrimination – Ontario –
  History.   I. Title.

  HV9960.C22O56 1998   364.3'4   C97-931359-7

University of Toronto Press acknowledges the financial assistance to its publishing
program of the Canada Council for the Arts and the Ontario Arts Council.

Contents

LIST OF TABLES   ix
FOREWORD   xi
ACKNOWLEDGMENTS   xiii

Chapter 1: Introduction   3
Minority-Group Crime   6
Police Bias in Dealing with Minority Groups   15
The Attention to Race and Crime Issues in Canadian Social Science   22
Plan of the Book   28

Chapter 2: Theoretical Perspectives and Methodological Approaches   32
Perspectives on the Sociology of Law   33
Review of Sentencing Literature   41
Canadian and British Literature on Criminal Justice Outcomes   42
Early Discussions of Minority-Group Crime and Criminal Justice Outcomes in the United States   47
Decision as Context   50
Victim/Offender Relationships   53
Spatial/Social and Temporal Context   55
Methodology   59
Data Sources   60
Qualitative Data   61

Chapter 3: Asians: Immigration and Restrictive Legislation   63
Immigration   64
Asian Lifestyles and Restrictive Legislation   73

Chapter 4: Blacks: Immigration and Restrictive Legislation 82
Early History 83
The U.S. Influence 87
Immigration 89
Access to Housing, Employment, and Services 95
Miscegenation 111
The Resistance to Change 115

Chapter 5: Criminal Courts and the Racialization of Crime in Ontario 119
The Social Contexts of Criminal Sentencing, 1892–1930 120
The Racialization of Crime 124
The Racialization of Crime: Asians 126
The Racialization of Crime: Blacks 129
The Social Contexts of Criminal Sentencing, 1930–1961 134

Chapter 6: Drug and Public-Order Crimes 138
Drug Legislation and Enforcement 139
Canada's Narcotics Legislation 140
The 1920s 144
The Policing of Narcotics Offences 146
Sentencing 151
Sentence Length 153
Public-Order Offences 160
Chinese and Gambling 166
Blacks and Public-Order Crime 170

Chapter 7: Property and Violent Crimes 175
Property Offences 176
Violent Offences 183

Chapter 8: Summary and Prospects for Change 196
Conclusion 203
Postscript 204

Appendix A: Data-Analysis Methods 205
Dependent Variables 205
Independent Variables 207
Analysis Strategies 212

Appendix B: Coding Classifications   215

NOTES   221
REFERENCES   231
INDEX   251

List of Tables

1.1 Number of Page References to Race and Racial Issues in Canadian Criminology and Criminal Justice Textbooks / 23

1.2 Convicts in Federal Penitentiaries, by Race, 1896–1938 / 27

6.1 Race of Offenders Arrested under the Opium and Narcotic Drug Act by the RCMP, 1924–1936 / 147

6.2 Descriptive Data: Drug Offences, 1908–1930 / 148

6.3 Logistic Regression on Imprisonment Decision: Drug Offences, 1908–1930 / 152

6.4 Regression on Sentence Length: Drug Offences, 1908–1930 / 154

6.5 Descriptive Data: Public-Order Offences, 1892–1961 / 161

6.6 Logistic Regression on Imprisonment Decision: Public-Order Offences, 1892–1961 / 163

6.7 Regression on Sentence Length: Public-Order Offences, 1892–1961 / 165

7.1 Descriptive Data: Property Offences, 1892–1961 / 177

7.2 Logistic Regression on Imprisonment Decision: Property Offences, 1892–1961 / 179

7.3 Regression on Sentence Length: Property Offences, 1892–1961 / 182

7.4 Descriptive Data: Violent Offences, 1892–1961 / 184

7.5 Logistic Regression on Imprisonment Decision: Violent Offences, 1892–1961 / 187

7.6 Regression on Sentence Length: Violent Offences, 1892–1961 / 190

A.1 Descriptive Data: All Offences / 213

List of Tables

Foreword

Clay Mosher's wide-ranging social and historical analysis of systemic racism in Ontario's legal and criminal justice system provides a revealing perspective from which to consider pressing contemporary problems. Like John Porter's *Vertical Mosaic*, Mosher's book is a myth breaker that forces us to look closely at stark social and historical truths that are often smugly denied. The reality revealed is that race and ethnicity have been prominent features of criminal justice in Ontario for more of our past, as well as our present, than most of us can comfortably admit. The larger problem is that as adept as many majority-group Ontarians have been in denying this record of discrimination against minorities, they could not control the awareness of these patterns by those who have been closer to and among its targets.

A result is that our system of criminal justice suffers in the regard and respect that it receives from the minority groups it often has victimized. Of course, some members of these groups, like some members of majority groups, are law-breakers, and it complicates matters to know that some will wrongly, as well as rightly, claim that the proportionality of their treatment is unjust. Mosher responds to this problem with care, struggling always to make comparisons, as much as possible, among 'like' cases. He is sensitive to the need to logically and statistically control for spurious attributions of injustice, and he exercises commendable care in doing so.

Meanwhile, the challenge for the justice system is that the legitimacy it is accorded must reach far beyond those who are immediately involved in its operations. For it is not only those caught up in this system who are aware of its injustices, but also the law-abiding citizens whom the justice system must count on to provide role models and leadership in the community. The problem is that when discrimination is falsely denied, it not only denies justice to those it punishes, but also undercuts the viability of the legal system as an institution that

xii Foreword

can generate public trust and confidence from the citizenry it wants and needs to bind to its goals.

The ultimate failing is therefore that our legal system has proved so stubborn in refusing to acknowledge and respond to these needs. Mosher drives this point home by establishing just how persistent the use of racial stereotyping and drug laws have been over this century in Ontario. At the end of this century, as at its beginning, we continue to demonize minority groups by stereotyping and exaggerating their involvement with drugs. This was true historically of the treatment of Asian Canadians as it is true today in the treatment of African and Caribbean Canadians. However, as pervasive as this tendency is, more remarkable is the insensitivity of majority groups to its consequences. A century of selective punitiveness has left us no freer of the drug problems we so feared at the outset.

One of Mosher's answers to this predicament is to urge that we at least make it possible to begin systematically to observe, record, and monitor the nature of our difficulties by collecting official statistics that are analysable in terms of race. The reluctance to enumerate crime in racial terms is an unexpected product of an odd coalition of forces that, for a variety of dubious reasons, bans the necessary data collection. An unfortunate and little-recognized result of this ostrich-like behaviour is complacent support for a posture of denial that pervades our justice system. If we are going to improve our social and moral vision of crime in Ontario, we will need at least to know more of the facts that Mosher has begun so ably to uncover. He offers a convincing argument that we would benefit by being more informed. This book is a major step towards understanding and confronting problems of criminal injustice that are a threat to us all.

John Hagan
Faculty of Law
University of Toronto

Acknowledgments

Several people have contributed to this book in both direct and indirect ways. For influencing my approach to sociological research, I would like to thank several teachers and professors, but in particular Bonnie Erickson, Rosemary Gartner, Ron Gillis, John Hagan, Charles Jones, John Lowman, Dennis Magill, Jeffrey Reitz, Lorne Tepperman, and Barry Wellman. For providing a supportive environment in which to initiate and complete this project, I would like to thank colleagues at the University of British Columbia and Washington State University. I would also like to acknowledge the financial assistance provided by the Commission on Systemic Racism in the Ontario Criminal Justice System, and in particular the efforts of Susan Addario and Amanel Iyogun, who recognized the importance and value of historical research into the experiences of minority groups in the criminal justice system. This work has also benefited greatly from the cooperation I received from staff at several libraries in Ontario and British Columbia, but in particular staff at the Ontario Provincial Archives of Ontario, who did not complain when I asked for yet another volume of jail records. For their comments on an earlier draft of the manuscript, I would like to thank Scot Wortley and two other reviewers for the University of Toronto Press. Virgil Duff and Margaret Williams at the University of Toronto Press provided guidance and prompt feedback on the numerous questions I had throughout the process.

Finally, I would like to thank Melanie Brown, who not only assisted in the collection of data, but also served as my first and most important critic, and provided a constant source of support.

CLAYTON JAMES MOSHER

DISCRIMINATION AND DENIAL:
SYSTEMIC RACISM IN ONTARIO'S LEGAL AND
CRIMINAL JUSTICE SYSTEMS, 1892–1961

1

Introduction

In the month of October last, Edwin W. Morgan, alias Newsome, Wilkins, Yorrick, etc., a colored man with a very long criminal record in the United States, was arrested in a house on St. Andrews Street where he was living with a prostitute he had brought over from New York after breaking jail. Two large calibre revolvers, both loaded, with a quantity of jewellery, as well as considerable narcotic drugs, were found in the premises they occupied. Investigation proved he had burglarized at least nine houses during his sojourn in Toronto. He was convicted on several charges and sentenced to five years in Kingston penitentiary, and ordered to be deported. (Toronto, *Annual Report of the Chief Constable*, 1926: 8)

On the floor lay the body of 17-year-old Sylvain Leduc, dead of asphyxiation after being tortured and beaten for three and a half hours. Beside him lay another teenage boy and two of his female cousins, still alive but also badly beaten – and one of the girls had been sexually assaulted with a curling iron. [All of the suspects in the case were linked to] Ace Crew, a Black street gang involved in prostitution and Ottawa's burgeoning crack-cocaine trade. (Fisher, 1995)

Despite the relatively widespread belief that race relations in Canada are characterized by tolerance and compassion and that Canada is a more egalitarian country than the United States, close examination of the empirical evidence suggests otherwise. We know, for instance, that members of visible-minority groups are discriminated against in employment, housing, and access to services in Canada (Henry, 1994; Henry et al., 1995). As evidence of this racial discrimination, a study by Multiculturalism and Citizenship Canada (1989) reported that 94 per cent of job-agency recruiters surveyed indicated that they had rejected job-seekers on the basis of racial characteristics; a 1986 survey

showed that thirty-one out of seventy-three landlords in the city of Toronto discriminated on the basis of race; and studies conducted between 1974 and 1989
demonstrated that 12 to 16 per cent of Canadians polled admitted to having a
strong racial intolerance.

In addition, minority-group relations in Canada have become particularly
strained over the last several years, with demands for restrictions on the immigration of particular groups, and growth in the presence and visibility of hate
groups (Sher, 1983). As Lee (1994) suggests, 'immigrants are defined by the
news media as foreigners who cheat on their taxes, steal from welfare, fraudu-
lently make refugee claims, drain school resources, peddle drugs, take jobs,
wear turbans in the legion hall, and want to kill Christmas. And these are some
of their better qualities.'

Another important, and comparatively underresearched, manifestation of the
unequal position of racial-minority groups in Canadian society is related to their
overrepresentation in the country's criminal justice system. In 1995, the Commission on Systemic Racism in the Ontario Criminal Justice System (Ontario,
1995) reported that the 1992/3 provincial incarceration rate for Black adult
males in Ontario was five times that for White adult males, proportionate to
their representation in the population. In discussing Blacks' overrepresentation
in the criminal justice system, the commission report asserted that this was 'a
relatively recent phenomenon' (ibid: 104). However, it is notable that, in 1911,
Blacks were incarcerated in Canadian federal prisons at a rate almost eighteen
times that of Whites, relative to their representation in the population. In the
same year, Asians were incarcerated at a rate four times greater than that of
Whites.

The purpose of this book is to examine systemic racism in Canada's social,
legal, and criminal justice systems, particularly as it applied to Asians and
Blacks in the province of Ontario for the period from 1892 to 1961. In later
chapters, I examine manifestations of this phenomenon with respect to several
aspects of social life in Canada. These include general attitudes towards Asians
and Blacks, and prevailing stereotypes of these groups that influenced their
treatment by Canadian legal and social institutions. As well, systemic racism
and xenophobia were prominent in restrictive Canadian immigration policies
and in discriminatory legislation that impeded minority-groups' access to
employment, public services, and housing. Most important for the purposes of
this book, these racist attitudes and racist institutions influenced the treatment
of Blacks and Asians by the criminal justice system.

In order to understand the current disadvantages Asians and Blacks face in
Canadian society in general, and in the criminal justice system in particular, it is
essential that we explore in detail the historical legacies of racism in this coun-

try. As Mann (1993) suggests, race is pre-eminently a sociohistorical concept – racial categories and the meaning of race in a particular society are given concrete expression by the specific social relations and historical contexts in which they are embedded.

In initiating this exploration of the importance of race in contemporary Canadian society and the historical antecedents of its current significance, a useful place to begin is with recent media discussions of the issues of race, crime, and criminal justice. While this 'racialization of crime' (Henry, 1994) has been promoted by sensationalistic media accounts, and has often been supported by unofficial and somewhat less than objective police commentaries regarding the extent of the minority-crime problem, the Canadian academic community has been virtually silent on the issue.

Over the past decade or so, there has been a growing tendency on the part of the Canadian media to attribute crime problems to minority groups, in particular Blacks and, to a lesser extent, Asians. These attributions of criminal tendencies to minority-group members have, implicitly at times, but often more explicitly, emphasized the threat to civil society posed by minority groups and their supposedly high rates of predatory crime. The alleged dangers created by minority crime have also been emphasized by certain politicians and critics of Canadian immigration policies to justify restrictions on the immigration of particular groups, and to impose more stringent requirements for those who are allowed into the country.

Concomitant with the media's racialization of crime has been an increase in the attention devoted to allegations of racial bias on the part of the police in their dealings with members of minority groups in several Canadian cities. This bias has been particularly apparent in police use of deadly force against Blacks in the cities of Toronto and Montreal. As is the case with respect to media discussions of minority overinvolvement in crime, Canadian social scientists have largely neglected these issues. In light of this nearly universal lack of attention to race and criminal justice issues in Canadian academic sources, a topic I address in more detail later in this chapter, we are forced to rely on media descriptions in assessing the extent of minority-group overinvolvement in the justice system and the possible existence of racial bias on the part of Canadian police.

While we should certainly view these media descriptions of the race–crime issue with a critical lens, such portrayals are vitally important to consider. Because of the marginalization of racial-minority groups from mainstream Canadian society, many Whites rely almost exclusively on the media for their information about these groups. As Henry et al. (1995) suggest, then, the relationship between the White community and racial-minority groups is largely filtered through the perceptions, assumptions, values, and beliefs of journalists and other media professionals. Given the nature of news reporting in contemporary society, the media often select events that are atypical, present them in a stereotypical fashion, and contrast them with 'White' behaviour.[1] Through this selective reporting, the media are able to influence the boundaries of social discourse from which policy priorities are set, and public agendas defined and perpetuated (Henry et al., 1995). In this chapter, I thus devote some attention to a consideration of the minority-group crime problem and allegations of police and justice system racial biases as reported in the Canadian media over the last decade or so, in order to contextualize my subsequent historical analysis of these issues.

Minority-Group Crime

Although this book will demonstrate that the racialization of crime has a long history in Canada, the phenomenon reached unprecedented levels in the late 1980s. In 1989, Inspector Julian Fantino of the Metropolitan Toronto police force released statistics alleging that Blacks, who comprised an estimated 6 per cent of the population in Toronto's Jane–Finch district, accounted for 82 per cent of robberies and muggings, 55 per cent of purse snatchings, and 51 per cent of drug offences in that area (*Vancouver Sun*, 1992).

Despite the obvious limitations of these statistics, at least some local and national politicians were apparently convinced that they were reflective of a larger Black crime problem. For instance, during her 1992 Toronto mayoralty campaign, June Rowlands claimed that Black youth were largely responsible for the high crime rates in the city, a view that was apparently shared by Alan Tonks, Council chair of Metropolitan Toronto (Henry, 1994). Similarly, Art Hanger, immigration critic for the federal Reform Party, was on a tour of Toronto's ethnic communities in 1994 when he commented to a storekeeper, 'Do you notice that in Toronto there has been increased crime from certain groups, like Jamaicans?'[2] Hanger claimed that he was only repeating what a Toronto shopkeeper had told him, and asserted that he was frustrated by lax immigration-law enforcement that allowed criminal gangs to cross national borders so easily. When Hanger's comments were repeated in the media, and concerns regarding their racist implications were expressed, Reform Party leader Preston Manning defended him, suggesting he was 'simply practising grassroots politics' (*Globe and Mail*, 1994a).

While the release of statistics on Black crime in Toronto, and politicians' reaction to the perceived problem, generated considerable controversy, even more clearly representative of the recent tendencies towards the racialization of crime is a series of articles that appeared in the *Globe and Mail* in 1991 and 1992, written by the newspaper's police reporter, Timothy Appleby (1991; 1992c; 1992d; 1992e). Appleby's first (1991) article addressed the controversial issue of the collection of crime statistics according to the race of offenders, and began with his assertion that 'perhaps half of those hanging around the cheerless hallways of Toronto's Old City Hall courtrooms are young Black men.' His observations revealed that, of the fifty-four people being processed in Courtroom 116 on the day he visited, 'seven [were] white, 37 [were] black, and the other 10 [were] members of other visible minorities.' Despite his admission that this constituted a 'wildly unscientific survey,' Appleby claimed 'there is no doubt that Metro Toronto's street-level arrest ratio is starkly at odds with its ethnic mix.'

Appleby's 1992 articles dealt more specifically with the issue of the extent of Black crime in Toronto, and relied on a series of anecdotes and quotations from often unidentified police officers and apparently law-abiding individuals in the Black community to make the point that Black crime was increasing, and was committed primarily by Jamaicans. In these articles, Appleby dismissed virtually all arguments pointing to social-structural explanations of this alleged Black-crime problem, and instead implied that Blacks were somehow characterized by an innate predisposition to crime.

In the first of his 1992 articles on this subject, Appleby (1992c) acknowledged the sensitive nature of the race–crime topic, but suggested, 'however offensive it is to say so, it is clear on the streets of Metro Toronto, and to a much lesser extent in Montreal, that this criminal subculture has been exported, blending into an array of negative Canadian factors to produce a lethal, racism-fomenting witches['] brew.' While asserting that the vast majority of Canada's Jamaican community was 'solid, hard-working and honourable,' Appleby notes that 'the presence of a small but volatile group of young Jamaican males has altered Toronto's criminal landscape significantly in the past three years, in an explosion of guns and crack cocaine.'

Appleby (1992c) quoted an anonymous member of the Metropolitan Toronto police hold-up squad, who suggested, 'You can't print the truth, and I don't see how the hell you're going to print this story.' However, the same individual contended that 'I guarantee that 90 to 95 percent of [Metropolitan Toronto's robberies] is Jamaican ... The reason I say that is from talking to Blacks.'

Just in case the reader is unwilling to accept these claims, Appleby (1992c) quotes Detective Dave MacLeod, an intelligence officer who specialized in Black organized crime, who will go on the record, 'perhaps because he was born in Jamaica.' The implication is that because MacLeod is Black, his views on Black crime have more validity. MacLeod suggests that 'it's a very small number, compared to the population, but within that number, violence within the Jamaican criminal element is very, very fierce. It's a type of violence where guns are fired off indiscriminately, where people not connected to the accused are shot and killed.' MacLeod also offers that Jamaicans tend to be more aggressive and violent, 'but if I say that publicly, I'll be taken to task for it.'

Appleby (1992c) was apparently unwilling to accept the views of those who are sceptical regarding the importation of Jamaican crime to Canada. For instance, after presenting the opinions of Carl Fuller, president of Toronto's Jamaican-Canadian Association, who claimed that posses exist only in Jamaica, and that 'the question of gangs is a misnomer,' Appleby immediately points out that 'others sketch a different scenario, describing how drugs and posse members are shipped to North America, while money and weapons flow the other way.' Similarly, while conceding that it is possible that a majority of young Jamaicans arrested in Toronto were born in Canada and that police racism and a lack of success in the educational system may be contributing factors to higher Jamaican crime rates, Appleby (1992c) contends that, 'equally, however, links between Canada and Jamaica are strong: the distance is short, back and forth travel is relatively frequent, and many of those born in Canada inherit a Jamaican accent.'

In another article in the series, entitled 'Identifying the Problem,' Appleby (1992e) relies extensively on commentaries from apparently law-abiding Blacks, seemingly to lend legitimacy to his claims and to underline the pervasiveness of the Jamaican crime problem. 'Trinidadian' Ruth Smith is quoted: 'I don't know why Jamaicans are different, they just are.' Another Trinidadian, interviewed in a Toronto park, 'grumbles ... "People don't come to this park the way they used to because of the violence. It's a minority that is responsible, and the minority is Jamaican."'[3] Similarly, Jamaican-Canadian Association president Carl Fuller apparently had serious concerns regarding how Metropolitan Toronto's police treat Blacks, but he 'nonetheless calls Jamaican-linked crime "alarming – there's a lot of it and it really worries leaders in the community."'

While acknowledging that factors such as the matriarchal nature of Jamaican society, the erosion of Church authority, and 'fierce social divisions created by Jamaica's political polarization' may contribute to the higher rates of Jamaican crime, Appleby (1992e) seems unconvinced by such explanations. He returns to descriptions of the extent of the Jamaican-crime problem, provided by police and other law-abiding Blacks, and focusing on violent and drug-related crimes. Police intelligence sources claimed that there were seven Jamaican posses in the Metropolitan Toronto area, with a hard core of about 350 members who 'routinely bring in new recruits from abroad and have strong links to the Colombian cocaine cartels.' In addition, although specific figures are not provided, 'Blacks are believed to have committed about 30 of Metro's record 87 homicides last year [1991].' To further emphasize Black overinvolvement in violent criminal activities, Appleby (1992e) repeats the assertion that appeared in the first article with respect to robbery – 'a Metro Toronto holdup squad officer says he can guarantee that 90 to 95 per cent of it is Jamaican.'

Concluding this article with comments by other Blacks on the Jamaican-crime issue, Appleby (1992e) asserts that, 'if the police exaggerate, there are other estimates ... "I'd say 70 to 75 percent of Black crime is Jamaican," says Guyana-born Ron Gaskin, who owns a barber shop on Pape Avenue. "I have no doubt whatsoever that 90 per cent of all this Black crime involves Jamaicans," says Barbados-born Netto Kefentse, 48, a Humber College business studies professor.' While these individuals' expertise with respect to the crime problem may legitimately be called into question, the main point is clear: Black crime is rampant, it is increasing, it poses a serious threat to the community, and even individuals in the Black community itself are concerned about it.

While the impetus for Appleby's 1992 articles was not specific acts of Black crime, a series of incidents that occurred in Toronto over a three-month period in 1994 involving Black offenders brought the issue to the attention of the public in a more forceful manner. On 5 April of that year, twenty-three-year-old Georgina Leimonis was shot and killed during a robbery in a café in Toronto's trendy Annex neighbourhood. This apparently random act of violence was portrayed as particularly problematic by the media, and pictures of two of the Black suspects captured by a video were prominently displayed in the coverage. Toronto police chief William McCormack referred to the incident as a 'cowardly, dirty, filthy act of "urban terrorism,"' and the acting head of Metro's homicide squad, Bob Clarke, appealed to the public to 'cut [the pictures] out, tape them to your car's visor, so that you will recognize [the suspects] when you see them' (Mascoll, 1994).

An article appearing in the popular magazine *Maclean's* (Corelli, 1994), entitled 'Murder Next Door,' described the Leimonis killing in the context of several other acts of 'random violence' that had occurred recently in Canada, and discussed the threat to 'the white middle class of Canada,' who 'are no longer just spectators. They have become targets as well.' Alluding to the fact that Leimonis's killer was a Jamaican immigrant, Corelli (1994) reported on the results of a *Maclean's*/CTV poll which revealed that, of those Canadians who felt more threatened by crime, 42 per cent looked upon increased immigration as a 'bad thing.' Interestingly, in detailed descriptions of two other murder cases to which the article refers, the race of the perpetrators (White) is not identified.

Approximately two months after the Leimonis shooting, Toronto police constable Todd Baylis was shot and killed, and another police officer injured, by

Clinton Junior Gayle, a Jamaican immigrant who had been under a deportation order. As a result of this shooting, the Metropolitan Toronto Police Association posted a notice of motion, stating that the death of Baylis was 'a direct result of breaches by members of the Federal Immigration Department in their statutory obligations to enforce the laws of Canada,' and urging that a legal action be commenced against the Immigration department on behalf of Constable Baylis's family. The motion was later amended to include the family of Georgina Leimonis (Valpy, 1994) in a $100-million lawsuit (Foster, 1996). Gayle was later found guilty of first-degree murder and attempted murder in the shooting of the two officers. Although Gayle, a 'cocaine dealer,' claimed that he had committed the crimes only after being fired upon by the constables, and was at the time 'blinded by pepper spray,' the jurors hearing the case rejected his claims (*Globe and Mail*, 1996a) and found him guilty of the crime. While the jury-selection process in the Gayle case included a screening for potential racial bias, and two males of 'apparent South Asian descent' sat on the panel, two Blacks who had passed screening were peremptorily challenged by the crown attorney (Claridge, 1996).

While there is no doubt that Gayle's crime was a serious one, it is notable that he was characterized as a particularly loathsome individual by the sentencing judge and by the press. Mr Justice David Watt of the Ontario Court's General Division, in sentencing Gayle to two life sentences, suggested that he was 'so devoid of humanity as to be incapable of expressing remorse for the grievous results of his misconduct' (Claridge, 1996). In a discussion of the case that appeared before Gayle's sentencing, Michael Valpy (1994) noted:

The greatest and most repulsive danger of all is that racial hatred is being stirred up against Jamaican-Canadians – the great majority of whom live law-abiding lives. Or perhaps we have failed to notice that we're not out on the streets screaming for a one-way plane ticket for the German immigrant who killed his wife and roto-tilled her ashes into the vegetable garden.

The fact that the Leimonis and Baylis murders were committed by Jamaican immigrants led to demands for restrictions on immigration, and the federal government acted quickly in an attempt to address the concerns. In July 1994, the immigration minister, Sergio Marchi, announced a change in priorities for the Department of Immigration's enforcement agency, which, instead of focusing on removing the largest number of people, as they had previously, were now ordered to deal first with those who 'posed the greatest danger to Canadians,' with foreign criminals being put 'at the top of the list for deportation' (Sarick, 1994).

Robert Mason Lee (1994), comparing the public's and government's reactions to Gayle's shooting of Baylis with a riot that had occurred in the city of Vancouver following a Stanley Cup hockey game in the same year, somewhat sarcastically noted, 'If the same analysis were applied to the riots as to the killing, then the solution would be obvious: Suburban white teens form criminal gangs. They should be deported back to the suburbs as quickly as possible. They should be allowed to return only when they have skills or dollars to invest.'

Despite the views of certain journalists and politicians that there is a direct connection between immigration rates and crime, a federal government report published a few months after the Leimonis and Gayle incidents called into question the immigration–crime relationship. Studying convicts serving time in, or on conditional release from, Canada's penitentiary system, the report found that, while immigrants comprised approximately 20 per cent of Canada's population, only 11.9 per cent of those incarcerated or on conditional release in 1991 were foreign-born. In addition, the report noted that only 18 out of every 10,000 Caribbean-born people were in Canadian penitentiaries in 1991 (*Globe and Mail*, 1994b). Despite the objective proof that Jamaican crime does not constitute a serious problem in Canada, the federal government has reacted to the agitation over high-profile cases of Black crime by 'deporting to the land of their birth people who have lived virtually all their lives in Canada' (Foster, 1996: 11). In one such case, a twenty-two-year-old man who had left Jamaica at the age of seventeen months was deported.

The alleged presence of violent Black criminals has not been restricted to the city of Toronto, and commentaries on the brutality of their acts and alleged threats posed by Black criminals have not been restricted to the media in that city.[4] In November 1995, *Maclean's* magazine, in an article entitled 'The Brutal Truth – Violent Gangs Instil Fear in Once-Staid Ottawa' (Fisher, 1995), displayed the pictures of two obviously Black suspects and described their 'heinous crimes.' Fisher's (1995) report on this case, which involved, among other crimes, the murder of a male and sexual assault against a female victim, notes 'the fact that the suspects still at large are Black and the victims are white has introduced a racial element to the case.' The supposed danger associated with these Black criminals is further emphasized in a description of events that occurred at the slain person's funeral, where 'several young Black men taunted mourners outside the funeral home where [Leduc's] body was lying, drawing the chalk outline of a body on the pavement and yelling "one down and three to go."' In addition, the victim of the sexual assault had been moved to a more secure part of a local hospital after police spotted 'two young men lurking near her room.' While Fisher did not attempt to offer explanations for the occurrence of these crimes, once again the message is clear – Black gangs and the crime associated with such organizations had spread to 'once-staid Ottawa' – Black criminals represent a serious threat to Canadian society.[5]

Although given somewhat less prominence by the Canadian media, the racialization of crime involving Asians has also become an issue in recent years, with a focus on the alleged influx of Asian triads and their participation in the drug trade, and Asian criminals' involvement in violent crimes such as home invasions and gang shootings. Similar to the media focus on Black crime which had been stimulated by Inspector Fantino's 1989 release of Black crime statistics in Toronto, media interest in Asian crime was influenced at least in part by the release of unofficial statistics on the extent and nature of the Asian-crime problem by a Toronto police official. In 1990, Metro police sergeant Ben Eng told the Toronto Crime Inquiry that 'phoney refugees' from mainland China and Vietnam were responsible for the vast majority of violent and vice-related crime in Toronto's Chinese community. Eng asserted that approximately half of the 3,000 offences committed in 1990 by Asian Canadians in Toronto involved Vietnamese refugees, and called for a 'targeting' of such individuals by Immigration officials (Hurst, 1993). In compiling these statistics, Eng relied on the surnames of offenders appearing on arrest forms and daily occurrence sheets, undoubtedly a questionable method in terms of its reliability in identifying Asian criminals.

Also drawing attention to the alleged Asian crime problem, Carrigan (1991: 335), in his book on crime and punishment in Canada, reported on the increasing number of Asian gangs in Canada, with the underlying message that with the high levels of Asian immigration Canada experienced in the 1970s and 1980s came the attendant problem of Asian crime.

In recent years the Chinese gangs have stepped up their drug trafficking and extortion activities. The influx of immigrants has provided fresh recruits as well as better contacts in the East for drug supplies. Also, the large number of students who come to Canada from Hong Kong to study has created an expanding market for extortion. The gangs contact parents of some of these students and demand protection money. While the Chinese have been the dominant Asian gangs for some time they are now being challenged by other ethnic groups.

While Carrigan (1991) asserts that these gangs and the violence and drug trafficking associated with them had spread to several Canadian cities, reports on their activities have been particularly prominent in the Vancouver media.[6] In an article entitled 'Enter the Dragons,' the *Vancouver Province* (Middleton, 1992) referred to 'New York's feared flying dragons gang' who had landed in

Vancouver and was 'putting heat on Asians ... The gangsters, and members of other Asian gangs, fly in, pull off a high-profit crime and catch the next plane out of town ... nowhere seems safe anymore.' This theme appeared once again in the *Province* in 1995, under the identical headline, with Chapman (1995) noting that triads 'had already established significant footholds in Canada.' 'Crime analysts' were reported as suggesting that 'we can expect a huge increase in imported gangsters ... who will be bringing their heroin network with them.'

In a similar focus on Asians and their connections with drug trafficking, McInnes (1994) quoted an RCMP drug officer in the Vancouver Island community of Nanaimo who attributed the 'massive increase' in the presence of high-grade heroin in that city to 'Vietnamese dealers.' The Reform member of Parliament from Nanaimo, Robert Ringma, offered his thoughts on the situation as well, stating, 'there's no question the drug trade stems from the Vietnamese community.'[7]

A series of incidents involving Asian criminals in late 1995 in several Canadian cities brought national media attention to the issue. In December 1995, a *Globe and Mail* article (Vincent, 1995) noted, 'kidnappings and home invasions by Chinese and Vietnamese gangs are increasing in frequency and brutality as gang members target both middle-class Canadians and recent immigrants ... Asian crime experts in Canada say they are alarmed by the growing level of violence and brutality against women and children who are victims of home invasions by Chinese and Vietnamese gangs.' Vincent emphasizes the violent nature of these crimes through reference to a 1991 Toronto case in which an Asian gang invaded a Toronto house and fastened a three-month-old baby to a wall with duct tape to pressure the family into giving up all their valuables. In another home invasion that occurred in Toronto two years later, gang members apparently stuck a gun into the mouth of a six-year-old and severely beat the child's mother to convince the family to surrender their valuables.

Similar to media reports of the allegedly increasing Black-crime problem, however, Vincent is unable to provide objective evidence on the actual frequency of such crimes. Noting that there are 'few statistics available because the police feel many home invasions go unreported in Asian communities,' she relies on the opinions of law enforcement officials in claiming that, 'over the past five years, home invasions have been increasing across the country ... Vancouver is increasingly targeted by gangs trying to extort small fortunes from students from Hong Kong and China. In recent months, several students have been threatened with violence, even death, unless they pay gangs as much as $100,000.'

While home-invasion crimes committed by Asians have thus received considerable media attention, the fact that they involve primarily Asian victims renders them somewhat less threatening to the larger society. However, reports of violent crimes committed by Asian gangs in public places are more effective in conveying to the general public the dangers posed by Asian gangs and the criminal members of such gangs. According to some media reports, these crimes have also become more commonplace in recent times. For instance, in December 1995, one Vietnamese man died and five others were either stabbed or shot in a downtown karaoke club in Nanaimo, British Columbia, as a result of 'a display of force by gang members.' A Vancouver police spokesperson suggested that Asian gangs had been involved in similar activities in other British Columbia cities, including New Westminster and Coquitlam (*Globe and Mail*, 1995).

Also in December 1995, a gunman opened fire outside a popular restaurant in Toronto's east Chinatown, leaving one man dead and two others wounded. Grange (1995) emphasized the danger associated with such crimes through interviews with Chinatown residents who expressed their concerns about the incident, and through reference to previous gang-related crimes that had occurred in the area. Mary Young, a Chinese Canadian who 'said she has shopped in the area for more than 20 years,' noted, 'it's scary when it happens so close to home.' Another 'long-time resident, who asked that his name not be used,' stated that 'it's going to keep happening.' Grange points out that the shooting was the area's second in two years: 'In December of 1993, two people were killed and two others wounded in a failed robbery at the Da Fu Ho massage clinic.'

In a follow-up article discussing the Chinatown murder, Hess (1995) places this 'execution-style' shooting in the context of 'a number of slayings in Toronto in recent years,' including the shooting of Georgina Leimonis by a Jamaican immigrant in 1994. The potential threat to members of the general public is underscored through Hess's reference to the fact that 'restaurants and clubs appear to be a favourite place for settling scores within the Asian underworld.'

While the threats posed to the larger society by both Asian and Black crime have thus received considerable attention in the Canadian media in the last several years, attempts to analyse the reasons for these alleged increases in minority crime have been lacking. Whether minority crime is attributable to inherent criminal tendencies on the part of these groups or is instead linked to their generally disadvantaged social position in Canadian society has not been sufficiently addressed in the media.

At the same time, however, there has also been some indication in the press that the police are biased in their treatment of minority groups, with allegations of racism in law enforcement officials' exercise of discretion and use of deadly force. Although seldom made explicit in these media accounts, there is an underlying suggestion that at least part of the minority-group crime problem may be attributable to biases in the criminal justice system.

Police Bias in Dealing with Minority Groups

In October 1991, alerted by police radio that two Black men had just robbed a pizza restaurant, Vancouver police officers pursued a car with a Black driver and Black passenger and, drawing their guns, arrested the two men. A Vancouver Police Board inquiry into the incident, reporting some four years after the occurrence, concluded that the police had done nothing wrong (*Vancouver Sun*, 1995a). In his report, Chuck Lew, chair of the Police Board panel, defended the police by stating that Blacks were unique because not many of them were seen in Vancouver. David St Pierre, a representative of the Vancouver Black Law Students Association, noted the almost cruel irony in the Police Board's report: 'Mr. Lew makes it perfectly clear that Black people are now potentially subject to unfair and discriminatory treatment not only because we are a visible minority, but because, according to Mr. Lew, we are also now an invisible minority' (*Vancouver Sun*, 1995b).

In its editorial response to the arrest of the two innocent Black males, the *Vancouver Sun* (1995a) questioned the need for police to draw their guns, but argued that 'proving racism in this case is difficult. The police had reason to stop the car and question the men inside. In a city with a small Black population, two Black men driving a vehicle not far from the scene of an armed robbery committed by two Black men quite reasonably would attract the attention of the police.'

Although Vancouver does not have a large Black population, and accounts of police racism in dealing with members of this minority group would thus be relatively infrequent, further evidence that Vancouver police are guided by racial concerns in their enforcement activities was provided by Stall (1995) in an article appearing in the *Vancouver Province*. Stall reported on the interactions with police of a mixed race couple in Vancouver. The wife, who was White, had not been stopped by the police in four years, but the Black husband, driving the same vehicle that his wife normally drove, had been pulled over more than fifteen times by Vancouver police officers for 'checks and minor infractions relating mainly to the vehicle's appearance.' Stall asserts that, 'if a Black male is in an expensive-looking car, police presume he's ... a pimp, drug dealer or driving a stolen car.'

In another incident from Vancouver, this time involving an alleged Asian criminal, the Vancouver Police Emergency Response Team entered the basement apartment of Feng Hua Zhang, responding to a tip that Zhang's residence contained guns and drugs. Operating under the assumption that he was being robbed, Zhang, who did not speak English, fled to his bedroom, locked the door, and hid in a closet. Police shot the door open and dragged Zhang to an alley outside, where he was kicked and punched by the police officers (Bellett and Young, 1992). After concerns regarding potential racial bias on the part of police were sparked by an amateur videotape of the incident, an unidentified Vancouver police source claimed that police had been getting an 'unfair rap' from the barrage of publicity. 'Was anyone shot? Was anyone killed? Everyone's taking this as being like the Rodney King thing ... So what if they kicked him? What's the difference between a blow from a foot, a hand, a club, as long as it's justified?' (Appleby, 1992a).

While reports from Vancouver have thus focused on the questionable exercise of discretion by officers in dealing with minority groups, the situation in the two Canadian cities with the largest minority populations, Montreal and Toronto, is far more serious. Although media reports of police racism in these cities has certainly included accounts of the questionable exercise of police discretion, there have also been more serious allegations of racial bias in police use of deadly force.

Blacks comprise approximately 6 per cent of Montreal's population, and relations between this minority group and the police have become increasingly tense over the last few years. As Dan Philip, president of the Black Coalition of Quebec, stated, 'there is a growing mistrust of the police and a growing mistrust of the manner in which they perform their duties' (*Maclean's*, 1992).

Farnsworth (1995) notes that Black youths in Montreal 'learn early about the realities of police zealousness,' and recounts the case of nine Black teenagers in that city who were offered free pizza by police officers, only to be taken to the local police station and placed in a line-up. Similarly, Picard (1992) reports on the arrest of three young Black males outside a convenience store in Montreal's predominantly Black Little Burgundy neighbourhood, where 'complaints of police harassment, brutality, intimidation, and racism are commonplace.' A resident of the community, emphasizing the discriminatory practices of police in dealing with Blacks, told Picard: 'every Black person in Little Burgundy is a moving target.' In an earlier incident in which witnesses complained that a fifteen-year-old Black youth was being subjected to racial taunts by three White men, Montreal police demonstrated their tendency to assume Blacks are criminals, and responded by ignoring the men and pulling a gun on the boy and taking him into custody (Picard, 1991).

The tensions between Blacks and the Montreal police force have been further exacerbated by a series of police shootings of minority-group members, with the force being involved in the deaths of eight men, including four Blacks and three Hispanics, between 1987 and 1994 (Henry et al., 1995). In November 1987, Constable Allen Gosset shot and killed Anthony Griffin, a nineteen-year-old Black male. Griffin, who was wanted for breaking and entering, was unarmed, and had apparently heeded an order to surrender after briefly bolting from police custody (Wood, 1989).

In November 1990, twenty-two-year-old Jorge Alberto Chavarria, a Salvadorean refugee, was shot to death by a Montreal police officer after stealing $10 worth of food from a corner store. Failing in several attempts to apprehend Chavarria, the police officer engaged in a struggle with him and, when he saw the blade of a knife, fired 'instinctively ... convinced his life was in danger' (Picard, 1991).

In July 1991, Marcellus François, an unarmed Black male, was shot and killed by Montreal police after being mistaken for a suspect in a drug surveillance operation (Poirier, 1992). Sergeant Michael Tremblay, the officer who killed François, was similarly convinced that his life was in danger, after François allegedly reached in his car for what Tremblay believed was a weapon (Picard, 1991).

In response to the François incident, the Quebec government appointed Harvey Yarosky, a Montreal criminal lawyer, as a special coroner to investigate the case. Yarosky noted that he was 'disturbed by certain signs within the MUC [Montreal Urban Community] police force of insensitivity to, ignorance about, and lack of respect for the members of the Black community' (Poirier, 1992). Following the special coroner's report, the Quebec government also commissioned a more extensive investigation of the Montreal Urban Community police force, under a retired Quebec Court of Appeal judge, Albert Malouf. According to Malouf's July 1994 report, the force was poorly supervised, insufficiently trained, inadequately equipped, and characterized by a 'totally unacceptable' level of racism (Farnsworth, 1995). As Andre Picard (1991) aptly concluded, 'the other constant pointed to by human rights activists in all the incidents is skin colour. Why, they ask, do police so fear visible minorities? Why do they immediately assume that Blacks and Hispanics are criminals? Why, when non-whites are alleged to have been involved in crimes, do police assume they will act violently?'

Allegations of racism have also plagued the Toronto police force in recent years. In August 1993, Audrey Smith, a Black woman on holiday from Jamaica, was apprehended by police and forced to strip naked on a downtown Toronto street corner as the police searched her for drugs. '"There I was, naked as the day I was born on the street. I have never felt so ashamed and humiliated in my life"' (Colbourn, 1993). The *Toronto Sun*, questioning the validity of Smith's version of the incident, quoted police sources as claiming that Smith stripped voluntarily, and that this was a 'common practice among Jamaican women rounded up in drug busts ... as a way of showing disrespect for the police' (cited in Colbourne, 1993).

Cuff (1994) provided further evidence of mistreatment of minority groups in Toronto by police and the criminal justice system. Reviewing a *Fifth Estate* television documentary on the wrongful murder conviction of Donzel Young, an illegal Jamaican immigrant living in Toronto, Cuff concluded that the show demonstrated that, 'if the suspect is Black and an illegal immigrant, the quality of justice proffered is inferior to that which is accorded anyone who is white or from a higher rung on the socio-economic ladder.' Pointing to the existence of systemic racism in the justice system, which Young's case reveals, and labelling it 'Southern Justice, Canadian Style,' Cuff noted that the police and prosecutors in the case ignored important evidence and refused to call witnesses who would refute their findings.

Although sceptics would argue that such incidents are isolated and not representative of pervasive racial bias in the Toronto police force, somewhat more objective evidence was provided in a Canadian Civil Liberties Association survey of teenagers conducted in 1993. This survey, although limited to 150 respondents, revealed that 71 per cent of visible-minority teenagers, as compared with 50 per cent of the White teenagers, who had been in contact with the police reported negative experiences. Even more disturbing, in a number of these encounters racial slurs were made when the teenagers were questioned by the police (Sarick, 1993).

As a result of their dealings with minority groups, the Metropolitan Toronto police have recently been subjected to a great deal of criticism, especially on the part of Black community activists in that city. The force has attempted to circumvent some of this criticism by initiating surreptitious investigations into the affairs of certain Black activists in that city, including, among others, Wilson Head, the founder of the Urban Alliance for Race Relations, and Kamala-Jean Gopie, a teacher who served on the Provincial Task Force for Race Relations (Barber, 1994). Constable Denny Dias, who conducted the investigations of Head and Gopie, sixteen other individuals, and thirteen activist groups, asserted that the purpose was to determine whether the groups were 'a threat to the community or terrorist groups.'

The Metropolitan Toronto police's questionable actions in dealing with Black activists was also evidenced in their treatment of Dudley Laws, co-founder of the Black Action Defence Committee and 'their most irritating critic' (Barber, 1994). Laws, who at various times had accused the Toronto police of 'shooting and beating [our people]' and who claimed '[they] are out of control' (Fennell, 1992), was arrested by police in 1991 for conspiring to smuggle illegal immigrants in and out of Canada. After police undercover officers posed as immigrants in trouble seeking Laws's assistance, essentially entrapping him, 'the police arrived accompanied by a phalanx of reporters and television cameras ... and fitted him with leg shackles' (Makin, 1994). Laws was eventually convicted of the offence, and members of the Black Action Defence Committee claimed that the police investigation cost more than $6 million and involved seventy-five people over a six-month period (Barber, 1994).

Toronto police also expressed their displeasure when Arnold Minors, a member of the Metropolitan Toronto Police Services Board, made comments to a Bermuda newspaper about the disproportionate number of Blacks who had been shot by the police. Art Lymer, the head of the Metro Police Association, called for Minors's resignation from the board, and suggested that he 'take his opinions elsewhere' (DiManno, 1993).

Similar to the situation in Quebec, police in Ontario have been involved in a disturbing number of shootings of Blacks in recent years. Between 1978 and 1994, on-duty police officers in the province shot sixteen Black people in Ontario, ten of them fatally, and in many of these cases the victims were unarmed. In nine of the cases, criminal charges were laid against the officers involved, but not one was convicted (Ontario, 1995).[8]

In the 1979 case of Albert Johnson, police responded to a complaint of a disturbance, and shot and killed Johnson as he descended the stairs of his house with what the officers apparently believed to be an axe, but what turned out to be a lawn edger. The two police officers were charged with manslaughter – the first time police officers had been charged with this offence in the history of the Toronto police force – but were eventually acquitted (Forcese, 1992). In August 1988, a Toronto police officer killed Lester Donaldson, a forty-four-year-old Black man, in a Toronto rooming-house. Constable David Denney claimed that he fired at Donaldson to defend his partner when Donaldson allegedly lunged at him with a knife (Wood, 1989).

In December 1988, seventeen-year-old Wade Lawson was killed after he and another Black teenager, driving a stolen car, were pursued by two plain-clothes Peel Regional Police Force detectives. The detectives involved in the case testified that they had attempted to stop the car, but the driver tried to run them down, so they fired shots to protect themselves (Forcese, 1992). The surviving teenager claimed that the police had not identified themselves and that, after they pulled him from the car, one of the officers kicked him and called him a 'nigger' (Fennell, 1992). Although these two officers were acquitted by a jury (Appleby, 1992b), it was later established that police in this case had used hollow-point bullets, which have greater 'stopping power' since they expand on impact. The use of such bullets had been prohibited by the Ontario Police Act (Forcese, 1992).

Despite the questions surrounding these and other instances of police use of deadly force against Blacks, it is important to stress that not one Toronto-area police officer has been convicted of an offence in any of the shootings. And while the Canadian media has certainly devoted some attention to allegations of police racism, the accounts are frequently tempered by discussions of the difficulties police face in the conduct of their duties. For instance, in a discussion of police use of deadly force in Toronto and Montreal appearing in *Maclean's*, Wood (1989) notes that 'a badge and uniform are no protection against daily dangers that range from a drunk's wildly thrown punch to the fear of AIDS infection through contact with an accident victim's blood. In addition, there is the ever-present risk of death from criminal gunfire. Between 1978 and 1987, 35 on-duty police officers have been killed in Canada.' Similarly, in a later article in *Maclean's* Fennell (1992) quotes Toronto Constable Bill McCormack, the son of then Toronto chief of police William McCormack, who claimed that 'the people who accuse us of racism have never been out on the street with us. We're trying to stop crime, and that is the bottom line.'

Probably no incident served more effectively to underscore the tensions between minority groups and police in Toronto than a civil disturbance that occurred in May 1992, sparked by a series of events related to police mistreatment of minority groups. While twenty-five off-duty (White) Toronto police officers, drinking and watching a hockey game, allegedly 'cheered' the acquittal of four Los Angeles police officers in the Rodney King beating case as it flashed on the screen (Appleby, 1992b), the Toronto-based Urban Alliance on Race Relations was planning a rally to protest the acquittal, and to emphasize parallels between the police use of force against minority groups in Los Angeles and Toronto. The announcement of the verdict in the King case coincided with the acquittal of the two Peel Region police officers in the killing of Wade Lawson, and the police killing of another Black in Toronto.

Raymond Lawrence, a twenty-two-year-old illegal Jamaican immigrant and suspected drug dealer, was shot and killed by an undercover Toronto policeman after allegedly threatening the officer with a knife in May 1992. Although Appleby (1992d) asserted that, if Lawrence had been killed by police in Kingston, Jamaica, 'he would barely have got a mention,' his death took on added significance in the context of the Lawson and Los Angeles verdicts, turning the planned demonstration into a major civil disturbance in which protestors and others vandalized and looted stores in Toronto's downtown area.

Responses to the riot were mixed, with some commentators suggesting it was virtually inevitable, and perhaps even justified, given the increasing tensions between Blacks and Toronto police, while others claimed racism was merely 'an excuse for riots and theft' (Amiel, 1992). Austin Clarke (1992) attributed the event to 'the historical use of unjustified police force against suspected Black youths' and argued that 'the boil of contained animosity and anger [on 4 May] was [therefore] no surprise.'

On the other hand, Walkom (1992), while noting that the complaints of Blacks regarding police harassment were 'too numerous to be shrugged off,' asserted that 'the fact that police tend to shoot proportionately more Blacks than Whites may have less to do with racism than the question of context – of who police run into.' Similarly, Appleby (1992b) labelled critics of the police 'armchair quarterbacks' and claimed that most people are 'oblivious to the extraordinary pressures police face in making split-second decisions with life-or-death consequences.'

Maclean's columnist Barbara Amiel (1992) attributed the riot to 'a fatally flawed liberal perspective on racism that for the past 30 years has sold Blacks in North America the notion that nothing in life is their fault, and that they are entitled to vent their unhappiness by stealing or destroying what belongs to others.' Referring to the police shooting of Raymond Lawrence, Amiel asserted that any man running towards the police with a knife in his hand and ignoring warning shots would be fired at, regardless of his colour. She lamented the persistence of a 'tired rhetoric' regarding systemic racism in Canada, and suggested that 'Canadians know themselves, and they know Canadian society is not racist.' Perhaps even more amazingly, Amiel claimed that 'some Black activists want to incite as much dissension and unrest as possible among us all, in order to build a power base for themselves. One sees a parallel in the Nazis who exploited the very real problems in Germany to build up their power.'

Despite conflicting interpretations of the causes of events such as the Toronto civil disturbance and disputes over the extent of the minority-crime problem in Canada, there is little doubt that minority crime, and the criminal justice system's treatment of minority groups, have become an increasingly important issue in Canadian society. While the press has provided relatively extensive coverage of these topics, as is the case with media treatment of other important social issues, detailed objective analysis and explanation of the causes of these problems has been lacking. Perhaps even more disturbingly, those looking to academic sources for answers to the problems of minority crime and racial bias on the part of law enforcement officials will only be disappointed, as there has been a decided lack of discussion of race and crime in Canadian social science in general, and Canadian criminology in particular.

The Attention to Race and Crime Issues in Canadian Social Science

While Canadian sociologists and criminologists have expended considerable effort in examining issues of aboriginal patterns of crime and differential treatment of Natives in the criminal justice system (see, especially, Silverman and Nielsen, 1992), there has been almost universal inattention to Asian- and Black-crime patterns and the criminal justice system's treatment of such groups. An informal survey of seventeen widely used Canadian textbooks published between 1982 and 1994 that deal with issues of Canadian crime, law, policing, and criminal and juvenile justice underlines the neglect of these topics by Canadian criminologists (see table 1.1).

The data in table 1.1 were compiled by examining the indexes of these texts for the total number of page references to Asians, Blacks, ethnicity, Natives, and racism. Although it is important to remain aware of the fact that this is not an exhaustive list, and that inadequacies and differences in indexing procedures may be a factor in the identification of racial issues in these texts, there is little doubt that Blacks and Asians have received scant attention in Canadian criminology. While the seventeen texts contained well over a hundred page references to Natives, there was a total of only seven page references to Asians, and seventeen to Blacks.

Most of these texts include the almost obligatory discussion of the overrepresentation of aboriginals in Canada's criminal justice system, but make no mention of Blacks or Asians. For example, texts such as Griffiths and Verdun-Jones's (1994) *Canadian Criminal Justice*, while containing a lengthy chapter on Natives in the criminal justice system, include absolutely no reference to Blacks or Asians. Similarly, Linden's (1992) book of edited readings contains a chapter by Hartnagel (1992) on the correlates of crime, which includes a specific section on the 'race' correlate, but this chapter provides no reference to any other racial minority group aside from Natives. Others, such as Ericson's (1981, 1982) two books on policing, as well as his co-authored book on the criminal justice process (Ericson and Baranek, 1983), similarly contain no reference to Blacks or Asians. A chapter in Jackson and Griffiths's (1991) *Canadian Criminology*, entitled 'Minorities, Crime and the Law' (Yerbury and Griffiths, 1991), restricts its discussion and analysis to aboriginals and Doukhobors. In short, anyone relying on these texts for information on the issue of race and crime would arrive at the conclusion that, while aboriginal crime and discrimination against aboriginals in the criminal justice system are important topics in Canadian criminology, there is no need for concern about Asian and Black crime, or the treatment members of these groups receive from the criminal justice system.

Table 1.1: Number of Page References to Race and Racial Issues in Canadian Criminology and Criminal Justice Textbooks

Author(s) and Subject	Asians	Blacks	Ethnicity	Natives	Racism
Brockman and Chunn (1993):					
Gender Bias in Law	0	0	0	8	0
Burtch (1992):					
Sociology of Law	2	9	4	15	14
Carrigan (1991):					
History of Crime	3	0	0	0	0
Ericson (1982):					
Policing	0	0	0	0	0
Ericson and Baranek (1982):					
Criminal Process	0	0	0	0	0
Forcese (1992):					
Policing	0	0	12	1	14
Gomme (1993):					
Crime and Deviance	0	3	6	6	6
Griffiths and Verdun-Jones (1994):					
Criminal Justice	0	0	4	30+	2
Hackler (1994):					
Crime and Policy	0	0	0	1	1
Hagan (1991):					
Crime and Deviance	0	0	1	0	0
Hudson and Roberts (1993):					
Criminal Justice	0	0	0	0	0
Hudson et al. (1988):					
Juvenile Justice	0	0	0	23	0
Jackson and Griffiths (1991):					
Criminology	1	0	2	30+	2
Linden (1992):					
Criminology	0	0	0	20	8
Sacco (1992):					
Conformity and Control	0	0	0	0	1
Schissel (1993):					
Juvenile Justice	1	5	4	30+	12
Vincent (1994):					
Policing	0	0	1	0	4

Note: 'Asians' includes Chinese and Japanese. 'Ethnicity' includes minority groups and visible-minority groups. 'Natives' includes aboriginal peoples, Indians, First Nations peoples, indigenous peoples. 'Racism' includes race and racial discrimination.

It is important to note that some other Canadian texts at least make passing reference to the issue of Black crime and criminal-justice processing of Blacks. For example, Gomme (1993) indicates that Blacks are significantly overrepresented in crime statistics in the United States, but that we know comparatively little about the situation in Canada, owing to the absence of official statistics on minority crime. Somewhat more promising is Burtch's (1992) *Sociology of Law*, which makes reference to discrimination against Blacks by police forces in Toronto and Montreal, and provides secondary data to discuss formal and informal discrimination against the Chinese in Canada. In addition, Forcese's (1992) book on policing in Canada refers to the lack of effectiveness of race-relations training for police officers in Canada, and pays some attention to the police shootings of minority-group members in Toronto and Montreal mentioned above. Schissel's (1993) book on juvenile delinquency also makes reference to the importance of racial variables in determining outcomes for young offenders.

Overall, however, the attention to these important issues of race, crime, and justice in Canadian criminology texts is disappointing, and perhaps disturbingly problematic. By neglecting the issue of minority crime and responses to it in the criminal justice system, Canadian criminologists have contributed to the prevailing societal view that anti-Asian and anti-Black racism in the Canadian criminal justice system are non-existent.

Given the neglect of these topics in Canadian criminological inquiry, it might be more fruitful to search for discussions of race and crime issues within the larger rubric of Canadian sociology. Canadian sociology has a strong tradition of identifying and analysing the importance of racial and ethnic variables in social stratification. This tradition began with the work of scholars such as Clark (1962), Breton (1964), and Porter (1965), among others, and has continued in more recent publications, including those of Anderson and Frideres (1981), Bienvenue and Goldstein (1985), Driedger (1989), Elliott and Fleras (1992), Reitz (1980), and Reitz and Breton (1994). These, and several other sources, have uncovered extensive evidence of racial and ethnic inequality in several spheres of Canadian society, and theorized about the causes and consequences of this inequality.

In addition, books devoted to the experiences of particular racial minority groups, including Asians (Anderson, 1991; Lai, 1988; Li 1988) and Blacks (Clairmont and Magill, 1987; Walker, 1980; Winks, 1971), have contributed to our understanding of the disparities in access to housing, services, employment, and the generally restricted patterns of social mobility for these groups. However, while the contributions of these scholars has certainly led to an erosion in the previously pervasive myth of Canadian egalitarianism, most have not devoted attention to minority-group crime and processing inequities in the criminal justice system as important dimensions of racial inequality. A notable exception to this rule is the recent work of Frances Henry (1994) and her colleagues (Henry et al., 1995), who have addressed in some detail the complex structural forces that contribute to minority-group crime, and responses to it by the criminal justice system.

While the Canadian academic literature has thus paid limited attention to the issues of crime, criminal justice, and race, recent developments signal a renewed attention to these important topics. In response to the 1992 civil disturbance in Toronto described above, then Ontario premier Bob Rae asserted that racism in Canada was a 'fact of life' and a 'scourge' (Wilkes, 1992), and responded to the events by appointing a commission to examine the issue of systemic racism in Ontario's criminal justice system. As a preliminary step, Rae appointed Stephen Lewis to examine the state of race relations in the province of Ontario. Lewis, in a 9 June letter to Premier Rae, noted the following:

First what we are dealing with, at root, and fundamentally, is anti-black racism. While it is obviously true that every visible minority community experiences the indignities and wounds of systemic discrimination throughout southern Ontario, it is the black community which is the focus. It is Blacks who are being shot, it is black youth that is unemployed in excessive numbers, it is black kids who are being inappropriately streamed in schools, it is black kids who are disproportionately dropping out, it is housing communities with large concentrations of black residents where the sense of vulnerability and disadvantage is most acute, it is black employees, professional and non-professional, on whom the doors of upward equity slam shut. Just as the soothing balm of 'multiculturalism' cannot mask racism, so racism cannot mask its primary target. (Lewis, 1992; cited in *R* v *Parks* (1993)

The subsequent report of the Commission on Systemic Racism in the Ontario Criminal Justice System (Ontario, 1995) presented extensive evidence of racism at virtually all levels of Ontario's criminal justice system. The report found that Black males were significantly more likely than Whites or Chinese to be stopped by the police (p. 353) and that a disturbingly high percentage of Blacks perceived that judges treat Blacks worse than they do Whites (p. 341). In a study comparing the criminal justice system's processing of 821 Black and 832 White adult male offenders charged with various crimes, the commission found that Blacks were less likely than Whites to be released by police before trial (p. 123), and were more likely to be refused bail (p. 124), even when other legally relevant factors such as prior record and seriousness of offence were controlled for. In the same sample of offenders, 49 per cent of Blacks convicted of possession of drugs, compared with 18 per cent of White offenders, were incarcerated (p. 279). As the commission report noted, these findings 'indicate that some Black convicted men were sentenced to prison when White convicted men with the same personal and case characteristics were not sentenced to prison' (p. 277).

These biases at the arrest and sentencing stage of the criminal justice system combined to produce a 1992/3 provincial incarceration rate for Black adult males that was five times the rate for White adult males, proportionate to their representation in the population, and an admission rate for Black women that was almost seven times that of White women (p. iii). In addition, evidence of the mistreatment of Blacks in Ontario's prison system, including racial segregation within institutions (p. 299), and the differential use of punishment powers by custodial officials against Black and White prisoners, were uncovered.

While the report prepared by the Commission on Systemic Racism in the Ontario Criminal Justice System thus leaves little doubt that racial differences in the treatment of offenders exists, it notes that the findings do not show direct racial discrimination in the full range of criminal charges (p. 280). In addition, at one point in the commission's report, it is claimed that the massive inequality in Ontario's prison admissions is 'a relatively recent occurrence' (p. 104). The data and arguments presented in this book indicate that the differential treatment of minority-group offenders was also prevalent in earlier periods in the province's history, and that this differential treatment applied to a wide range of offences.

Although national and provincial data on the numbers of minority-group members arrested in the period from 1892 to 1961 are not available, table 1.2 provides evidence that, relative to their proportion in the general population, both Asians and Blacks were overrepresented in Canada's federal-prison population for the 1896–1938 period.[9] Blacks, who comprised only 0.22 per cent of the total population of Canada in 1911 (Census of Canada, 1911), constituted 2.8 per cent of all federal prisoners in the same year, which translates to an incarceration rate of 3.21 per 1,000 (Black) population. While the corresponding rate of incarceration for Chinese was 0.75 per 1,000 in 1911, the rate for Whites was only 0.18 per 1,000. In 1931, Blacks comprised 2.0 per cent of the federal prison population, and their rate of incarceration was 3.85 per 1,000. The incarceration rate for Chinese had increased to 1.74 per 1,000 in that year, largely due to lengthy sentences meted out to Chinese drug traffickers. The federal imprisonment rate for Whites had also increased by 1931; however, at 0.35 per 1,000 population, it was less than one-tenth the rate for Blacks, and less than one-fifth the rate for Chinese. These figures thus leave little doubt that

Table 1.2: Convicts in Federal Penitentiaries, by Race, 1896–1938

Year	Black	Chinese	White	Total
1896	56 (4.1)	14 (1.0)	1,306 (92.9)	1,376
1897	55 (4.0)	10 (0.7)	1,287 (93.6)	1,375
1898–9		NOT AVAILABLE		
1900	75 (5.3)	12 (0.8)	1,306 (92.2)	1,415
1901	54 (3.9)	10 (0.7)	1,281 (93.3)	1,372
1902	49 (4.1)	8 (0.7)	1,106 (92.5)	1,195
1903	53 (4.2)	7 (0.6)	1,131 (90.4)	1,250
1904	54 (4.1)	11 (0.8)	1,207 (90.8)	1,328
1905	55 (4.0)	14 (1.0)	1,244 (91.0)	1,367
1906	51 (3.5)	16 (1.1)	1,325 (92.1)	1,439
1907	51 (3.6)	17 (1.2)	1,298 (91.2)	1,423
1908	54 (3.7)	20 (1.4)	1,357 (91.9)	1,476
1909	62 (3.5)	22 (1.2)	1,635 (92.6)	1,765
1910	53 (2.9)	20 (1.1)	1,738 (93.5)	1,859
1911	52 (2.8)	21 (1.1)	1,747 (93.7)	1,864
1912	52 (2.7)	27 (1.4)	1,777 (93.8)	1,895
1913	62 (3.2)	29 (1.5)	1,831 (93.0)	1,968
1914	57 (2.8)	41 (2.0)	1,867 (93.2)	2,003
1915	62 (3.0)	39 (1.9)	1,929 (93.5)	2,064
1916	63 (3.0)	47 (2.2)	1,970 (93.0)	2,118
1917	56 (3.3)	38 (2.3)	1,553 (92.0)	1,688
1918	64 (4.4)	29 (2.0)	1,333 (91.1)	1,462
1919	52 (3.1)	24 (1.4)	1,585 (94.0)	1,686
1920	57 (3.0)	22 (1.1)	1,820 (94.3)	1,931
1921	67 (1.1)	25 (1.2)	2,019 (93.9)	2,150
1922	83 (3.1)	30 (1.1)	2,489 (94.3)	2,640
1923	87 (3.5)	49 (2.0)	2,303 (92.8)	2,483
1924	63 (2.8)	51 (2.3)	2,065 (92.9)	2,224
1925	54 (2.3)	40 (1.7)	2,198 (93.8)	2,343
1926	48 (1.9)	44 (1.8)	2,327 (94.1)	2,473
1927	42 (1.7)	41 (1.7)	2,354 (94.9)	2,480
1928	43 (1.7)	58 (2.3)	2,409 (94.1)	2,560
1929	60 (2.2)	71 (2.6)	2,589 (93.5)	2,769
1930	60 (1.9)	80 (2.5)	2,995 (94.0)	3,187
1931	75 (2.0)	81 (2.2)	3,499 (94.2)	3,714
1932	79 (1.9)	81 (1.9)	3,923 (94.2)	4,164
1933	66 (1.4)	78 (1.7)	4,376 (95.4)	4,587
1934	50 (1.2)	51 (1.3)	4,068 (96.4)	4,220
1935	51 (1.4)	36 (1.0)	3,417 (96.2)	3,552
1936	45 (1.5)	24 (0.8)	2,972 (95.9)	3,098
1937	43 (1.3)	29 (0.9)	3,130 (95.9)	3,264
1938	58 (1.6)	30 (0.8)	3,426 (95.7)	3,580

Source: *Canada Year Book*, Report on Penitentiaries, 1896–1938
Note: Figures in parentheses represent percentages of the totals and may not add up to 100 per cent because of unincluded groups and rounding error. Figures broken down by race are unavailable after 1938. Figures in 'Total' column may not equal sum of 3 columns because of missing data.

minority-group offenders have been overrepresented in Canada's federal-prison populations for quite some time.

Of course, these figures provide us with little information regarding whether this overrepresentation of minority-group offenders in prison populations was due to their differential proclivity to be involved in criminal activities or whether, instead, it was the result of racial biases in the criminal justice system. In order to determine the causes of this minority-group overrepresentation, it is necessary to utilize both qualitative and quantitative historical data, as is done throughout this book.

Plan of the Book

The purpose of this book is to examine the historical antecedents of systemic racism in Canada's legal and criminal justice systems, with a particular focus on the experiences of Asians and Blacks in the province of Ontario for the 1892–1961 period. The importance of such historical exploration should not be underestimated, for, as Monkkonen (1995) suggests, the analysis of racial inequality in diverse historical contexts allows us to establish a perspective from which to view contemporary problems.

My discussion of these issues will be informed by recent scholarly commentaries on race and racism. First, it is important to recognize that, while biological factors are frequently invoked in order to establish racial hierarchies and to justify differential treatment of individuals on the basis of their race, race is a social construct that is defined in specific social and historical contexts. In addition, recent theorists (Mann, 1993; Henry 1994) have noted that racism comprises various components (individual, institutional, systemic, and cultural/ideological), and that each one of these may have different implications for the treatment of minority groups in social and legal systems.

Individual racism is related to what is more commonly known as 'race prejudice,' and is rooted in the belief that one's own race warrants a positive attitude and that other races should be viewed negatively (Henry, 1994). Racial prejudice and individual racism thus involve a general feeling of dislike for people, perhaps even hatred of them, based upon their race, and may manifest itself in acts of discrimination against individuals from racial minority groups.

Institutional racism is manifested in the policies, practices, and procedures of a variety of societal institutions. Such policies, practices, and procedures may, directly or indirectly, consciously or inadvertently, promote, sustain, or entrench differential advantage to people of diverse races (Henry, 1994). Garcia (1996) asserts that, while institutional racism has its origins in the beliefs and actions of individual people, this form of racism appears to be capable of continuing, even after individual racism has largely disappeared. Systemic racism is similar in form to institutional racism, but refers to the laws, rules, and norms of a social system that result in an unequal distribution of economic, political, and social resources and rewards among various social groups. The Commission on Systemic Racism in the Ontario Criminal Justice System (Ontario, 1995: 39) defined it this way: 'by systemic racism we mean the social production of racial inequality in decisions about people and in the treatment they receive ... It is produced by social constructions of race as real, different, and unequal; the norms, processes and service delivery of a social system and, the actions and decisions of people who work for social systems.'

Cultural/ideological racism, on the other hand, is often more difficult to identify and isolate as it is embedded in the cultural systems of a group or society, and is expressed through language, religion, art, and literature. As Henry (1994: 25) suggests, 'cultural racism ... represents the tacit network of beliefs and values that encourage and justify discriminatory actions, behaviours, and practices.' This form of racism is most commonly manifested in the stereotypical images of racial-minority groups produced in mass-media sources, and will be a major focus of this book.

In distinguishing among these various components of racism, it is important to realize that, if racist consequences are the result of institutional laws, practices, or procedures, the institution is racist, whether or not the individual actors responsible for those practices have racist intentions (Williams, 1985). And, while institutional or systemic racism is the usual focus of attention for theorists, we cannot neglect manifestations of racism at the individual level, as racist institutions are composed of individuals who create policies and implement them. In short, institutional and systemic racism are the result of a series of interactions between individuals who function in official roles within those institutions.

In this book, I present extensive evidence of racism against Asians and Blacks in Canada's immigration policies, and in several spheres of social and economic life, including access to housing and property, employment, and services. The analysis demonstrates that Canadian law has been used through direct action and interpretation, but also through silence and complicity (Kobayashi, 1990), to control and disadvantage Asians and Blacks in Canada.

When discussing the treatment of minority groups in the criminal justice system, it is clear that a consideration of the interrelationships between that system and other societal institutions is fundamental to an adequate understanding of racial inequality and disadvantage. The tendency of racial-minority groups to be concentrated in lower-status and low-paying occupations, and the existence of racial segregation in housing, which are both the result of racist policies and practices, lead to the overrepresentation of Asians and Blacks in 'catchment areas' which receive disproportional police attention. All these factors play a significant role in the production of what are usually negative outcomes for members of racial-minority groups in the criminal justice system.

In my historical analysis of the experiences of Asians and Blacks in the criminal justice system, I demonstrate that differential police attention to such individuals resulted in their experiencing higher rates of arrests, particularly for drug and public-order crimes. In addition, the negative views of criminal-court officials towards minority-group offenders affected their generally more severe treatment in the criminal courts. The analysis demonstrates that stereotypical images of Asians and Blacks that frequently appeared in popular-media sources served to define them as 'other' and threatening to the larger society, particularly when their crimes involved White victims, and were used to justify and rationalize discrimination against them.

It is important to note that, although there is certainly a need for a comprehensive theory of the relationship of race, crime, and criminal justice outcomes, I do not offer one here. My objective in this book is somewhat more limited, and involves laying a framework for such a comprehensive theory by emphasizing the historical patterns of discrimination against Blacks and Asians in Canadian law and criminal justice, with a specific focus on the province of Ontario.

Chapter 2 outlines the theoretical perspectives that inform my approach in examining racial inequality in Canadian society, and draws from literature on the sociology of law, the sociology of crime and deviance, and the sociology of race and ethnic relations. With an emphasis on conflict-theoretical perspectives, the chapter also presents a review of the United States, Canadian, and British literature on criminal justice outcomes for minority groups, addressing important methodological issues in this literature. Given the historical focus of this book, I also devote attention to the relationship between sociology and history, and outline my specific methodological approach and data sources in addressing issues of racism in Canadian law and criminal justice over the period from 1892 to 1961.

Chapters 3 and 4 examine several dimensions of inequality for Asians (chapter 3) and Blacks (chapter 4) in Canadian society for the period from 1892 to 1961, focusing in particular on attitudes towards these groups and the popular media's negative stereotypical portrayals of their qualities and behaviours, which had an important impact on legislation enacted to restrict the immigration of such groups. These negative images of Asians and Blacks also limited their access to housing and employment opportunities, and resulted in discrimination against them in their access to social services.

Chapters 5 through 7 are concerned with minority groups' experiences in the criminal justice system. Chapter 5 examines the characteristics of criminal courts in Ontario for the period from 1892 to 1961 that influenced the dispensation of justice for criminal offenders in general, and minority-group offenders in particular, and discusses in some detail the popular media's stereotyping of Asian and Black offenders.

Chapter 6 presents analyses of the treatment of minority-group offenders in Ontario's criminal courts for drug and public-order crimes. The chapter begins by examining the racist foundations of Canada's initial drug legislation, and emphasizes that, for victimless drug and public-order crimes, bias against minority groups manifested itself most clearly at the level of policing. Chapter 7 examines the processing and treatment of minority-group offenders for property and violent crimes, and indicates that, for these offences, considerations of the context of the crime and race of the victim are the most important factors to consider in assessing the extent of racial bias and its causes.

Chapter 8 contains a summary of the major findings of my historical analyses, and suggests that recent developments indicate that the situation for minority groups in Canada, in particular Blacks, is not improving. Certain criminal justice system officials continue to deny the existence of systemic racism, and legislators in Ontario have shown no signs of acting on the recommendations of the Commission on Systemic Racism. As a result, potentially ameliorative policies have not been implemented. The chapter concludes with the suggestion that policy responses to issues of racism in Canadian law and criminal justice would benefit from the collection of criminal justice statistics on the basis of race.

2

Theoretical Perspectives and
Methodological Approaches

The real challenge is to find a model of historical explanation which accounts for (institutional) change without imputing conspiratorial rationality to a ruling class, without reducing institutional development to a formless, ad hoc adjustment to contingent crisis, and without assuming a hyperidealist all triumphant humanitarian crusade. (Ignatieff, 1983: 185)

Most sociological theories offer monolithic explanations of control, assuming that the dimensions of inequality such as race or social class influence the forms and levels of control in a unidirectional and consistent manner, regardless of the social contexts or historical periods in which they occur (Bridges and Myers, 1994). In this book, I present a detailed examination of the diverse historical and social contexts and manifestations of racial inequality in Canada for the period from 1892 to 1961, with a particular focus on the situation in the province of Ontario. The analysis draws variously from theoretical perspectives in the sociology of law, the sociology of deviance, and the sociology of race and ethnic relations in analysing the treatment of Asians and Blacks in Canadian legal and criminal justice institutions.

   In the first section of this chapter, I review a number of perspectives on the sociology of law that inform my analyses in subsequent chapters. While most of these arguments have focused on the importance of social class, as opposed to racial inequality, in law formation, and deal primarily with criminal legislation, they are instructive in terms of their emphasis on the importance of social conflict in producing legislation that worked to the disadvantage of relatively powerless groups. In a more specific discussion of the literature on the formation of narcotics laws in Canada, I outline the shortcomings in traditional conflict approaches to law formation and argue for more detailed historical analyses of legislative enactments and their effects on socially disadvantaged groups. It is important to move beyond analyses that focus only on the law in theory to analyses that assess the impacts of the law in action. I thus suggest that analyses of law should also direct attention to law enforcement practices and the interpretation of laws as manifested in the decisions of judicial officials.

The second section of this chapter provides a more specific context for the findings presented in later chapters through a review of the rather limited Canadian and British literature on the topic of minority-group crime and racial differences in criminal sentencing. It then moves to a consideration of the far more extensive U.S. literature on criminal justice outcomes, with a particular focus on explorations and explanations of the impact of race that appeared in the early and middle 1900s.

In outlining my methodological approach to issues of racial inequality in Canadian law and criminal justice, the third section of the chapter addresses the relationship between history and sociology. Given that the primary focus of this book is historical, I emphasize the need for empirical approaches that utilize methodological principles from both history and sociology and that rely on diverse forms of data in assessing the extent of racial inequality and its determinants in Canadian society.

Perspectives on the Sociology of Law

There are profound differences of opinion in the literature on the sociology of law concerning the foundations and origins of law. Some commentators argue that law evolves from social consensus and that it represents commonly held social values; this is what is known as the 'consensus,' or 'moral functionalist,' approach (Hagan, 1980). Competing arguments focus on the importance of social conflict in the formation and enforcement of laws, stressing that laws emerge when certain powerful groups in society are able to impose their definitions of deviance on less powerful groups. As will become clear from the discussion below, however, there are several variations in this 'conflict,' or 'moral Marxist' (ibid.), approach.

Both the consensus and conflict approaches have originated with the founders of the discipline of sociology. The source of the consensus approach lies with Durkheim (1938), who asserted that crime was a normal phenomenon, and who saw law as the embodiment of the normative order of society. Importantly for Durkheim, however, legal constraint arose, not from the state or the ruling classes, but from society itself (Hall and Scraton, 1986) as an expression of the collective conscience of the community.

This Durkheimian perspective was dominant in much of the early writings on the sociology of law. For instance, Savigny, writing in the early nineteenth cen-

tury, argued that the law was a product of the national spirit of a particular people (Hopkins, 1975). Similarly, Sumner (1906) noted that 'acts of legislation
come out of the mores ... Legislation ... has to seek standing ground on the
existing mores and it soon becomes apparent that legislation, to be strong, must
be consistent with the mores' (as quoted in Sawer, 1965: 172).

This consensus tradition continued with Pound's (1942) 'sociological juris-
prudence,' which focused on an examination of the external influence of social,
economic, psychological, and other non-legal factors on the concrete content of
legal propositions. While Pound characterized these influences in terms of the
different interests that had an impact on the formation of the law, his analysis
presumed that law rests upon a consensus of values and the rationally imposed
authority of the state (Boyd, 1986).

In contrast to these consensus approaches to the sociology of law are conflict
theories, which have their roots in the work of Marx and Engels. While Marx
and Engels wrote extensively about law and crime, they did not develop a consistent theoretical analysis of either. They did argue, however, that crime was a
product of the competitive and exploitative nature of capitalism and that the law
often constituted an instrument of class domination. Law was an important
component of the superstructure of institutions and the ideology created by the
ruling class to further its own interests.

While the seeds of a more critical analysis of law were thus planted by Marx
and Engels, the disciplines of sociology and criminology were dominated from
the early 1900s to the 1960s by the structural-functional and liberal-pluralist
traditions. Criminology was primarily concerned with the causes of criminal
behaviour, with attempts to explain crime through the delineation of various
biological, psychological, and sociological factors occupying the efforts of
most criminologists.

Beginning in the 1960s, a shift in the liberal-pluralist traditions of criminology began to occur, and criminologists began to pay attention to the fact that the
concept of criminal behaviour itself was problematic. Initially, deviancy theory
offered only an implicit critique of the consensus theories of social order by
focusing on the individual social worlds of various deviant actors, the relativity
of social rules, and the meaningful, as opposed to the pathological, nature of
the deviant act itself (Lemert, 1951). The advent of this 'labelling' perspective
in criminology marked something of a departure from objectivist perspectives which sought to explain why deviance occurred, to more subjectivist
approaches. By denying that crime and deviance are intrinsically distinct
behaviours, such theories became interested, instead, in 'the activities of individuals and groups making assertions of grievances and claims with respect to
some putative condition' (Spector and Kitsuse, 1977: 75).

Beginning with the work of Tannenbaum (1938) and Lemert (1951), then, a central concern for the study of deviance has been the delimitation of factors that affect the decisions and actions of deviance-controlling agencies, and the consequences of these decisions and actions for persons officially identified as deviants. This concern is motivated by a more general theoretical interest in the way in which discretion is manifested in the societal reaction to deviants (Becker, 1963; Chambliss and Seidman, 1971; Turk, 1969), and a methodological interest in the role of discretion in the production of crime statistics (Ditton, 1979; Kitsuse and Cicourel, 1963), for instance.

Other developments in sociology and criminology over the last three decades have led to more basic concerns about the creation of the law itself, and have directly challenged the consensus views regarding law formation. For example, group-conflict theory, associated with the work of Vold (1958), asserted that the legislative enactment of criminal law represented the triumph of a particular group over other groups. Turk (1969) expanded on these ideas, and argued that different segments of society, including both economic and cultural interests, compete to create and enforce definitions of crime. As Turk points out, however, this competition is not one between equals – some groups have a greater capacity to influence both law creation and law enforcement than do others. Although theories such as Turk's are appealing because they see social power as something not exclusively reducible to class position, they have been criticized for not adequately specifying the relationship between the dynamics of social stratification and the actual content of law.

The work of Quinney (1970, 1974) is perhaps most explicitly Marxist in its orientation in addressing the issue of law creation.[1] Quinney (1970: 16, 35) asserts that 'the criminal law describes behaviours that conflict with the interests of segments of society that have the power to shape public policy ... Law incorporates the interests of specific persons and groups; it is seldom the product of the whole society.' Further, Quinney (1974: 52) contends that

contrary to the dominant view, the state is created by the class that has the power to enforce its will on the rest of society. The state is thus a political organization created out of force and coercion. The state is established by those who desire to protect their material basis and who have the power to maintain the state. The law in capitalist society gives political recognition to powerful private interests. Moreover, the legal system is an apparatus created to secure the interests of the dominant class. Contrary to popular belief, the law is the tool of the ruling class.

Similar views have been expressed by Chambliss (1974: 37), who maintains that 'the criminal law is first and foremost a reflection of the interests and ideologies of the governing class.'

Perhaps more relevant to analyses of racial inequality in the formation of law and processing of law violators is Blalock's (1967) threat hypothesis. Blalock argues that, as the percentage of non-Whites in a particular society or jurisdiction increases, they constitute a growing political and economic threat to Whites. In Blalock's view, racial discrimination, in both its political and its economic forms, can be conceptualized as an attempt by Whites to control a threatening non-White population. This perspective would predict a positive association between the relative size of a minority population and the imposition of repressive measures by the majority to control non-Whites and protect their own privileged social position. However, as Tolnay and Beck (1992) point out in a criticism that is also relevant to instrumentalist Marxist theories more generally, tests of the threat hypothesis that focus too heavily on the relative size of the minority group risk neglecting the possibility of heterogeneity in the majority-group's attitudes towards and interests in minority groups. As will become clear in the analyses of law implementation, enforcement, and processing in later chapters of this book, the threat hypothesis is somewhat too simplistic as a means of explaining racial inequalities in Canadian law.

In general, then, the instrumentalist Marxist perspective is predicated on the assumption that the state in capitalist societies is an instrument used by the ruling class to further its own interests. While this perspective (see also Miliband, 1972; Taylor, Walton, and Young, 1973) employs a more restricted, political-economic view of power than that provided by Turk (1969), it can be seen as something of an improvement over group-conflict theory by virtue of the fact that it relates the content of law to the dynamics of social stratification. However, this form of Marxism views the law as an instrument or tool that the ruling class uses on behalf of its own interests, and critics have correctly asserted that Marxist instrumentalism reintroduces a functionalist, albeit a revised functionalist, interpretation of the law. For instance, Hinch (1983) notes that Quinney's contention that crime is defined solely in the interests of capital leads to the absurdly romantic assumption that all criminal acts are instances of resistance against capitalism.

This vision of the law as unilaterally serving the interests of the ruling class has thus been criticized by Marxian and non-Marxian theorists alike for failing to address the often contradictory nature of law, and for viewing the state as representing the interests of capital only. As Tittle (1994) notes, a key question that needs to be addressed in conflict analyses of law concerns whether only élite groups or the larger society benefits from the existence of specific laws and the imposition of sanctions on those who violate them. A growing body of historical research has demonstrated that the law has been used *against* groups holding power, and that, while the actions of the state can certainly be shown to represent particular vested interests, they also often represent more general interests.

Such criticisms led to the development of a structuralist Marxist sociology of law. This perspective opposes the instrumentalist view that the capitalist state is a pliant tool of the ruling class, and asserts that the state exercises relative autonomy in its relationship with capitalist-class members and their specific interests (Greenberg, 1981). Thus, the French structuralists' interpretations of Marx, particularly those of Althusser (1971) and Poulantzas (1973), see the law as an essential component of class formation in capitalist societies, but do not view the law as a simple reflection of the interests of any particular class. Similarly, Balbus (1977) contends that the law is relatively autonomous from the will of particular social actors and groups, and asserts that the complex structure of capitalist societies, with their various competing components, prevents one class from gaining total control of the society and imposing its will. Although the existence of law is seen as being rooted in class relations, especially class formation, structuralists argue that its content is not necessarily controlled by a single, dominating class.

Structuralist Marxists assert that the state best serves the interests of capital by remaining relatively aloof from any one faction or class – in short, the state maintains relative autonomy. Structuralists further maintain that the content of substantive law may routinely favour the interests of the working class over capitalists, because, in the long run, such legislation is functional for the capitalist system. This perspective asserts that 'correspondences' among the state, law, and economy cannot be explained by examining individual actors exclusively, since these spheres are linked by structural connections. Thus, Poulantzas (1973) claims that the state is neither an instrument nor a tool; it must be understood, not as a unified 'thing,' but as a relation. By this Poulantzas means that, through the state, different relations in society are organized into a definite system of power. Most important for Poulantzas, the state is the arena where popular consent for specific laws is organized – in particular, the consent of the dominated classes to the continuity and legitimacy of the dominant.

These structuralist Marxist perspectives are not without their own flaws, however. Critics (Greenberg, 1981; Hinch, 1992) have pointed out that such approaches do not provide a full understanding of how real people create and sustain social systems, and that, by placing an undue emphasis on the capitalist system, structuralist arguments lose contact with the real people involved in the struggle over law. Other critics (Beirne, 1979; Spitzer, 1983) have noted that the functionalist 'system needs' explanations of structural Marxists, like functionalist reasoning in general, are tautological and much too vague. Structuralist analyses do not adequately explain why the overall and long-term interests of the capitalist class are embodied in the form of law. As Samuelson (1985: 272) has argued, 'Simply, why must the capitalist class rely on the legal form in order to perpetuate capitalism?'

Attempts to address these shortcomings have led to a focus on the mechanisms by which the state produces conformity and ideological consensus. Much of this theory draws on Gramsci's (1971; as cited in Jessop, 1982: 148) concept of hegemony, which he defined as follows: 'Hegemony involves the successful mobilization and reproduction of the "active consent" of dominated groups by the ruling class through their exercise of intellectual, moral, and political leadership.' As Hall et al. (1978: 202) have argued in their discussion of legal and societal responses to 'mugging' in Britain in the 1970s, 'society clearly works better when men learn to discipline themselves; or where discipline appears to be the result of spontaneous consent of each to a common and necessary political order.' In analysing law formation, then, these approaches draw attention to the importance of searching beyond the immediate influence of ruling-class groups to consider how consent over the legal order is generated in society. An important element to examine in this context is the media (Hagan, 1980), whose portrayal of crime problems and subordinate groups is essential in the production of hegemony.

Despite the diversity of positions within conflict theory and the problems associated with each, they share in common the premise that the processes of law creation and law enforcement cannot be understood apart from the structures of political and economic power in society. In combination, all of these perspectives, by problematizing the consensus model of law formation that characterized positivist and functionalist sociologies of law and crime, have pointed to the necessity of examining the interests served by law and the conflict over what its purpose and content should be.

This premise has been the point of departure for analyses of the creation of several different forms of law. For instance, Chambliss (1974), in discussing the enactment of vagrancy legislation in thirteenth-century England, argues that such laws were a legislative innovation which reflected the necessity of providing an abundance of cheap labour to England's ruling class during a period in which the previous social system of serfdom was breaking down and the pool of labour had been depleted. With respect to early juvenile delinquency legislation, Platt (1974: 398) has argued that 'the juvenile court system was part of a general movement directed towards developing a specialized labour market and industrial discipline under corporate capitalism by creating new programs of adjudication and control.' Conflict analysis has also been applied to theoretical interpretations of sexual psychopathy and prostitution laws (see Hagan, 1980), and Canadian anti-combines legislation (Goff and Reasons, 1978; Smandych, 1985), among other forms of law.

One of the most fruitful areas of inquiry for conflict theorists has been explorations of the formation of narcotics laws in North America in the early twentieth century, a topic addressed in more detail in chapter 6 of this book. The literature on narcotics legislation is particularly salient to discussions of racial inequality and law formation, as commentators on both the U.S. and the Canadian experience have emphasized the racist foundations of these laws. Here, I briefly review some of the shortcomings in this literature that are common to conflict interpretations of law formation more generally, and that indicate the need for a revised methodological approach in addressing racial inequalities in the law.

The literature pertaining to the implementation of narcotics legislation in the United States (Becker, 1963; Bonnie and Whitebread, 1974; Helmer, 1975; Musto, 1987; Reasons, 1976) has largely employed an instrumentalist Marxist interpretation, emphasizing that such laws were primarily an expression of hostile attitudes towards minority groups – in particular, Asians, Blacks, and Hispanics – who were associated with the use of drugs.

In Canada, the interpreters of narcotics legislation (Boyd, 1984; Chapman, 1979; Comack, 1985; Cook, 1969; Solomon and Madison, 1976–7; Trasov, 1962) have also generally relied on an instrumentalist Marxist perspective, stressing that certain socially and economically powerful groups within Canada were influential in generating legislation that was directed primarily against Canada's immigrant Chinese population.

While both the Canadian and American literatures on the topic of drug-law implementation have generally done an admirable job of explaining the role of social and racial conflict in the passage of this legislation, the analyses suffer from several of the common problems associated with instrumentalist Marxist approaches to law. In many cases, the literature on narcotics-law implementation has attempted to depict narcotics policies as direct reflections of consciously articulated conspiracies on the part of ruling-class groups or specific individuals. For instance, while the influence of 'moral entrepreneurs' on the passage of narcotics legislation in both the U.S. (Abel, 1980; Becker, 1963; Lindesmith, 1967) and the Canadian (Cook, 1969) contexts has been well documented, it is difficult to establish whether the influence of these individuals was direct or indirect, conditional or unconditional. More specifically, while then deputy minister of labour Mackenzie King's prominence in the debates surrounding narcotics legislation in Canada should not be underestimated (see chapter 6), it is important to emphasize that anti-opium legislation would have been enacted even without his presence, a point which is often neglected by commentators. Thus, when delineating the factors that influence the implementation of laws and their subsequent enforcement and interpretation, it is essential to examine the role of all significant actors and agencies, including the police and various government bureaucracies that had a vested interest in the process of legislative enactment and revision.

Yet another weakness in the extant literature on narcotics law is that it has rather uncritically accepted the notion that, in the United States, these laws were enacted as a measure to control Asians, Blacks, and Hispanics, whereas, in Canada, the legislation was implemented to control the immigrant Chinese. While there is indeed considerable empirical evidence to support the claim that Canadian narcotics laws were enacted in response to the Chinese use of opium, most of the studies that assert this causal link do so without providing sufficient evidence. A limited number of studies (see Boyd, 1984; Green, 1979) provide some evidence to indicate that, in the early period of the legislation, Asians were more likely to be charged for narcotics violations. However, these studies do not go beyond noting this overrepresentation of Chinese in the arrest statistics, and have generally failed to examine the actual enforcement of narcotics legislation by police and the sentencing of narcotics-law violators by the courts. As such, the apparent support of such studies for conflict interpretations of the law is incomplete.

A final problem with the Canadian literature on the implementation of narcotics law in particular, and in conflict interpretations of the law more generally, is that, for the most part, they have relied on a static view of history. The studies generally examine an abbreviated period surrounding the initial enactment of legislation, and seem to assume that it is unnecessary to explore issues beyond this limited period. As such, there is no allowance for discussions of change, both legislative and in terms of the enforcement of such legislation, and in the criminal justice system's punishment of drug-law violators. One of the primary goals of this book is to overcome the general historical myopia of conflict theory by addressing criminal justice system responses to Asians and Blacks for a seventy-year period, for a wide range of offence types in six Ontario cities. The discussion and analyses demonstrate that, while the relative lack of social power of these minority groups was certainly important in determining racially discriminatory criminal justice responses towards them, there was considerable variation across a number of relevant dimensions, including the type of offence, where and against whom offences were committed, and the prevailing societal views on racial issues. The analyses thus call into question a strict conflict-theory interpretation of racism in the adminstration of justice, and underline the importance of examining contextual issues.

However, before presenting these findings, it is necessary to review the literature on minority-group crime and racial differences in criminal sentencing, as this will serve to inform the interpretation of findings that appear in chapters 6 and 7.

Review of Sentencing Literature

Obviously, judicial decisions are not made uniformly. Decisions are made according to a host of extra-legal factors, including the age of the offender, his race, and social class. Perhaps the most obvious example of judicial discretion occurs in the handling of cases of persons from minority groups. Negroes, in comparison to whites, are convicted with lesser evidence and sentenced to more severe punishments. (Quinney, 1970: 141–2)

Much of the impetus for studies of criminal sentencing has arisen from concerns, primarily expressed by conflict theorists, regarding the differential treatment of Blacks and Whites by the criminal justice system in the United States. In general, conflict theory explains racial disparities in the administration of justice as products of broader patterns of social, economic, and political inequality. Thus, the overrepresentation of members of racial-minority groups in arrest, prosecution, and imprisonment is both the product of these broader inequalities and an expression of prejudice against minority groups.

There have been numerous studies in this genre that provide often conflicting results. Several studies have found that the race of offenders affects sentencing outcomes – that is, Blacks are sentenced more severely than Whites (Clarke and Koch, 1976; Garfinkel, 1949; E. Johnson, 1957; G. Johnson, 1941; Kelly, 1976; Lizotte, 1978; Sellin, 1928; 1935; Unnever, Frazier, and Henretta, 1980). However, other studies have found somewhat reduced effects, or even contradictory results, when legal variables are controlled for (Bernstein, Kelly, and Doyle, 1977; Bullock, 1961; Burke and Turk, 1975; Gibson, 1978; Green, 1961, 1964; Hagan and Bumiller, 1983; Kleck, 1981; Levin, 1972; Spohn, Gruhl, and Welch, 1981–2). Research from U.S. jurisdictions has also demonstrated that Hispanics are especially vulnerable to conviction for certain offences and receive harsher sentences than do other offenders (Lemert and Rosberg, 1948; Moore et al., 1978; Sissons, 1979; Unnever, 1982). Overall, however, the empirical evidence regarding the effect of race on the sentencing of convicted offenders is, at best, contradictory. As Zatz (1984: 147–8) argues, 'the sum of our knowledge is that for some offences, in some jurisdictions, controlling for some legal and extra-legal factors, at some historical points, and using some methodologies, some groups are differentially treated.'

The inability to establish unequivocally the effects of racial variables on sentencing outcomes has been attributed to methodological shortcomings in the extant studies (Hagan and Bumiller, 1983; Kleck, 1981) and to the neglect of a variety of contextual factors that are important to consider in sentencing. While there certainly have been methodological problems in several of the sentencing studies, Hawkins (1987) argues that the lack of consensus regarding the impact of race stems as much from a lack of theoretical clarity as from the methodological problems identified in several reviews of the literature. He asserts that the work of early conflict theorists such as Quinney (1970) and Chambliss and Seidman (1971) does not support the proposition that Blacks or other minorities will receive more severe punishment than Whites for all crimes, under all conditions, and at similar levels of disproportion over time. Hawkins further argues that such anomalies can be explained through a revised and more sophisticated conflict theory which takes into account relevant contingencies such as the type of crime and the race of the offender relative to the race of the victim.

Such considerations have led researchers to address the more complex question of under what contexts, and with respect to which types of offenders and offences, the effects of race variables are most likely to manifest themselves (Myers and Talarico, 1987). Implicit in this question is the assumption that the significance of race variables is not constant, but instead varies as a function of the type of decision being made, victim/offender relationships, and time and social space (Peterson and Hagan, 1984).

Canadian and British Literature on Criminal Justice Outcomes

Similar to the situation in the United States, although perhaps not to as great an extent, Blacks are overrepresented in crime and incarceration statistics, relative to their proportion in the population, in both Britain (Hood, 1992; Hudson, 1989; McConville and Baldwin, 1982; Reiner, 1989; Walker, 1983) and Canada (Nova Scotia, 1989; Ontario, 1995). Although as mentioned above, there is an extensive literature on the differential treatment of minority groups in the U.S. criminal justice system, there is comparatively little systematic research on the British and Canadian experiences. This lack of research in Canada is attributable at least in part to an underlying belief that Canada is a kinder and gentler nation with respect to a number of issues; this notion includes the country's social welfare system and extends to the idea that Canada has historically not been overly severe in its treatment of minority groups in society in general, or in its criminal justice system in particular. For example, one of the most thorough historical accounts of Black experiences in Canada argues that Blacks 'were punished in no harsher a manner than any other criminals' (Winks, 1971: 251).

A second, and possibly more important, reason for this lack of attention to racial disparities in the Canadian criminal justice system is the absence of sufficient data that would allow researchers to explore this issue. Despite recent debates surrounding the collection of information on the race of criminal offenders (Gabor, 1994; Hatt, 1994; Johnston, 1994; Roberts, 1994), Canada has not collected national sentencing data since 1973, and information on the race of offenders as a variable in the data collected was removed well before that. Although there are a considerable number of studies on the police and criminal-court treatment of aboriginal persons (Alberta, 1991; Griffiths and Verdun-Jones, 1994; Manitoba, 1991; Nova Scotia, 1989; Schissel, 1993), on the sentencing of minority-group narcotics offenders for the period from 1908 to 1960 (Mosher, 1992; Mosher and Hagan, 1994), on public-order offenders for the period from 1890 to 1930 (Mosher, 1996), and, more recently, on the treatment of minority-group offenders in the province of Ontario (Ontario, 1995), research on the impact of racial characteristics on criminal justice outcomes in Canada is almost embarrassingly sparse.

There is little doubt from the rather limited evidence that exists, however, that racism in the administration of justice in Canada is widespread and has existed throughout Canada's history. Studies focusing on the history of the Canadian criminal justice system have provided evidence of discriminatory enforcement practices against minority groups on the part of the police, particularly with respect to morals offences. For example, Fingard's (1984) research on prostitution in Halifax in the late nineteenth century reveals that Black women were vastly overrepresented among the population of convicted prostitutes in that city. While Blacks constituted only 3 per cent of the recorded population in Halifax in the 1860s, 40 per cent of the prostitutes arrested were Black. Bedford's (1981) study of prostitution in Calgary between 1905 and 1914 similarly indicated discrimination against Blacks in the enforcement of prostitution laws and in the sentencing of offenders in that city. Backhouse's (1985) research on prostitution in nineteenth-century Toronto also points to the overrepresentation of Blacks in arrest statistics.

Daniel Hill's (1960) PhD thesis, which focused on Black life in Toronto in the 1950s, does not deal extensively with the issue of Black crime, and justice system reactions to it. However, he does present several anecdotal examples of Blacks being mistreated by the Toronto police. For example, in his presentation of a case-study of a Black male he refers to as 'Joey,' Hill reveals that this individual was apprehended by the police at a restaurant while in the company of a White woman. The police, who apparently believed Joey was a pimp, took him to the station and 'beat him across the room and back again,' referring to him as a 'damned nigger' and 'black bastard' (p. 403).

Weaver's (1995) historical analysis of crime and courts in Hamilton indicates that the police in that city believed that racial-minority groups were inclined to engage in certain types of criminal behaviour, in particular, morals offences.[2] Suggesting that 'racial prejudice was rampant among the police,' Weaver indicates that the Hamilton police 'chose routes of least resistance and hauled in members of visible but marginal groups,' in enforcing morals legislation, which resulted in a large number of arrests of 'Afro-American' prostitutes, and 'an extraordinary number of Chinese for gambling' (p. 116).

More contemporary analyses have also provided evidence of discrimination in Canada's criminal justice system. A study of court outcomes in the province of Nova Scotia, for instance, found that sentencing patterns were associated with the defendant's race, even when restricted to first offenders charged with summary-conviction offences (Renner and Warner, 1981). While not one Black first offender in Renner and Warner's sample received a discharge, Whites received discharges in 23 per cent of the cases. However, these findings should be treated with caution, as there were only twenty-eight Black defendants in the sample, and, in the authors' multiple-regression analysis of sentencing, race failed to emerge as a significant predictor of sentence.

Studies conducted for the royal commission on the Donald Marshall case (Nova Scotia, 1989) also demonstrated disproportional lenience in the treatment of White offenders. Among a sample of 177 offenders receiving theft convictions, including 51 Blacks and 126 non-Blacks, 11.1 per cent of the Whites received an absolute discharge, whereas none of the Blacks did. In addition, 15.7 per cent of Blacks received a conditional discharge, while, among Whites, the percentage granted the same disposition was 27. Despite these findings, the Nova Scotia commission was concerned about reliability issues connected to the small sample size of the study, and funded a second study on court outcomes for Blacks. This study examined cases involving 221 males, 22 per cent of them Black, convicted of assault in 1987–8 in the Halifax–Dartmouth area. While Blacks in this study were more likely to be incarcerated for assault than non-Blacks, the relationship between sentence severity and race was not statistically significant, and was substantially reduced when other legal factors such as prior convictions and the extent of injury suffered by the victim were taken into account. Donald Clairmont, author of the assault study, suggested that, although conclusions of racial bias in the criminal justice system were not warranted on the basis of these findings, the possibility of such bias should not be ruled out. Clairmont noted that studies employing larger sample sizes, using different methodologies, and focusing on decision points at different stages of the criminal justice system would allow for a more detailed analysis of the impact of race on criminal justice system outcomes.

This research has shown that the race impact on sentencing either directly or indirectly is quite weak ... More attention has to be given to the laying of charges itself, stays of prosecution, discharges overall, and implicit understandings and expectations of Blacks, lawyers, and court officials. Racism in a system of formal rationality cannot be but subtle and cumulative. Statistical analyses of the sort done here may be too blunt a tool to capture this well. (Nova Scotia, 1989: 191)

A more recent examination of the treatment of Black offenders in Ontario's criminal justice system (Ontario, 1995) concluded that there was widespread discrimination against Blacks. From 1986 to 1993, the number of Blacks imprisoned in the province increased by 204 per cent, compared with a 23 per cent increase for Whites, and, while Blacks comprised only 3 per cent of Ontario's population, they accounted for 15 per cent of the prison population. In addition, a survey of youth found that nearly half of Blacks between the ages of eighteen and twenty-four were stopped at least twice by the police in the two years prior to the survey, compared with fewer than a quarter of White youths. Analysis of police and bail decisions found that the proportion of accused Whites released by the police was significantly greater than that of accused Blacks.

While the empirical evidence regarding racial discrimination against Blacks in the Canadian criminal justice system is certainly not extensive, the extant data and commentary suggest that there is little doubt that racial bias exists.

Britain

Although Blacks are overrepresented in Britain's criminal justice system, as has been the case in Canada scholarly attention to the issue was limited until quite recently. In addition, there is some dispute regarding the very existence of discrimination against Blacks in the British system (Crowe and Cove, 1984; Halevy, 1995). In an early commentary on the British situation, McConville and Baldwin (1982) noted that as of 1982 no empirical research had been conducted into the relationship between the race of offender and severity of sentence received. Their study of courts in Birmingham and London found no support for the proposition that Black defendants were sentenced more severely than Whites, but McConville and Baldwin noted that it should not be assumed that racism did not exist at other stages in the criminal justice process, such as policing, arrest patterns, bail status, and jury selection.

Monica Walker (1983) also noted the lack of attention to racial issues in British criminal justice studies, and asserted that this inattention was at least in part attributable to inadequacies in the available data. Walker's own research examined the outcome of London court prosecutions for males aged fourteen to six-teen, and found that, of those prosecuted, relatively more Blacks had their cases dismissed without trial owing to insufficient evidence. Walker interpreted this finding as indicative of a tendency on the part of London police to more readily arrest and prosecute Black people. However, when convicted, a higher propor-tion of Blacks were given a custodial sentence.

In a more recent British study, Hudson (1989) examined courts in the greater London area, and found that, for offences against the person, race had a direct effect on sentencing. Blacks were more likely to receive custodial sentences in circumstances in which Whites would receive non-custodial outcomes. How-ever, for very serious offences, the gravity of the offence exerted the strongest effect on sentencing. Hudson also found that those boroughs which produced the highest custody rates also had the greatest concentrations of ethnic-minority groups – in particular, Black residents.

In a 1992 study of approximately 1,500 convicted minority-group offenders sentenced in five British courts, Hood (1992) suggested that 80 per cent of the overrepresentation of Black male offenders in the prison population was attrib-utable to legal factors such as the type and circumstances of the offences of which they were convicted. The remaining 20 per cent of the overrepresentation was apparently the result of differential treatment and other factors such as the tendency of Blacks to plead not guilty.[3]

In short, the limited number of Canadian and British studies on race and crimi-nal justice indicate that, while racial disparities in the processing of offenders may exist, they do not appear for all offence types, at all stages of the system, and in all sociohistorical contexts. Given the paucity of data and commentary on the issue of racial biases in the Canadian and British criminal justice sys-tems, I will now move on to a more detailed consideration of the U.S. literature on race, crime, and criminal justice. I begin with a discussion of the literature published from the early to middle 1900s, in part because this is the historical period with which I am most concerned in the analyses of sentencing that appear in chapters 6 and 7, but also because this literature, despite some of its methodological shortcomings, offers significant insights into the dynamics of the race-and-crime equation. I then proceed to a discussion of the importance of considering the various contexts of criminal justice system outcomes in exam-ining racial disparities – including the context of the decision itself, victim–offender relationships, and social and historical contexts. Although this litera-ture is based on data collected in the United States, it will be clear that many of the arguments are applicable to explanations of the Canadian historical experi-ence with respect to racial issues in criminal justice.

Early Discussions of Minority-Group Crime and
Criminal Justice Outcomes in the United States

The principal thing is always ... the stifling of the primitive, wild instincts. Even if he [the Negro] is dressed in the European way and has accepted the customs of modern culture, all too often there remains in him the lack of respect for the life of his fellow men, the disregard for life which all wild people have in common. To them, a murder appears as an ordinary occurrence, even a glorious occurrence when it is inspired by feelings of vengeance. This mentality is furthered in the Negro by his scorn of white fellow citizens, and by bestial sexual impulses. (Lombroso, 1899; as quoted in Bonger, 1943, pp. 48–9)

While early criminologists such as Lombroso pointed to certain unidentified biological differences that allegedly contributed to higher rates of Black crime, others such as Root (1927) suggested that the 'Negro criminal' was the victim of a 'vicious cycle' of social, biological, and economic causes. As Root asserted, 'forced to live in discarded houses of the dominant race, restricted in employment and social opportunity, the Negro is forced daily to feel inferiority and humiliation in a thousand ways. All this must be given consideration in judging his status in the criminal world' (p. 46). Similarly, in Sutherland's 1934 textbook, *Criminology* (as cited in Hawkins, 1995: 111), sections on immigration and race were included in the discussion of the causes and correlates of criminal behaviour. Importantly, Sutherland urged caution in concluding that the actual rate of crime among Blacks was greater than that among Whites. 'These statistics reflect a bias against the Negro because of the prejudice against that race ... even if the statistics are completely reliable, they involve a comparison of groups that differ economically, educationally, and socially, as well as racially.'

Willem Bonger (1943) was another early criminologist who identified social-structural factors as being the key to understanding differential rates of Black and White crime. While accepting some of the prevailing stereotypes regarding Blacks, including their 'sensuality, tendency to servile imitation, childlike nature, lower level of intelligence, lack of initiative, horror of solitude, instability, inordinate love of singing and dancing, and unconquerable taste for glitter and ornament,' Bonger noted that 'the circumstances in which Negroes live are strongly conducive to crime' (p. 45). Similarly, Moses (1947), in a comparison of Black and White crime rates in four areas of Baltimore, asserted that poverty played an important role in the genesis of Black crime. This poverty was pervasive in Black communities, and manifested itself in bad housing, overcrowding, restricted areas of settlement, and low levels of employment.

One of the most extensive and insightful studies of Blacks' social and economic situation in the United States was Gunnar Myrdal's (1944) *An American Dilemma*. Myrdal, a Swedish social economist who had been commissioned by the Carnegie Foundation to conduct studies on the Black experience in the United States, noted that American Whites believed that Blacks were somehow innately addicted to crime, a presumption that he argued was connected to two more basic beliefs: first, the notion that Blacks could not control their passions, and hence were prone to commit crimes against the person; second, the idea that Blacks were lacking in important moral qualities, which led them to commit crimes against property.

While at least some early criminologists thus emphasized the importance of social-structural factors in explaining Black crime rates, another important contributor to the allegedly higher levels of crime among Blacks were biases on the part of criminal justice system officials. However, there was certainly no consensus in the early literature that minority-group offenders were universally treated more severely.

In the early part of the twentieth century, writers such as Kavanaugh (1928) and Murphy (1909) suggested that Blacks were treated in a disproportionately *lenient* fashion by the criminal justice system. In asserting that many crimes committed by Blacks were often ignored by police officers, Murphy noted that 'the world hears broadly and repeatedly of the cases of injustice, it hears little of those more frequent instances in which the weaknesses of a child-race are accorded only amused indifference by their stronger neighbors' (p. 105). Myrdal (1944) similarly acknowledged the possibility of lenience towards Blacks, but offered a different interpretation, focusing on the importance of economic issues. He noted that, when White employers were experiencing labour shortages, they would inform local sheriffs, who would suddenly begin to enforce vague laws such as those against vagrancy, particularly against Blacks. These White employers would then appear in court and 'make a deal with the Negro defendant to pay his fine if he will work a certain number of days' (p. 551). Johnson (1941: 102) also connected pardons and lenient sentences for Black offenders to the economic interests of powerful Whites. 'He receives a light sentence for manslaughter, and he has scarcely begun to serve this when his employer obtains his parole because he is anxious not to lose the Negro's services.'

Despite arguments that Blacks were treated more leniently by the criminal justice system, however, individual cases of injustice towards Blacks were sometimes revealed in academic and popular-media sources. For example, the *Negro Yearbook* (1931–2) reported on the case of a Black woman in Richmond, Virginia, who was convicted on three counts of forgery and sentenced to thirty years in prison, despite the fact that the total amount of money secured through the forgery was $185. The same source reported on a Black male in Atlanta, Georgia, who stole a watch and fifty-five cents and was given a sentence of from twelve to sixteen years' imprisonment.

In addition to such anecdotal revelations of injustice, the relatively more sophisticated empirical analyses of Blacks' treatment by the criminal justice system generally concluded that the system was racially biased. In an interesting interpretation of this bias, the Black scholar Monroe Work (1913) argued that it was not necessarily the case that Blacks were treated overly severely by the system, but rather that Whites were dealt with in an overly lenient fashion. Citing the address of an Alabama judge to the Southern Sociological Congress, Work noted:

It is not that the Negro fails to get justice before the courts in the trial of the specific indictment of him, but too often it is the case that the native white man escapes it. It must be poor consolation to the foreign-born, the Indian, the Negro, and the ignorant generally to learn that the law has punished only the guilty of their class or race, and to see that the guilty of the class, fortunate by reason of wealth, learning, or color, are not so punished for like crime. (p. 79)

While Work's arguments regarding a positive bias on the part of the justice system towards Whites are indeed intriguing, and are of assistance in explaining at least part of the racial differences in court outcomes (see chapter 6) that occurred in Ontario in between 1892 to 1961, later analyses were more likely to identify negative bias towards Blacks as the most important factor in explaining their disproportionately severe treatment. For instance, Steiner and Brown's (1927) study of more than 1,500 chain-gang prisoners in North Carolina concluded that there was a much higher percentage of Blacks serving comparatively short sentences, and that at least part of this difference was attributable to the inability of Blacks to pay fines. However, these authors also noted that Blacks were more than twice as likely to be serving sentences greater than three years, 'suggesting that justice is not blind to the color of a man's skin' (p. 59).

Thorsten Sellin (1935: 214), while asserting that 'the Negro is regarded as inferior in native intelligence and prone to certain types of crime, especially sexual crimes,' pointed to a 'decided discrimination against the Negro on the part of agencies of criminal justice' that contributed to the higher crime rates of Blacks. Although his rather unsophisticated methodology did not allow him to statistically control for the effects of other important variables such as prior record and seriousness of offence, Sellin found that approximately 31 per cent of Blacks, compared with approximately 15 per cent of Whites, were sentenced to imprisonment in Detroit courts.

In a second study, Sellin (1935), using data on U.S. federal prison populations, noted that the rate of imprisonment for Blacks was approximately ten times that of foreign-born Whites, and three times that of native-born Whites. In one of the first explicit identifications of the importance of contextual factors in criminal justice decision making, Sellin attributed these disparities to geographic differences in the administration of justice. He noted that prejudice towards Blacks was greater in the northern United States than in the South, and argued that the extant caste system in the South led to greater paternalism in dealing with Black offenders. In the northern states, Blacks were perceived as economic competitors and 'outsiders,' and were thus dealt with more severely by the criminal courts.

Johnson's (1941) study constitutes a significant contribution to the early literature on race, crime, and criminal justice. As did several of the other authors of this period, Johnson acknowledged that Blacks had higher rates of crime, but identified several social factors that contributed to these rates. For instance, referring to 'scapegoats and frameups,' Johnson noted that it was not uncommon for White men to blacken their faces before committing crimes. With respect to sexual offences committed by Blacks, Johnson claimed that 'a white woman may try to avoid the consequences of sexual delinquency by raising the cry that she has been raped by a Negro ... a neurotic woman may "imagine" that she has been raped by a Negro, or she may interpret the same innocent action as an insult or "attack" by a Negro' (p. 96). Johnson also asserted that many acts which would not be considered crimes if committed by Whites were seen in a different light when committed by Blacks. Included in this category were such acts as 'forgetting to say mister' to a White man, 'looking at' a White woman, entering the wrong waiting room, 'sassing' the landlord, disputing a White man's word, and taking the wrong seat on a bus or streetcar (p. 95).

This brief review of the early literature on race, crime, and criminal justice thus indicates that several commentators were aware of the impact of social-structural factors on minority-crime rates, and expressed concern regarding the influence of criminal justice system biases on these rates. Several of the other important points these early authors made with respect to explanations of criminal justice system biases are addressed in the discussion of the contexts of criminal justice decision making that follows.

Decision as Context

The literature on criminal justice outcomes has pointed out that racial discrimination is more likely to occur in the earlier stages of the criminal justice system, for example, in police decision making, than in the later stages. There are, of course, strong theoretical reasons to predict that bias is more likely to occur at the police stage of processing than at the level of the court. First, a relatively large amount of discretion is endemic to police work, and action must often be taken without adequate knowledge of the relevant facts. As Skolnick (1975) argues, police work constitutes the most secluded part of an already secluded criminal justice system, and therefore offers the greatest opportunity for arbitrary behaviour. Goldstein (1960) notes that many police decisions have low visibility, and, as such, few of these decisions are subject to legal review. As Ericson and Baranek (1982: 23) suggest, 'the ordering of the criminal process is very much under the influence of the police because their versions of the truth are routinely accepted by the other criminal-control agents, who usually have neither the time nor the resources to consider competing truths.' The importance of the above considerations, as Hagan and Zatz (1985: 106) argue, is that

the low visibility of street-level policing contrasts with the more formal and symbolic character of later stages in the process. [Our] point is that the environment of the courtroom may be more conducive to equality and due process than the environment of the street ... The implication is that the police are most likely to play fast and loose with the law, prosecutors less so, and the courts least of all.

There is an abundance of evidence, dating back to the earliest studies of police, documenting racial prejudice as a prominent aspect of street-level policing. For example, Sellin (1928: 52) argued that the actual amount of Black crime was unimportant compared with the belief that people, including law enforcement officials, held that Blacks had higher rates of crime. 'Regardless of its basis in reality, it is a significant element in the creation of racial attitudes toward [him] on the part of the white.'

Further evidence of police bias towards minority groups was provided by Hopkins (1931: 339), who, in a statement that applies to Canadian policing in the early 1900s, asserted that 'many years ago the American policeman undertook to make enemies of the vast numbers of foreign-born people whom we were inviting to our shores ... Perhaps nothing is more directly responsible for the violent character of much present-day crime than the lawless police work that was visited upon the immigrant in the past.'

The Chicago Commission on Race Relations (1922: 345) also observed that police officers in that city shared in the general public opinion that Blacks were more criminally inclined than Whites, 'and also [felt] that there is little risk of trouble in arresting Negroes, while greater care must be exercised in arresting Whites.' Even more relevant to considerations of the Canadian situation, where

Blacks were far fewer numerically and proportionally, the Chicago Commission on Race Relations suggested that Blacks were more easily identified and more likely to be arrested, with the knowledge of the criminal's colour making it possible for the police to limit their search to what in some communities constituted a very small group.

Myrdal (1944: 526) reiterated these claims of police bias towards minority groups, noting that, in most northern communities of the United States, Blacks were more likely than Whites to be arrested 'under any suspicious circumstances.' Myrdal further asserted that 'probably no group of whites in America have a lower opinion of the Negro people and are more fixed in their views than [Southern] policemen. To most of them no Negro woman knows what virtue is ... and practically every Negro man is a criminal' (p. 540).

Lukas (1945: 273) also focused on police bias in explaining higher rates of Black crime, asserting that police activity was 'greater in relation to the Negro than to the white. Everywhere, in the North and in the South, police arrest Negroes on slight suspicion, and do not hesitate to use force against Negroes.' Johnson (1941), referring to the police 'custom' of arresting Blacks on slight suspicion or of staging mass 'round-ups' of Blacks, similarly asserted that Blacks were more exposed to the police misuse of power than any other group.

More recent studies of criminal justice in the United States have presented analogous arguments. For instance, Irwin (1985) argues that a tendency on the part of the police to characterize lower-class persons and Blacks as disreputable and dangerous may lead them to watch and arrest such individuals more frequently than is warranted on the basis of their actual criminal involvement. Although focusing more explicitly on socio-economic status as opposed to race, Sampson (1986) provides further evidence of police bias in arrest decisions. In a study examining the police processing of juveniles in the Seattle, Washington, area, Sampson found that for the bulk of offences committed by juveniles, official police records and referrals to court are structured, not simply by the act itself, but by the socio-economic and situational contexts of such acts.

Supporting the view that much of the difference between minority and Whites crime rates is the product of discrimination on the part of police is the fact that the disproportion tends to be greatest in offence categories that are maximally open to police discrimination and stereotyping, such as public-order and drug offences (Reiner, 1989) a topic addressed in more detail in the analysis of drug and public-order crimes in chapter 6.

In short, although the literature on criminal justice outcomes generally indicates that the effects of offender characteristics such as race on sentence length may not be particularly large in magnitude, it shows that these characteristics possibly affect outcome decisions indirectly through bias in police practices.

In relation to the importance of the context of criminal justice outcome decisions, it is essential to note that the initial court decision of whether to find an offender guilty is separate from the decision regarding the type and duration of punishment imposed. The implication of this consideration is that data sets drawn at later stages of the criminal justice system may produce biased estimates of the influence of independent variables, including that of race, on sentencing; this may, in fact, be one reason why the measured influence of race on sentencing is small (Hagan and Bumiller, 1983).

Bernstein, Kelly, and Doyle (1977) provide an example of the importance of considering the type of court decision as a contextual variable in research on criminal justice outcomes. In their analysis of 1,213 male arraignments in New York for the years 1974 and 1975, the authors first examined as a dependent variable the likelihood of an individual's case being dismissed. They found that cases were more likely to be dismissed if: (1) the defendant's most serious arrest charge was a burglary or assault; (2) the defendant's total number of arrest charges was higher; (3) the defendant was detained in jail while awaiting his final disposition; and (4) the defendant's felony charge was reduced to a misdemeanour at the latest possible opportunity. Bernstein, Kelly, and Doyle found that extralegal factors such as age, education, employment stability, marital status, and race explained more variance in sentencing-severity decisions than in prosecution and adjudication decisions, although the effects of these variables on sentence length were not great. In the analyses of court outcomes that follow in chapters 6 and 7, separate analyses of the conviction and sentence-length decision are conducted to take into account the fact that the racial characteristics of offenders may have an impact on conviction and sentence-length decisions differentially.

Victim/Offender Relationships

The importance of context in explaining racial differences in criminal justice outcomes also extends to victim/offender relationships. Specifically, the sentencing literature suggests that Black offenders who victimize Whites in property and violent crimes may be treated more severely by the courts than Blacks who victimize other Blacks.

Sellin (1928) was one of the first commentators to allude to the fact that police did not devote as much attention to offences committed by Blacks against Blacks. Myrdal (1944: 969) reinforced the contention that intraracial crime was viewed differently by the criminal justice system, suggesting that, especially in the American South, Black-against-Black crime was handled by White policemen by 'letting [the Negro] off with a warning or a beating, and the court will let him off with a warning or a relatively light sentence.' Conversely, when offences were committed by Blacks against Whites, Blacks 'often [found] the presumptions of the courts against them, and there [was] a tendency to sentence them to a higher penalty than if they had committed the same offence against Negroes' (p. 526).

In a similar vein, Lukas (1945), writing in the *Journal of Criminal Law and Criminology*, referred to the frequency of intraracial homicides in the American South, and asserted that the high rates were attributable to the fact that 'life was cheap' in Southern Black communities, because the courts dealt with Black-on-Black crime so leniently. Similar observations were made by Moton (1929) and were also referred to by Garfinkel (1949), who, in recounting a conversation he had with a court official, noted that 'no [Guildford County] jury would give a nigger the chair for killing another nigger. It just doesn't seem worth it' (p. 380). Or, consider the comments of a chief of police in a southern U.S. jurisdiction in the early 1900s: 'We have three classes of homicide. If a nigger kills a white man, that's murder. If a white man kills a nigger, that's justifiable homicide. If a nigger kills another nigger, that's one less nigger' (as quoted in Friedman, 1993: 375).

There was thus an implicit realization on the part of several theorists that the victim/offender relationship was important to consider in assessing the differential treatment of Black and White offenders. The salience of the victim/offender dyad was stated most explicitly by Johnson (1941: 98), who contended that differentials in the treatment of Black offenders existed, but these were obscured by the fact that crime statistics took into account only the race of the *offender*.

If caste values and attitudes mean anything at all, they mean that offences by or against Negroes will be defined not so much in terms of their intrinsic seriousness as in terms of their importance in the eyes of the dominant group. Obviously the murder of a white person by a Negro and the murder of a Negro by a Negro are not at all the same kind of murder from the standpoint of the upper caste's scale of values.

Johnson was thus one of the first theorists to suggest a rank of crime seriousness based on the offender/victim dyad. He asserted that crimes would rank in seriousness from high to low, with a Black offender and White victim the most serious, a White offender and White victim being the second most serious, Black and Black third, and White and Black fourth.

While Johnson initially outlined these categories of seriousness, it was left to later commentators to explicate the theoretical basis for the hypothesized differential seriousness of crimes based on the victim/offender dyad. Thus, Spohn (1994) outlines two possible theoretical explanations for disproportional treatment based on the victim/offender dyad. The first stems from conflict theory's premise that the law is applied to maintain and reinforce the power of the dominant group and to control the behaviour of individuals who threaten that power. This explanation suggests that crimes involving Black offenders and White victims are punished most severely because they pose the greatest threat to the system of 'racially stratified state authority' (Hawkins, 1987: 226).

Spohn's (1994) second explanation for these differences emphasizes the race of the victim rather than the racial composition of the victim/offender dyad. This explanation suggests that crimes with Black victims are not viewed seriously by the criminal justice system because the lives of Black victims are devalued relative to the lives of White victims. Spohn suggests that it is possible that predominantly White jurors and judges are more able to identify with White as opposed to Black victims.

Spohn's research on the processing of violent offenders in Detroit found that Blacks who sexually assaulted Whites were incarcerated at a much higher rate than Blacks who sexually assaulted other Blacks. Eighty-six per cent of Blacks convicted of sexually assaulting Whites were sentenced to prison, compared with only 66 per cent of Blacks convicted of sexually assaulting Blacks, and 54 per cent of Whites convicted of assaulting Whites. Spohn concludes that sexual assaults involving White offenders and White victims are punished more leniently, not because crimes with White victims are deemed less serious than crimes with Black victims, but because crimes involving White offenders are regarded as less serious than crimes involving Black offenders.

Similar findings have been reported by LaFree (1980), who, analysing data for suspects charged with the commission of 'forcible sexual offences,' found that Black men who assaulted White women were charged with more serious offences and received longer sentences. Even stronger relationships between the victim/offender dyad and sentencing outcomes were found in studies focusing on rape cases in earlier periods (Partington, 1965; Wolfgang and Riedel, 1973).

These studies thus suggest that it is important to take into account the race of the victim in analysing sentencing outcomes for minority-group offenders, a practice that is followed in the analysis of court outcomes for violent and property offenders that appears in chapter 7.

Spatial/Social and Temporal Context

The contextual issue of central importance to the court-outcome analyses appearing in chapters 6 and 7 of this book involves context as a spatial/social and temporal variable. As Levin (1977) points out, courts are part of the community, and what they do is in part a function of what the community expects them to do and whom it supplies to staff them. In order to properly understand the operations of courts, then, it is necessary to locate them in a larger context – to see them not only as systems which have their own internal dynamics, but also as institutions which are responding to their environments (Feeley, 1979).

The first sentencing studies to give attention to the issue of context as a spatial/social variable, albeit not in a direct and conscious sense, were Sellin's (1928, 1935) early studies of the impact of race on sentencing. In his 1935 study, Sellin focused on the length of sentence received by native-born Whites, foreign-born Whites, and Blacks, for ten different offence categories. He concluded that, in states employing determinate sentences, Blacks received a longer sentence than Whites in only three of the ten offence categories. In states employing indeterminate sentencing, however, Black offenders received longer minimum sentences for all types of offences, with the exception of homicide, and longer maximum sentences for all offences with the exception of assault and burglary.

Although it has not commonly been recognized as such in the literature, another early sentencing study that took contextual variables into account was Hood's (1962) examination of magistrates' sentencing practices in Britain for the years 1951 to 1954. Hood concluded that imprisonment policies of magistrates were related to the social characteristics of the areas they served, the social constitution of the bench, and its particular view of the crime problem.

This focus on social context has continued in contemporary sentencing studies. For instance, Kleck (1981), in an assessment of all scholarly empirical studies of race and criminal sentencing conducted prior to 1980, points to the importance of social and temporal context in interpreting the frequently conflicting results of sentencing studies. Kleck first addresses studies of capital punishment, and asserts that every study consistently indicating discrimination towards Blacks was based on older data from the southern United States, and that all of these studies failed to control for the prior criminal record of the accused, for the defendant's social class or income, or for the distinction between felony and non-felony killings. Kleck argues that 'the evidence considered as a whole indicates no racial discrimination in the use of the death penalty for murder outside the South, and even for the South the empirical support for the discrimination hypothesis is weak' (p. 788). Regarding the use of capital punishment for rape offences, Kleck argues that discrimination in such cases is of historical significance with respect to capital punishment in the South, but has limited relevance to current debates over capital punishment.

From his own analysis of execution rates for Blacks and Whites over the period from 1930 to 1967, Kleck argues that 'Blacks in the United States, both in the recent and more remote past, have been less likely than whites to receive a death sentence if they committed a homicide' (p. 799).

Kleck provides a number of possible explanations for the more lenient treatment of Blacks. Similar to the previously addressed arguments of Spohn (1994), Kleck points out that the most plausible explanation of the lenient treatment of Black offenders who commit predominantly intraracial crimes is that crimes with Black victims are considered by the criminal justice system to be less serious offences, representing less of a threat to the community than crimes with White victims. Kleck also provides alternative explanations, including 'white paternalism,' and what he refers to as 'sociology-based tolerance,' or the idea that, since Blacks commit crimes because of their disadvantaged socio-economic position, they are deemed to be not as responsible for their acts as are Whites (p. 800). Clearly, the social context of sentencing is central to Kleck's analysis.

In another study underlining the importance of social and historical context, Peterson and Hagan (1984) analysed the treatment of drug offenders sentenced between 1963 and 1976 in New York. The authors focus on three temporal/social contexts: 1963–8, 1968–73, and 1974–6. Peterson and Hagan note that, historically, American drug-prohibition ideology portrayed minorities as the villains behind the drug problem. However, with increases in drug use by middle-class youth beginning in the 1960s, a shift in attitudes towards drugs occurred. 'Big dealers' became the new villains, and both middle-class youth and non-Whites were reconceived as victims. As a result of this change in philosophy, there was a peak in the punitive treatment of big dealers and the lenient treatment of non-White offenders between 1969 and 1973. Peterson and Hagan note that, 'while there may be a trend toward equality in American criminal sentencing, there are also patterns of differential leniency and severity that can only be revealed when changing conceptions of race and crime are taken into account' (p. 56).

Myers (1989) analysed the sentencing of drug offenders in the state of Georgia for the years 1977 to 1985, and found that Blacks were consistently more likely to be incarcerated than Whites, and that this difference was particularly pronounced for Black drug traffickers, who were 25 per cent more likely to be imprisoned. These results are thus consistent with those of Peterson and Hagan (1984), who found that differential treatment by race was dependent simultaneously on both the nature of the offence and the political and social climate surrounding drug use.

Pruitt and Wilson (1983) used a random sample of 1,512 criminal defendants charged with armed robbery or burglary in the courts of Milwaukee between

1967 and 1977. They found that race had an independent effect on sentencing outcomes at time 1 (1967–8), when Blacks were both more likely to go to prison and to serve longer sentences if sentenced to prison. However, in the later two periods examined (1971–2 and 1976–7), being Black had no significant effect on the chances of going to prison or on the length of prison term. Pruitt and Wilson assert that the reduced impact of race is attributable to changes in judicial ideology, a greater bureaucratization of the prosecutorial and defence bar, and the rise of decision-making rules that reduced the effect of judicial ideology on court outcomes.

Myers and Talarico (1986) used a stratified random sample of almost 17,000 felons convicted between 1976 and 1982 in Georgia in their analysis of sentencing outcomes. Focusing on both type of sentence and sentence length as dependent variables, Myers and Talarico found evidence of lenience towards Black offenders, which was explained by 'contemporary white paternalism or in perceptions of the differential political value of crime victims' (p. 248). Myers and Talarico conclude that, for the initial decision to incarcerate, race becomes a meaningful variable only when considered in conjunction with the specific act committed by the offender and the racial composition of the community where sentencing occurred. For decisions about the length of incarceration, race is a consistently meaningful consideration, unaffected by the crime, the offender's social background, or structural aspects of the surrounding community.

Yet another important aspect of the contexts of criminal sentencing involves a consideration of rural/urban differences. Research on the effects of contextual variables such as rural or urban location has demonstrated that rural courts are more likely to discriminate against minorities in sentencing than are urban courts (Clayton, 1983; Hagan, 1977; Pope, 1975). Pope (1975) in a study of nearly 33,000 offenders sentenced in California between 1969 and 1971, found that, when type of sentence is the dependent measure, rural courts sentence Blacks more severely than they do Whites. This finding of discrimination in rural but not urban courts has a parallel in Hagan's (1977) Canadian study, where it was found that the differential treatment of Native Canadians was more pronounced in rural courts.

The literature reviewed above has identified a number of offence- and offender-related characteristics that affect criminal justice system decisions, and has underlined the importance of the consideration of social and temporal context in the analysis of these decisions. The strength of the analyses of criminal justice outcomes in Ontario courts presented in chapters 6 and 7 is that they incorporate offence-related variables, offender-related characteristics, and structural factors in examining criminal justice outcomes for a large number of offenders for a seventy-year period. The final part of this chapter outlines the methodological approaches employed in this book.

Methodology

The type of historical sociology employed in my analyses of Asians' and Blacks' experiences in Canada's legal and criminal justice systems over the period from 1892 to 1961 is informed by Weber's (1949) and Skocpol's (1984) suggestions. Weber's historical sociology, while recognizing the uniqueness of events, sought in addition to delineate certain patterns in history. The basis of Weber's comparative study and generalization was that unique and diverse actions, events, and persons might also have a great deal in common within their several classes. Similarly, Skocpol has argued that the agenda for historical sociology is to ask questions about social structure or processes that are concretely situated in time and space. Such analyses examine processes of change over time, and explain outcomes in temporal sequences; focus on the way in which individual actions and their structural contexts interact to produce both intended and unintended consequences; and highlight both the uniformity and the variation in particular social situations and patterns of change.

While my theoretical and methodological approach in analysing the experiences of Asians and Blacks in Canadian society and the Canadian legal and criminal justice systems is thus specifically guided by these notions of historical sociology, and by conflict theories of law formation, it is also influenced by more general concerns regarding the importance of a 'grounded' sociological theory. Coleman (1986: 1310), in support of a new type of 'action' theory for the social sciences, argues for theories in which large-scale macro changes in society are understood as occurring through the purposeful action of individuals:

Social theory with this kind of ground [makes] ... possible a connection between the individual and society, and it even [makes] ... possible a conception of how social systems might be shaped by human will. Perhaps most important it [makes] possible a link between positive social theory and normative social philosophy, by connecting individual interests with their realization or lack of realization.

Thus, Coleman essentially rejects sociological theories which fail to examine micro-level processes. In place of a solely macro-level explanation, Coleman is proposing an analysis in which theories begin at the macro level, move down to the micro level of individual actions, and then go back up again. This is the approach adopted in this book.

Data Sources

In the examination of the experiences of Asians and Blacks in Canada's social, legal, and criminal justice systems, I relied on a diversity of historical sources in the collection of both quantitative and qualitative data. The quantitative data on criminal offences analysed in chapters 6 and 7 were obtained from jail records for the Ontario cities of Hamilton, London, Ottawa, Toronto, Thunder Bay, and Windsor for the years 1892 to 1961. These cities were chosen because they were among the largest in the province over the period examined, and represent a reasonable geographical spread, covering central, eastern, western, and northern sections of the province. I analyse a systematic sample[4] of approximately 23,000 criminal cases from these six jurisdictions for this seventy-year period. The collection of this quantitative data involved the perusal of approximately 600 individual jail-record volumes, each one comprising, on average, some 3,000 individual criminal cases.

Jail records were chosen over court records as the former were more available and complete. Jail records were accessible for all six cities over the entire seventy-year period; this was not the case for court records. As all offenders charged under the Criminal Code in the period studied would have initially been apprehended by police and placed in a local jail before court appearance, I have confidence that, with the exception of possible coding errors, the sample is representative of apprehended criminal offenders in these six cities.[5] Furthermore, to derive a sample of criminal offenders in these six cities using court data, one would have to examine courts at several different levels, including provincial, district, and Supreme courts, as criminal cases were tried at all of these levels. The advantage of jail records is that they reported on the sentence of the accused, regardless of the court level at which the particular case was tried.

The jail records also contain information on a number of different offence- and offender-related variables that are not consistently available in court records. These variables include the offender's age, sex, marital status, race, country of birth, religious affiliation, education, occupation, number of offences charged, type of offence charged, and sentencing judge. Clearly, the measurement of these variables in the jail records will be subject to reliability and validity problems, and for several of the cases I was unable to collect information on all variables. However, there is no evidence to suggest that there were any systematic biases in the reporting of this information, and for a large proportion of the cases independent verification of these variables was possible through examination of provincial jail records and newspaper accounts of the relevant cases.

Qualitative Data

Longitudinal research of the type being conducted in this book faces the problem of applying modern interpretations to patterns that can be adequately understood only by considering information about the actions and beliefs of those responsible for generating the data. As Lempert (1990: 322) suggests, 'applying consistent interpretations to data, which is the natural way of theorizing, is itself problematic in longitudinal research because different forces generate similar patterns at different points in time or similar forces may generate different patterns.' One method of compensating for this feature of longitudinal research is to acquire what Lempert (p. 323) refers to as 'local knowledge' of the legal culture existing in any particular jurisdiction or court. In the discussions that follow in chapters 5 through 7, this local knowledge was attained through a systematic and comprehensive examination of qualitative historical data about police courts in the six cities. These data were collected primarily from local newspapers,[6] and also from annual police department reports, criminal casebooks, legislative debates, various government commissions and reports, popular magazines, and academic literature.

The tradition of newspaper reporting of crime and police-court proceedings is one that reaches back at least to 1820, when such reports first appeared in British newspapers (Harris, 1932; Surrette, 1992). North American newspapers of the late nineteenth and early twentieth centuries also devoted a great deal of attention to crime and criminal justice issues. Craven (1983) notes that the Toronto press devoted a considerable amount of space to coverage of the local police court, and a perusal of newspapers from the early to middle 1900s in the cities of Hamilton, London, Ottawa, Thunder Bay, and Windsor indicates that they were no exception. These daily reports of police-court proceedings often provided detailed information regarding a substantial proportion of the criminal cases heard by the courts in each city. This was particularly true of major crimes such as murder, but even relatively minor offences were frequently included in the reports.[7]

Owing to limitations in the availability of newspapers and incomplete coverage of all cases in newspaper sources, a systematic sampling of cases was not possible. Instead, a combination of 'typical' and 'deviant' case sampling (Patton, 1990) was applied to the newspaper materials. The first type of sampling was concerned with identifying the most common types of criminal cases that occurred in each year in each city. Names of offenders and dates of court appearance were taken from the jail records, and individual newspapers were searched for reference to these cases. The second type of sampling focused on cases that were expected to be rich in information because they differed from predominant patterns. Here, I paid particular attention to cases involving members of racial-minority groups (as identified in the jail records), women, and offenders who received disproportionately severe, or lenient, sentences.

Based on microfilm newspaper collections in the University of Toronto's Robarts Library, the Provincial Archives of Ontario, and the Metropolitan Toronto Central Reference Library, these two types of sampling produced information on several thousand criminal cases. While individual court reports commonly appeared in the first few pages of the newspapers examined and were prominently displayed with identifying headlines, in many cases these appeared in the later pages of newspapers and were not as easily located.

In several instances, the qualitative information collected included extensive details on the circumstances of arrest in individual cases, and commentaries by police officers, prosecutors, defence lawyers, and the court reporters themselves. Following Hagan's (1980: 624) call for research in the area of law and society that simultaneously demonstrates 'syntheses of description and explanation' and details 'qualitative-historical exposition with quantitative multivariate analysis,' I combine this qualitative material with quantitative data to analyse criminal justice system outcomes for racial-minority-group offenders for a variety of criminal-code offences in a way that separate use of such sources has not allowed in previous historical work.

Before proceeding to a detailed examination of the criminal justice system's treatment of Asians and Blacks, however, it is necessary to examine the disadvantaged social positions these groups occupied in Canadian society. Chapters 3 and 4, through an examination of popular and academic literature, case law, statutes, and legislative debates at the municipal, provincial, and federal levels, provide evidence of pervasive and systemic racism against Asians and Blacks in several spheres of Canadian society over the period from 1892 to 1961.

3

Asians: Immigration and Restrictive Legislation

Between Nordics and Asiatics lie differences fundamental and deep, differences in moral outlook and philosophy. Humanity may have had the same common origin back in the dim mists of the past, but all history is against the theory that races can ever revert back again to a common kind. (Hope and Earle, 1933)

Canada's early history was characterized by xenophobic attitudes towards several immigrant groups. Asians, owing to their obvious physical differences and alleged differences in moral philosophies and habits, were particularly likely to be subject to negative stereotyping and formal legislation that prevented their immigration. In addition, several laws imposed restrictions on the employment, business, and social activities of those Asians who were allowed into the country. As Peter Li (1988) notes, and as this chapter will demonstrate, 'anti-Orientalism' was common among politicians, union leaders, White workers, and employers across Canada, even though each group benefited directly or indirectly from the presence of the Chinese.

The chapter demonstrates that opposition to Asians in Canada and the array of restrictive legislation directed towards them were given justification on the basis of the economic threat they posed to White Canadian workers and the supposed moral inferiority of Asians, which was often portrayed as being rooted in their biological characteristics. After examining the debates surrounding Asian immigration that occurred in Canada in the late 1800s and early 1900s, I discuss specific non-criminal legislation that was enacted to control the existing Chinese population, particularly as manifested in provincial laws and municipal by-laws aimed at restricting Chinese businesses. While such legislation appears on the surface to be economically based, another important component of these laws was their attempt to prevent the allegedly corrupting influences of Asian males on White women.

Immigration

Although this chapter focuses on issues of Asian immigration to Canada, and chapter 4 on those of Black immigration, it is important to realize that there was a more generalized opposition to certain types of immigrants in Canada in the early 1900s. Clifford Sifton, who served as the minister of immigration in the late 1890s and early 1900s, noted in a 1922 *Maclean's* article (Sifton, 1922) that the immigrants who had entered Canada from the United States during his tenure were 'of the finest quality, the most desirable settlers, and did not need sifting.' Offering his view of 'the immigrants Canada wants,' Sifton noted that, 'When I speak of quality ... I think of a stalwart peasant in a sheep-skin coat, born on the soil, whose forefathers have been farmers for ten generations, with a stout wife and a half-dozen children.' Clearly, such a definition would exclude most Asians, and in this 1922 article Sifton lamented the fact that, since his retirement from office, Canada had not followed a selective immigration policy. 'It is quite clear that we received a considerable portion of the off-scourings and dregs of society. They formed colonies in Ottawa, Montreal, Winnipeg, Toronto, and other places, and some of them and their children have been furnishing work for the police ever since.'

William Byron (1919), also expressing opposition to the increased immigration which was occurring in early-twentieth-century Canada, argued that the West 'has made up its mind very definitely about two or three things, and one of them is that no more alien population is required or wanted.' Included in Byron's list of undesirables were Bolsheviks, who were 'disciples of the torch and the bomb,' owing to their apparent 'red' tendencies, and Hutterites, who 'maintained queer little communities.'

While there was thus a general opposition to immigration of a variety of groups, many of the strongest anti-immigration pronouncements were reserved for visible-minority groups such as Asians, and in contrast to the situation with other immigrants these sentiments often had a more direct influence on specific legislative measures to deal with the alleged problem.

The source of this xenophobia lay at least part in the alleged biological and moral deficiencies of Asians, which received widespread coverage in the Canadian popular press in the late 1800s and early 1900s. In emphasizing these biological differences and their influence on Asians' moral thinking, Byron (1919) asserted that they 'go deeper than the color of the skin and the cut of the jib. They go right into the cells of the brain, where thought originates, into the roots of being where instincts are evolved and nursed.' Byron cited the experience of Edmonton judge Emily Murphy, who had suggested that it was 'comparatively easy to plumb what is transpiring in the mind of the average Anglo-Saxon ... but these same questions bring strange results sometimes when fired at a dusky-skinned fellow whose father, and all his ancestors before that, herded goats on the Carpathians.'

In an article appearing in *Canadian Magazine*, Nichol (1900)[1] focused more exclusively on the moral shortcomings of the Chinese in describing the peculiarities of a Chinese domestic servant he employed. Claiming that his servant had stolen food from the house to supply his friends, Nichol notes that 'we could never muster sufficient courage to take the almond-eyed humbug by the throat and force him to have a little consideration for his employers and a little less for his friends.' Referring to the predilection of Chinese to use opium, and the deleterious effects of the substance on them, Nichol continued:

for there are Chinese dens in Vancouver where opium is smoked and unspeakable infamies are practised, and no matter how meek and mild your Chinaman may look, no matter how gentle his voice and confiding his manner, Saturday night is almost certain to find him 'doped' in his bunk, weaving dreams under the poppy's subtle spell. From this debauchery he arises haggard and worn in the pale dawn and returns to his work with a million memories in his heavy eyes and about him the painful odour of unutterable things.

In his final assessment of the utility of the Chinese, Nichol concludes that 'my own experience leads me to believe that the good Chinese are something like the good Indians – dead ... but such as he is, he solves the great servant girl problem in British Columbia, ... without him housekeeping would be an impossibility.' As is discussed in more detail in chapter 6, such stereotypical portrayals of the Chinese and their supposedly peculiar and immoral habits were quite common in media sources of the early 1900s and served to socially construct Asians as alien. These descriptions of Asians' distinctive and overwhelmingly negative qualities were frequently invoked to justify their exclusion from Canadian society, and to assert the necessity of controlling those who remained through discriminatory legislation and law enforcement practices.

The first Chinese immigrated to Canada in the 1850s to work in the gold mines in the province of British Columbia. The majority of these first arrivals moved up the west coast of North America from California, but within a few years of their first appearance in the province, direct immigration from the Chinese province of Kwangtung began to occur (Woodsworth, 1941). The majority of these Chinese immigrants were middle-aged male labourers, who immigrated with the intention of making enough money to improve their economic situation at home (Ward, 1978). As Willmott (1970: 42) points out, the Chinese immigrant 'left in order to remit whatever savings he could afford to aid his family in China. In effect he left to sojourn elsewhere, with the clear intention of returning to his home, of supporting it in the meantime, and of eventually being buried in his village.'

As the British Columbia gold rush subsided and employment opportunities in the industry became scarce, many of these Chinese immigrants began to work as farm labourers and domestics. Further employment opportunities arose with the discovery of coal in the province in the 1860s, the rapid development of the fishing industry in the 1870s, and the construction of the Canadian Pacific Railway. The report of the Royal Commission on Chinese Immigration (Canada, 1885) estimated that, of 9,870 Chinese adult males resident in the province of British Columbia in 1880, more than 7,200, or 72.9 per cent, were involved in menial labour. As Comack (1985: 74) suggests, 'by the end of the 1870s the Chinese were shouldering much of the unskilled work in British Columbia.'

By the late 1880s, employment opportunities were not as abundant, and the Chinese, who were willing to work for less money than White labourers, increasingly became the object of public animosity. Clear evidence of the lower wages paid to Chinese workers was provided by the Royal Commission on Chinese and Japanese Immigration (Canada, 1902). Examining wages in the lumber and sawmill industries, for example, the commission reported that Chinese were paid $1.00 per day, while Whites were paid $2.00 to $2.50 per day for the same work. In the mining industry, wages were $1.25 for Chinese, compared with $4.00 per day for White workers. In the cannery industries, Chinese pay ranged from $3.09 to $33.09 per month, while Whites averaged $80.91 per month. Roy (1989: 154) notes that a geography textbook published in 1906 for use in British Columbia elementary schools made specific reference to the problems posed by Chinese labour. A passage in the text remarked, 'The presence of a large proportion of Chinese among the population of the province has added to the difficulty of the labour problem. The Chinese work cheaper, live on less, and send more money out of the country than any other class of labourer.' At least in part as a result of their acceptance of these lower wages, then, the Chinese, who had earlier been welcomed as a cheap source of labour in the province of British Columbia, were now resented for this very reason. 'White labour could not compete with the Chinese workers, who were unmarried and lived frugally. It was not the white businessman who was blamed, but the Chinese labourers he hired, for they were willing to work for a salary a white man could not live on' (Solomon and Madison, 1976–7: 240).

Branches of the Asiatic Exclusion League were formed in several Canadian cities, and these groups attempted to force the passage of more stringent laws to prevent the immigration of Asians and East Indians. In response to these demands, in 1875 the federal government imposed a tax of $50 on Chinese brought into the country by employers, and passed a restriction that allowed vessels to land only one Chinese for every fifty pounds of ship weight (Giffen, Endicott, and Lambert, 1991). While this legislation acceded to the demands for some form of action, in reality it amounted to a symbolic gesture, since the tax was not sufficiently high to prevent the immigration of more Chinese if their labour was required by employers (Comack, 1985).

For groups such as the Anti-Chinese Association of Victoria, British Columbia, the 1875 legislation did not go far enough in reducing Asian immigration. This association, which claimed to have the support of the mayor and all municipal councillors in Victoria, sent a petition to the federal government calling for immediate restrictions on Asian immigration.

We being still determined to oppose the terrible evil of Mongolian usurpation, monopoly of all our industries, and, with cheap labour, the future deprivation of our lands, thus dispossessing our own flesh and blood and congenial races, and to guard against a miscarriage, wrong presentation, misapprehension, and to avoid the possibility of failure in any shape of our obtaining the happy result of British Columbia and the Dominion of Canada for the white man; ... We respectfully ask your Honourable Body to pass such a measure, Resolution, or Bill as you in your wisdom shall decide, in order to abate the evil complained of and stop the future immigration of Chinese to this country. (British Columbia Sessional Papers, 1880: 406)

However, the federal government seemed reluctant to act more forcefully to quell the opposition to Chinese immigration through the passage of more stringent legislation. Prime Minister Macdonald held views on the Chinese which were consistent with those of many other Canadians, referring to them as an 'inferior race, ... semi-barbarians,' and 'machines with whom Canadians could not compete' (Canada, *House of Commons Debates*, 1882: 1471). Clearly, Macdonald was a racist, but, as Roy (1989) notes, he was also a practical politician and a nation-builder, and his government was apparently more concerned with the completion of the railway: 'At present this is simply a question of alternatives – either you must have this [Chinese] labour or you cannot have the railway' (Canada, *House of Commons Debates*, 1882: 1477). As Comack (1985: 78) suggests, 'in short, the position of the federal government on the "Chinese question" was one of expediency; as long as their labour was needed, the "immoral" habits of the Chinese could be tolerated.'

Frustrated by the federal government's reluctance to deal with Asian immigration in what they deemed to be an effective fashion, British Columbia legislators attempted to act on their own. The provincial legislature disenfranchised the Chinese in the 1870s, and, eventually, the Chinese were legally excluded from participation in the electoral process at all three levels of government. In fact, the provincial franchise was not restored until 1947. As Roy (1989: 46) suggests, 'free of any worry about the Chinese vote, politicians could readily agitate and legislate against them.'

Between 1878 and 1899, more than twenty statutes with the aim of preventing or restricting the settlement of Asians were passed in British Columbia. Legislation passed in 1878, for example, prohibited Chinese from working on projects sponsored by the province, and also required every Chinese person over the age of twelve to obtain a licence for $10, payable every three months. Failure to secure this licence would result in a fine of $100 and/or imprisonment (Henry et al., 1995). In 1884, the British Columbia government introduced bills to prohibit the exhumation of Chinese bodies, and to ban the use of opium for non-medical purposes (Roy, 1989). The province also passed a male minimum-wage law, which was designed to reduce Chinese and Japanese employment. By setting the wage above that normally paid to members of these minority groups, the law served to diminish the attractiveness of cheap labour to employers in the lumbering industry and led to the hiring of White labourers (Henry et al., 1995). Another British Columbia law prohibited all workers whose hair was more than a specified number of inches in length from working in underground mines. This law was clearly directed against Chinese labourers, who at the time frequently wore pigtails.[2] The justificatory preface to a proposed provincial immigration law starkly illustrated the racist sentiments of the British Columbia legislators.

Whereas [they] are not disposed to be governed by our laws; are dissimilar in habits and occupation from other people; evade the payment of taxes ... are governed by pestilential habits; are useless in instances of emergency; habitually desecrate graveyards by the removal of bodies therefrom; and generally the laws governing the whites are found to be inapplicable to Chinese, and such Chinese are inclined to habits subversive to the comfort and well-being of the community ... (as quoted in Kobayashi, 1990: 451–2)

Another law passed in 1900 required every immigrant in the province, when ordered, to write an application to the provincial secretary in some European language, with failure to comply being punishable by a $500 fine, one year's imprisonment, or deportation (Henry et al., 1995). While much of this legislation was eventually overturned by the federal government since it was outside provincial jurisdiction, federal legislators did not question the racial foundations of such laws. As Kobayashi (1990: 452) notes, it 'was therefore based upon a natural acceptance that people can be legally designated according to their race. No one at that time, and for many decades thereafter, would have questioned either the concept of "Chinese origin" or the fact that their rights might be relegated to a status below those of Europeans.'

With the completion of the railway in the 1880s, unemployment became even more widespread in British Columbia, and in response to continued concerns over increasing Asian immigration the federal government established a royal commission on Chinese immigration in 1885. Despite the imposition of a $50 head tax on Asian immigrants, and an increase in this amount to $100 in 1899, Asian immigration into the province of British Columbia continued, with 4,402 Chinese arriving in 1899. In response to continued agitation on the part of Whites, the federal government appointed another royal commission in 1902, which raised the tax on Asian immigrants to $500. This tax was specifically aimed at restricting the labouring class of Asians (Comack, 1985).[3]

The imposition of this head tax had a somewhat paradoxical effect on Chinese immigration, however. By temporarily restricting Chinese immigration, the tax raised the wages for Chinese labourers, thereby providing those already in Canada with greater wealth, which enabled them to send for friends and relatives. One Chinese merchant from British Columbia was reported to have declared: 'I always thought the white people fools. You pay the tax in higher wages, and we make more money out of financing the immigration' (as quoted in Tolmie, 1929: 12). Mackenzie King, who became minister of labour in the Laurier cabinet of the 1910s, was also aware of the fact that the imposition of the head tax was not having its intended effect of reducing Chinese immigration (Roy, 1989).

Despite this further increase in the head tax, then, Chinese continued to arrive in the province of British Columbia,[4] resulting in intensified racial strain. The Asiatic Exclusion League, inspired by the economic concerns of White workers, held a protest rally in the city of Vancouver in the fall of 1907. A large crowd converged on City Hall, and a full-scale riot ensued, resulting in substantial damage to the Chinese and Japanese districts of Vancouver (Green, 1979). Ward (1978: 69) suggests that this riot represented a 'spontaneous outburst' and was by no means planned, but it had the effect of 'asserting west coast radicalism in a clear and emphatic way.' The federal government's investigation of the circumstances surrounding this riot had a direct impact on the passage of Canada's first narcotics legislation, which is discussed in more detail in chapter 6.

Concerns over Asian immigration continued into the 1910s and through the early 1930s, primarily fuelled by the alleged threat posed by the concentration of Asians on Canada's west coast. H.H. Stevens, federal member of Parliament for the Vancouver riding, presented an address to the Canadian Club in Toronto in February 1912 in which he underlined the importance of assimilating the

Chinese, while ironically asserting at the same time that the assimilation of Asiatics was simply not possible.

I want you to get fastened in your mind this fact, that unless you assimilate your immigrants you are laying up a problem which will equal the Negro problem of the south. On the Pacific coast our primary objection to the Oriental is that he will not assimilate ... I contend that the Oriental, be he Japanese, Chinese, or Hindu, is entirely different in ideals, political, economic, social, religious, intellectual; in fact in every way his traditions and history are entirely different from ours. So, that in view of that fact the process of assimilation is a waste of time. (Stevens, 1911–12: 141–2)

Similar sentiments were expressed in more élite forums, such as the *Canadian Law Times and Review* (1908: 13), a source presumably read by many of the leading legal authorities in the country. Although this article specifically addressed the necessity of restricting Japanese immigration on the basis of the supposed moral inferiority of that group, the comments are reflective of the more general anti-Asian sentiments prevailing in Canada during this period.

[We] concluded that the door of entrance into the Canadian community must open only to those races who are capable of fusion with the native stock, so that absolute national unity may be attained in a generation or two; and only to members of the races indicated who are physically and morally sound. We believe that the science of eugenics looks askance at the blending of Aryan blood with the Turanian, even if white and coloured racial antipathies could be overcome; therefore it is of immense importance that the orientation of the west [by the Japanese] should be nipped in the bud ... The moral character of the Japanese would need to be vastly improved before it reaches Anglo-Saxon standards, imperfect though they may be ... The Oriental, accustomed for ages to oppression and deceit, has become a past master of craftiness and guile.

Hope and Earle (1933), referring to an 'invasion' of Asiatics, and employing 1921 census figures to support their claims, suggested that the fact that there was one 'Asiatic' to every twelve Whites[5] in British Columbia was 'catastrophic.' In response to these disturbingly high proportions of Asians in British Columbia's population, W.G. McQuarrie, a member of Parliament from the Vancouver area, sponsored a resolution demanding the complete exclusion of Asians and declaring that the influx of Oriental aliens and their 'rapid multiplication' had become a 'serious menace' to the living conditions of British Columbia (*Toronto Daily Star*, 9 May 1922). British Columbia members of Parliament from all political parties were apparently 'pregnant with celestial fire' and cited 'Japanese invasion of the fishing industry, Oriental inroads upon the fruitlands of the beloved Okanagan,' and the 'alarming dimensions of the drug traffic in Vancouver,' among other things, as justifications for exclusionary measures. It was also asserted that the social, political, and economic conceptions of the Asian races were so different from those of Canadians that Asians threatened the integrity of the social order of the regions to which they were freely admitted. The minister of immigration apparently agreed with the British Columbia members, asserting that what was needed was 'as homogeneous a white population as possible' (*Toronto Daily Star*, 9 May 1922).

In the 1920s, Western concerns began to focus more specifically on Japanese immigration. Although in the early part of the century Prime Minister Laurier had indicated that the Japanese were more desirable than the Chinese because they had adopted Western ideals of government and differed 'from them as the fully developed man from the child' (Roy, 1989: 203), sentiments began to change in the 1920s. Nelson (1921a) placed less emphasis on the issue of the 'bland and passive Chinese' and argued that the Japanese were the 'key of the problem,' owing to the immigration of significant numbers of Japanese women, and the consequent high birth rate among the Japanese population. Nelson (1921b) noted, 'A Vancouver daily paper carried on its front page in June a statement that in the municipality of Richmond, adjoining the city, out of 12 births registered, only one was that of a white child.' The Japanese were now considered to be more of a threat than the Chinese, because of their 'racial pride and national self-consciousness, and [their] insistence upon race equality and demand for political rights ... from childhood, the Japanese is taught that he is a God-ruled race, designed to dominate other races.' Nelson also alleged that more sinister forces were responsible for the influx of Japanese, noting that 'some declare that the Japanese government financed its people in many of the British Columbia enterprises.' Hope and Earle (1933) echoed these claims, noting, 'with the Japanese, penetration appeared to be ordered and controlled as though from some central source.'

The strong anti-Asian sentiment in British Columbia, coupled with restrictions on Asian immigrants' rights to work in various trades and factories in that province, was at least in part responsible for a fairly substantial eastward migration of Asians. Thompson (1989) notes that, in 1881, 99 out of every 100 Chinese residents in Canada lived in British Columbia, while, in 1901, 86 out of every 100, and, by 1921, only 59 out of every 100, lived in that province. Associated with the eastward migration, Chinatowns of various sizes arose in several Ontario cities in the early 1900s, primarily because of cultural barriers and economic factors, but also from the conscious actions of Chinese immigrants themselves. As Li (1988: 35) suggests, 'voluntary segregation resulted in the birth of a Chinatown, which was a kind of self-defense measure used by the Chinese to avoid open discrimination and hostility.'

Not surprisingly, this increased concentration of Asians in Ontario cities led to the expression of anti-Asian sentiments in that province as well. Roy (1989: 97) notes that agencies such as the Toronto and Hamilton Trade and Labour Council were calling for restrictions on Chinese immigration in the early 1900s, and the Toronto *Globe*, which had initially questioned the utility of restrictions, suggested immigration laws needed to be altered. Similarly, the *Toronto Telegram* argued that, while the Chinese were still something of a curiosity in the eastern part of Canada, in British Columbia, they were a 'positive menace to labour.'

Also representative of the emerging anti-Asian sentiment in the East was a series of articles in the late 1800s and early 1900s that appeared in *Saturday Night*, a magazine published in Toronto. An 1892 editorial (8 October) asserted, 'It will be time enough to accept [the Chinese] as an equal when he develops into something remotely like an equal ... Coming in here he may introduce new vices, but he is not likely to infuse new virtues in the social body ... He would entirely displace women in many of their lines of occupation, and displace men in all their lighter and less intelligent tasks.' However, not all readers of the magazine were in agreement with its editorial policy. One respondent from British Columbia, disputing the magazine's stance that Canada should be a 'white man's country,' and emphasizing the economic benefits associated with Asian labour, wrote: '[Your article] was not at all what the majority of employers in this province think. We need 10,000 more Chinese to do the work we cannot get white labourers to do. But we do not want any Hindus,[6] who are worthless, lazy dirty fanatics; one Chinaman is worth a dozen of them' (*Saturday Night*, 27 October 1906). The editor of *Saturday Night* magazine's response to this letter, which essentially denigrated and dehumanized the Chinese as a race, was representative of the prevailing sentiments towards minority groups in general, and the issue of Chinese immigration in particular:

The dispute is not as to the respective demerits of two inferior races – keep them both out of this white man's country. This will only be a white man's country if we make it so. It was once ranged by the red man, but we took it from them, and it is ours, if we can keep it. The employers in British Columbia are favourable to the admission of Chinese because these yellow fellows are great workers, cheap, docile, reliable ... Like the horse and the mule, they are considered indispensable. However, they are not horses, nor are they indispensable. They are an inferior race of men like the Africans who were brought over in thousands to the southern states and now constitute a serious and permanent danger to the neighbouring republic ... We can get Chinese labour [but] these people will not possess value as citizens, and when once fastened to the country will retard its development. (*Saturday Night*, 27 October 1906)

These strong anti-Asiatic sentiments culminated in 1923, when the federal government passed legislation refusing the entry of all Chinese to Canada. This act, which was not repealed until 1947, had the effect of reducing the Chinese population in Canada from 46,519 in 1931 to 34,627 in 1941 (Anderson and Frideres, 1981) and only 47 Chinese legally entered the country from 1923 to 1947 inclusive. And while this act was repealed by the federal government in 1947, concerns surrounding illegal Chinese immigration to Canada following its repeal led to a full-scale investigation by the Royal Canadian Mounted Police in the late 1950s. Thompson (1989: 103) indicates that the continuing sinophobic attitudes of the Canadian government during this period was typified by the Canadian minister of immigration, who noted in a speech: 'In Hong Kong we had conversations with the British, Americans, Australians, and United Nations officials as well as with our own staff ... All agreed that almost every [Chinese] migrant is lying about something, either because he or she is an imposter, is covering for someone else, or is trying to create new "slots" for future use.'

Asian Lifestyles and Restrictive Legislation

While the views of journalists and (especially British Columbia) politicians regarding Asians were thus influential in generating restrictive immigration legislation, it is also important to examine the conditions experienced by those Chinese who were allowed into and remained in Canada. Until the 1950s, there was no requirement for special legal protection for individuals in Canada on the grounds of their race or nationality, and there were thus several formal laws and informal practices in existence that restricted minority-group members' access to social services and employment opportunities.

Given the concentration of Chinese and locus of much anti-Chinese sentiment in the province of British Columbia, it is not surprising to find several examples of such discriminatory practices and laws in that province. British subjects of Asian descent resident in British Columbia were excluded from eligibility for elected office and employment in the public service for many years (Angus, 1931). Until the 1940s, Asians were also specifically excluded from practising the professions of law and pharmacy, and from serving on juries (Thompson, 1989).

Asians thus were formally restricted from access to several types of employment, and undoubtedly were subject to more subtle forms of exclusion on the part of other potential employers. In part as a result of such formal and informal restrictions, specific occupational enclaves, particularly in the restaurant and laundry business, formed in Asian communities across Canada. As Li (1988) reports, in 1885 the number of Chinese engaged in laundry and restaurant work in Canada represented less than 5 per cent of the total Chinese population. By 1921, this figure had increased to 32 per cent, and, by 1931, 40 per cent of Chinese were employed as servants, cooks, waiters, and laundry workers, with a significant proportion of these being self-employed. However, provincial and municipal legislative activity with respect to the regulation of these businesses worked to the decided disadvantage of the Chinese employed in them.

Several forms of restrictive legislation were enacted in various provinces and municipalities to curtail the ability of Chinese to conduct their businesses. Some of these laws were not specifically directed at Asian businesses and were seemingly egalitarian in their intent, but were often disproportionately enforced against these groups. An example of this is snow-removal by-laws, passed in Toronto and several other Ontario cities in the early 1900s, which required business owners and residents to keep the public areas outside their establishments free of snow. An analysis of the enforcement of these by-laws in Toronto for the year 1903, violations of which were accompanied by $1 fines or ten days in jail in default, found that approximately 40 per cent of the charges were laid against Chinese (Mosher, 1995).

Immigrants, particularly Chinese, were also seen as prone to violate social and religious conventions regarding the conduct of business on Sundays. For instance, Shaw (1924: 336) noted that 'observance of the Sabbath is to the white man simply a matter of decency. The white farmer does only the absolutely essential things on Sunday, because he thinks that is the right thing to do. The Oriental has no such code.' In response to immigrants' tendencies not to observe such conventions, the city of Toronto passed a Lord's Day Act, which prevented the conduct of business on Sundays (Toronto, *Annual Report of the Chief Constable*, 1901). These laws were also vigorously enforced against the Chinese, and although Toronto's Lord's Day Act was declared *ultra vires* by the Ontario Privy Council in 1902, the chief constable noted that 'it may be found more difficult to enforce Sunday observance than heretofore, but the police will not relax their efforts' (Toronto, *Annual Report of the Chief Constable*, 1903).

While these laws and the disproportional enforcement focus on immigrant violators of such legislation thus served to restrain Chinese businesses, activities that resulted in the exposure of White women to Chinese males were deemed even more worthy of regulation. Writing in the early 1920s, Nelson (1921a) expressed concern that Chinese were working in packing houses in the British Columbia interior, 'sometimes [serving] as bosses over white women and white girls.' The threat posed by interracial mixing was even more prominent with respect to service occupations, with Nelson noting that there were fifteen Chinese and sixty Japanese barber shops in Vancouver, each with two or more assistants, 'many of whom were [White] women.'

Discriminatory legislation was passed in several Canadian jurisdictions to control the activities of Asian restaurant and laundry owners.[7] While such laws were, to a certain extent, based on economic principles of restricting Asian businesses, they were also an attempt to control the Chinese, who were viewed as potential corruptors of the White females they employed in particular, and White women more generally. In Saskatchewan, for example, where 1908 legislation had earlier disenfranchised the Chinese (Li, 1988) an act passed in 1912 explicitly prohibited Asians from employing White female labour in restaurants, laundries, or other businesses they owned, with violations of the act being punishable by fines of $100 or two months' imprisonment.

A 1914 case from Moose Jaw (*Quong-Wing* v *The King*, 1914) involved an appeal of a Chinese restaurant owner's conviction under this statute. The Supreme Court of Canada's decision in not allowing the appeal emphasized the importance of the law in protecting White females from the corruption of Chinese males. The counsel for the accused claimed that the statute was *ultra vires* of provincial jurisdiction, and that the aim of the act was to deprive the defendant, and Chinese more generally, of the rights ordinarily enjoyed by other inhabitants of Saskatchewan. In his decision, the Chief Justice of the Supreme Court argued that the legislation may have affected the civil rights of 'Chinamen,' but the fact that it was primarily concerned with the protection of women and girls, 'in a geographical area where Orientals were disproportionately concentrated,' convinced the court to uphold the legislation.

Orientals are not prohibited in terms from carrying on any establishment of the kind mentioned. Nor is there any ground for supposing that the effect of the prohibition created by the statute will be to prevent such persons carrying on any such business. It would require some evidence of it to convince me that the right and opportunity to employ white women is, in any business sense, a necessary condition for the effective carrying on by Orientals of restaurants and laundries and like establishments in the western provinces of Canada. Neither is there any ground for supposing that this legislation is designed to deprive Orientals of the opportunity of gaining a livelihood. In the sparsely inhabited western provinces of this country the presence of Orientals in comparatively considerable numbers not infrequently raises questions for public discussion and treatment, and, sometimes in acute degree, which in more thickly populated countries would excite little or no general interest. (p. 465)

Similar laws prohibiting Asians from employing White females were enacted in Ontario in 1914, and British Columbia in 1923 (Li, 1988). Although the specific Ontario legislation was apparently infrequently enforced, municipalities in the province passed by-laws, and police engaged in surveillance of Chinese businesses, to prevent the corruption of White women.

Weaver (1995: 116), quoting the chief of the Hamilton, Ontario police force, notes that Chinese restaurants in that city were attracting official attention because they stayed open into the early hours of the morning and were 'becoming the resorts of objectionable characters at night.' The discovery of a drugged White woman in a Chinese café in 1917 led to an increased focus on controlling such establishments in Hamilton, and, in November 1920, the city's new police chief instructed all members of the department to report any instances of 'White girl(s) being employed in a laundry or restaurant owned or controlled by a Chinaman.'

Municipal and police officials in Toronto also devoted considerable effort to regulation of Chinese businesses. In 1908, the city solicitor advised the Board of Police Commissioners to refuse licences for Chinese restaurants where female labour was employed (Toronto, *Minutes of the Board of Police Commissioners*, 1909). However, in response to a petition from Chinese restaurant-keepers in Toronto, indicating that their businesses would suffer irreparable damage if they were not allowed to employ women, the board decided to 'leave the matter in the hands of the police to discriminate where females should and should not be employed.'

In addition to their employment in restaurants, a second major occupational niche of the Chinese was in the laundry business, and several municipalities enacted legislation to stem the spread of these businesses as well. In 1881, only twenty-two Chinese lived in the entire province of Ontario, but in that year four of the sixteen laundries listed in Toronto's city directory were owned by Chinese. By 1901, there were ninety-five Chinese laundries in Toronto, and three-quarters of all laundries in the city were owned by Chinese (Thompson, 1989). As a 1905 *Saturday Night* (23 December) article, somewhat disparagingly, but none the less accurately, noted, 'the chief occupation of the Toronto Chinaman is washee-washee.'

Toronto passed a laundry by-law in 1902, allegedly to prevent infection from the gambling and opium smoking that was believed to occur in such establishments. In discussing the necessity for this by-law, the chief constable of Toronto indicated that the impetus for the legislation was sanitation. However, he suggested that, 'in this connection, I would point out that the Chinese are invading districts where their presence is considered objectionable by the residents. I think the location of such laundries should be subject to police control' (Toronto, *Annual Report of the Chief Constable*, 1903: 13). As Boritch (1985: 151) concludes, it is quite clear that the real reason for this legislation was that 'Chinese laundries were largely increasing to the detriment of White people engaged in the business.' In addition, and similar to the laws with respect to restaurants mentioned above, Chinese laundries in Toronto that employed women were not granted licences (Toronto, *Minutes of the Board of Police Commissioners*, 1909).

In Hamilton, a by-law required all Chinese laundrymen to renew their licences every year and stated that renewal would be denied if any resident objected (Li, 1988). As a result of these by-laws, Chinese laundrymen were restricted to establishing their businesses in or near the small Chinatown in Hamilton. In 1913, for example, fifteen Chinese laundrymen applied to relocate their laundries to other areas of the city, but the requests were refused after local residents objected to the relocation (Lai, 1988).

While legislation directed at Chinese businesses thus had the effect of further marginalizing the Chinese and limiting contact between Asians and Whites, interracial mixes between White women and Chinese males still occurred. Media commentary on the supposed dangers of these interracial unions, and the legal responses to the Chinese males found guilty of attempting to initiate such interactions, are reflective of perhaps the most virulent form of racism directed towards the Chinese in Canadian society during this period.

In his 1910 report, the chief constable of Toronto (Toronto, *Annual Report of the Chief Constable*, 1910) drew attention to this issue in noting that immorality among young girls was increasing, and that this was 'caused by too much liberty on the streets ... [and] the lure of the Chinaman is also developing among this class of girls to their utter demoralization in many instances.' The *Toronto Daily Star* (16 August 1909) had earlier expressed concern regarding the fact that 'some of the Chinamen are taking an interest in white girls, and as a result of the finding of a letter on Wah Lee, the police are looking for the girl to whom the missive was addressed. A photo of another white girl was found in one of Ling Hen's pockets.' A series of court cases from Ontario demonstrates how Asians involved in such morally questionable unions were treated.

In 1913, Horace Wing, a Chinese resident of Toronto, wrote to a White girl (Minnie Wyatt) in answer to a newspaper advertisement she had published seeking employment as a stenographer. In the letter, Wing indicated that he had two rooms, that he desired a girl for the purpose of the business he was conducting, and that she could live in the rooms. Wyatt's suspicious parents forwarded the letter to a Toronto police officer, who sent another girl to meet with Wing. A charge of attempting to procure the woman for immoral purposes was eventually laid against Wing, and the crown attorney supervising the case indicated that there could be no doubt as to Wing's object in writing the letter – he wanted to get the girl to his rooms for an immoral purpose. The crown's evidence in support of this contention consisted of the fact that Wing had engaged in two false representations: first, that he had the rooms, and, second, that he wanted the girl for an honest purpose. 'It is manifest from the evidence that it was in the mind of the prisoner to procure girls who were seeking employment to come to the office, or place where he was living, for the purpose of his having carnal connection with them' (*Rex* v *Wing*, 1913). Despite what appeared to be rather questionable proof regarding Wing's supposedly immoral intentions, the Supreme Court of Ontario upheld his conviction for the offence, emphasizing that such attempts to initiate interracial unions were not to be condoned.

In a similar case from the southwestern Ontario city of Sarnia, a 'Chinaman' followed a 'respectable girl of fifteen' and offered her $5 to 'go with him for an immoral purpose.' Although Louie Chong appealed his conviction on indecent-assault charges on the grounds that the young woman had consented, the Ontario Supreme Court upheld his conviction (*Rex* v *Louie Chong*, 1914).

There were also a number of attempted bribery cases that arose from Chinese males who were attempting to avoid being arrested for their involvement with White females. Such cases were portrayed in the media as being relatively common among the Chinese, and descriptions of their actions allowed for a further questioning of their moral values. In the case of Sen Boo, 'a small and apologetic Chinese,' who had allegedly tried to bribe a Hamilton police officer after being apprehended as a result of his involvement with a White female, Magistrate Jelfs 'gave him to understand that the majesty of the Hamilton police force is not to be corrupted with filthy lucre.'

When Sergeant Bainbridge caught Sen Boo in Tonie You's laundry with two white girls, Boo tried to contaminate the officer's fingers with the base bribe of $5. The Sergeant recoiled with mingled horror and scorn that he could be bought for a lowly five spot. (Magistrate Jelfs) 'We pride ourselves upon the incorruptibility of the police force. No man shall be allowed to sap the foundations of the administration of justice.' (*Hamilton Spectator*, 3 August 1918)

In a similar case, two White 'girls' were found on Lee Sing's 'premises,' and he apparently attempted to bribe Constable McBride of Hamilton not to lay charges (*Hamilton Spectator*, 15 January 1919). Lee Sing denied the charges, claiming the police officer had asked him how much he made per day, producing money as evidence. 'The constable contradicted this statement as he had no interest in this phase of Lee's life.' The accused was sentenced to $50 or two months in jail for the bribery offence.

While situations in which Asians were seen to be the initiators of such questionable unions were generally dealt with quite severely by the courts, moral opprobrium was also attached to what, on the surface, appeared to be more voluntary unions, that is, cases of marriages between Asians and Whites. Nelson (1922) quoted the superintendent of Oriental Missions for the Methodist Church pointing out the threats posed by such racial intermixing: 'I strongly discourage [intermarriage]. Even in those unfortunate cases where matrimony between a white and yellow is invoked in a vain attempt to save a woman's name.' Nelson (1921a) also suggested that 'most observers think the offspring of such intermarriage is inferior to either of the parents. Herbert Spencer long ago declared them incompatible, protested against an ethnological impossibility, and decried any attempt to bridge the racial gulf as leading the way to social chaos.'

Stevens (1911–12), the member of Parliament from Vancouver, was also opposed to intermarriage, especially if its goal was to achieve assimilation. 'I say assimilation must mean intermarriage ... [but] are you prepared to adopt that course to give your own sons and daughters in marriage to these races? History tells us this fact, that the offspring of intermarriage of Occidentals and Orientals shows detriment of both races, that there seem to gather within that offspring the vices of both races and the virtues of neither' (p. 142).

Ontario magistrates also apparently viewed such interracial marriages rather unfavourably. For instance, the case of Ralph Lee, 'a young Toronto Chinese' who married a White woman, was described by his lawyer in the *Border Cities Star* (13 March 1937) as follows: 'He married this girl out of a sense of chivalry. She threatened to go down and jump in the river if he didn't ... "Perhaps" suggested the magistrate "it might have been wiser for him to let nature take its course."'

Given the prevailing societal attitudes towards marriages between Chinese men and White women, it is perhaps not surprising that priests and ministers from conventional religious denominations displayed a marked reluctance to preside over such marriage ceremonies. And, when these marriages were performed by others, the legal system intervened to question the credentials of such individuals and attempted to nullify the marriages. For instance, in 1907, the *Toronto Daily Star* (28 March) reported on a marriage ceremony performed by Robert Brown, 'missionary to the Chinese,' and official of the Chinese Christian Church, 'by which Jessie Stock became the wife of Charles Hing.'

The chief inspector of the Toronto police force was concerned that Brown did not possess the requisite qualifications to conduct marriage ceremonies: 'Missionary Brown has to show me his authority for performing a marriage service before I can believe that the ceremony is binding.'

Brown was charged under section 311 of the Criminal Code, one of the few reverse-onus clauses in Canadian law. This section read: 'everyone is guilty of an indictable offense ... who, without lawful authority, the proof of which shall lie on him, solemnizes or pretends to solemnize any marriage.' The Ontario Supreme Court justices hearing the appeal of Brown's conviction were not in favour of the interracial marriage, and expressed their scepticism regarding the religious validity of Brown's Chinese Christian Church. One justice noted that the church had 'grown up like Jonah's gourd in the night'; another argued that he 'did not think that the so-called First Chinese Christian Church is a church within the meaning of the Act.' Justice Meredith delivered the majority opinion of the Court, upholding Brown's conviction, and invalidating the marriage:

It is quite true that some modern churches and religious denominations have had their origin in some such manner, but it is not every mushroom, nor indeed every acorn, that becomes an oak, nor does every mustard seed eventually become a lodging place for the fowls of the air; it is to be hoped that the 'First Christian Chinese Church, Toronto' is of the good seed and that it may develop into a great tree in the branches of which the fowls of the air may even build their nests, but it must await the growth of at least a character- istic quality if not some branches in which, with at least some degree of caution, nests may be builded, before entering on the business of mating. (*Rex* v *Brown*, 1908)

In the 1940s and beyond, however, as Asian communities in Canada began to stabilize and immigration levels declined, several of the previously held stereotypes regarding the Chinese began to be challenged in at least some sources. For instance, Sutherland (1941), in an article describing the *Shing Wah Daily News*, Toronto's Chinese community newspaper, noted that one of the positive qualities of the Chinese was that it was 'rare to find [a Chinese] in this country having to ask for relief.' In addition, the Chinese, according to Sutherland, were a 'kindly, intelligent people, well worth knowing and a privilege to count as friends.'

In a 1949 *Maclean's* article titled 'What, No Opium Dens? – No Secret Tunnels Either, in Vancouver's Chinatown – It's Exotic Enough without the Dime Novel Trappings,' Gilmour (1949) questioned many of the extant myths surrounding the Chinese. In providing readers with a positive image of Vancouver's Chinatown and its residents, Gilmour noted that violent crime was virtually non-existent in the Chinese community, and that opium use was no longer common.

Despite some indication of the emergence of more positive commentaries on the Chinese in the mid-1900s, however, negative attitudes towards interracial mixing and the legal decisions that followed from such beliefs, combined with the previously addressed restrictions on Chinese immigration and business activity, resulted in an almost complete isolation of the Chinese community from the mainstream society. It is important to realize that these restrictions were legally sanctioned by the state, and thus formally institutionalized. As Li (1988: 33) suggests, 'the resulting discrimination was systematic and legal, and its practice was rationalized by an ideology stressing the superiority of White over non-White.' In chapters 6 and 7 of this book, I discuss how such stereotypical attitudes towards the Chinese led to their differential treatment in Ontario's criminal justice system.

4

Blacks: Immigration and
Restrictive Legislation

Finding that their record is clean, and seen to be clean, they may like Caesar's wife be
expected to find much ill and little good in those who are so clearly unclean. (Winks,
1968: 291)

Blacks have a long and fascinating social history in Canada, despite the relative
inattention to this group in Canadian historical sources. And while Canada's
admission of fugitive American slaves is often seen as representative of the
country's admirable level of racial tolerance, this chapter will demonstrate that,
once they arrived in Canada, Blacks experienced racial discrimination throughout the country and in virtually every aspect of their social and economic lives.

In this chapter, I focus on negative stereotypes of Blacks that were frequently
invoked by influential public figures in order to justify discriminatory practices
and legislation in several spheres of Canadian society. Such practices and legislation played an important role in Blacks' disadvantaged social positions in
Canadian society, and contributed to their disproportional involvement in the
criminal justice system.

The chapter begins with an examination of the Blacks' early history in Canada, focusing on the situation in the province of Ontario from the middle to
late 1800s. The second section of the chapter concentrates on the tendency
among commentators on racial issues in Canada to assert that the country was
more egalitarian in its treatment of Blacks than the United States, and to
attribute the racial problems that did exist to American influences on Canadian society. I also address the discourse surrounding Black immigration to
Canada in the 1910s and 1950s that emphasized the necessity, in order to
avoid racial problems, to keep Canadian society White. The chapter then
considers issues surrounding Blacks' restricted access to housing/property,

employment, and services in Canadian society over the period from 1900 to 1960. I also examine concerns related to the intermixing of Blacks and Whites, which constituted one of the most prominent aspects of racism in Canadian society. As a growing racial consciousness emerged in the 1950s, there were some indications that the situation for Blacks in Canada would change for the better. However, as this chapter concludes, this consciousness resulted in something of a backlash against Blacks and little actual change in their social and economic situation. This chapter will thus examine in some detail the various contexts of institutional and systemic racism in Canadian society, and thereby engage in a comprehensive attack on the 'myth of equality.'

Early History

Although most Canadians believe that slavery has never existed in their country, Riddell (1919: 375) notes that, in 1790, the Parliament of Great Britain passed an act authorizing 'any subject of ... the United States of America' to bring into Canada 'any Negroes, household furniture, utensils of husbandry or cloathing [*sic*] free of duty.' The household furniture, utensils, husbandry, and clothing were 'not to exceed in value 50 pounds for every white person in the family and two pounds for every Negro, any sale of Negro or goods within a year of the importation to be void.' This bill was passed in the legislature of Upper Canada by a vote of eight to four, the main justification for its enactment being the scarcity of the labour supply in the province, and the fact that it was deemed necessary to allow intending immigrants the same privileges with respect to slavery that they had in U.S. jurisdictions.

The myth of the absence of slavery in Canada's history is further eroded by evidence that Peter Russell, who had been head of state in Canada for three years in the late 1700s, advertised for sale at York (Toronto) 'a Black woman named Peggy, aged 40 years, and a Black boy, her son, each being servants for life – the woman for $150 and the boy for $200, 25 percent off for cash' (Riddell, 1919: 384). In fact, Henry et al. (1995) report that at least six of the sixteen legislators in the first Parliament of Upper Canada owned slaves. It was not until 1834 that all slaves in the British Empire were freed and slavery was declared officially illegal in Canada.

Although slavery thus became illegal in the mid-1800s, this development should not be interpreted as evidence of racial equality in Canada. As Black immigration to Ontario in the mid-1800s increased, racial tensions and conflicts intensified. And as the number of Black competitors for the limited jobs available in the depressed economy increased, the hostility of White workers in response to this perceived threat was magnified. In addition, as Black–White social interaction became more common, Whites had more opportunity to express their hitherto repressed prejudice (Walker, 1980).

Although Blacks have had the same general legal status as other Canadians since 1834, several examples from the mid-1800s suggest that Blacks' rights existed only in theory, and that the prejudice towards and stereotyping of Blacks were deeply entrenched in Canadian society. Several southwestern Ontario communities that received large numbers of Blacks who had migrated to the region from the United States through the 'underground railway' drafted various proposals to restrict Black immigration and legal rights in reaction to the perceived threat Black settlers posed. For instance, in 1849, the *Amherstburg Courier* (27 October) printed a resolution passed by the District Council protesting against a proposed Black-fugitive settlement in the neighbouring county of Elgin. 'There is but one feeling, and that is of disgust and hatred, that [they] should be allowed to settle in any township where there is a white settlement. The increased immigration of foreign Negroes into this part of the province is truly alarming' (as quoted in Landon, 1925: 6). The resolution also proposed a prohibition on the sale of lands to Blacks, suggested the imposition of a poll tax on Blacks entering the country, and included a requirement that 'Negroes shall furnish good security that they will not become a burden' (ibid.).

Similar concerns surrounding Black immigration were expressed in the neighbouring southwestern Ontario community of Chatham, where it was argued that property values would decrease because Blacks, 'being lazy, would let their farms run down ... Crime would increase, White Canadians would suffer from the Black odour. Blacks would try to marry white girls, with the result that a "mongrel" population would be produced and the white race would be downgraded' (Walker, 1980: 80).

Although proposals to restrict Black immigration and property purchases were not successfully enacted into law in the 1800s, Whites were successful in limiting Black access to public schools. With the exception of the city of Toronto, Blacks were barred from the public schools in all of Upper Canada, as a result of the passage of the 1850 Common School Act of Ontario (Hill, 1979). This act provided for the subdivision of school districts in the province, and the separation of schools along religious and racial lines. Section XIX of this act stated, in part:

It shall be the duty of the municipal township, and of the Board of School Trustees of any city, town, or incorporated village, on the application, in writing, of 12 or more resident heads of families, to authorize the establishment of one or more separate schools for Protestants, Roman Catholics, or coloured people. (as quoted in Walker, 1980: 110)

In short, a relatively small number of Whites could make the decision to create a separate school for Blacks, and legal challenges to these segregated schools were not successful. Winks (1971) notes that, by 1859, school administrators agreed that, where no separate school was established for Blacks, they had the right to attend the common school, whereas, if a separate school had been established for them, all Blacks could be compelled to attend. In the city of Windsor, one Black resident pointed out that a coop measuring sixteen by twenty-four feet was used for thirty-five Black pupils, while the White school remained unfilled. Interestingly, the legislation allowing for segregated schools remained on the statute books in Ontario until 1964.

Unlike other minority groups, in particular Asians, Blacks were legally allowed to vote and to serve on juries in Canada. However, these rights were not always appreciated and respected by some Whites. In the early 1850s, a group of Whites in Essex County, Ontario, physically prevented Blacks from voting in an election. When the injured parties filed a grievance before the county magistrate, he insisted that they be allowed to vote.

Similarly, although Blacks served on juries throughout the province of Ontario in the 1850s, attempts by Blacks to exercise this right often resulted in controversy. At an 1851 trial in Toronto, for instance, White jurors objected to a Black serving with them, although the judge presiding over the trial ultimately did not heed their wishes to have the Black juror removed. When White jurors in Windsor voiced a similar objection, the presiding judge threatened them with jail terms unless they agreed to serve with a Black man. As Walker (1980: 86) points out, there is something of a double message revealed in these reactions to Black voting rights and service on juries. On the one hand, Blacks were legally citizens like all others, but, on the other hand, general public opinion and common practice frequently influenced Blacks' exercise of these legal privileges.

The few positive commentaries on Black settlers that did appear during this period were decidedly condescending in their tone, as is revealed in Landon's (1925: 6) quotation of the 'traveller' Benjamin Drew's description of the Black households he visited in Amherstburg in the 1830s:

Cooking, eating, and sleeping are not done in the same room, but in separate ones. They are tidily furnished, and some have carpets on the floors and curtains on the windows. It is pleasant to see the feeble dawnings of taste in rude pictures, and simple attempts at ornament ... It is evident that they spend more money upon their households than foreign immigrants do. They live better, and they clothe their children better. They say, indeed, that this is the reason they do not lay up so much money as many Irish and Germans do.

Animosity towards Blacks was not restricted to the province of Ontario, but was also evidenced in other areas of Canada to which Blacks migrated.[1] For instance, the city of Victoria, British Columbia, had a fairly substantial Black colony of 400 to 600 people who had immigrated to Victoria from San Francisco in the 1850s (Winks, 1971), and Weber (1971) suggests that resentment towards these immigrants increased as their numbers grew. Although there were certainly individual success stories for Blacks in Victoria,[2] a letter to the editor of the Victoria *British Colonist* (13 June 1859) recounted the hostility Blacks endured and the denial of services they experienced in that community.

We have not conquered that mildew-like feeling that lurks in the hearts of our enemies, i.e., prejudice. All the hotels, inns, and wiskey [sic] shops are closed against us, and a colored gentleman was ordered out of the cabin of the steamer Governor Douglas the other day – he had a cabin ticket. They shut us out from concerts, and a member of the church says give him $500 and he will build a gallery in the English Church, in which to huddle us together. The position we hold in this country is not only humiliating in the extreme, but degrading to us as a class. The obnoxious seeds of prejudice are so deeply rooted in the white man's heart, which he directs against us with such burning force, biting like an adder and stinging like an asp, that we naturally suffer from its deadly effects.

That this author's claims regarding the existence of prejudice and discrimination in Victoria were not unfounded was revealed in an incident that occurred in November 1860. In this case, two Blacks were denied admission to Victoria's Colonial Theatre, and a disturbance involving fights between Black and White patrons of the theatre ensued. In a decidedly biased account of these events which placed the blame on the Blacks involved and completely neglected their legitimate claim to be admitted to the theatre, the *British Colonist* (7 November 1860) noted that a 'large number' of Whites were 'knocked down ... kicked and otherwise abused' by the 'Negroes who rejoiced over their victory ... [while] only one Black man was injured.' The *Colonist* concluded: '[This] was the result of an organized plan on the part of the colored population, who, it is asserted, came fully prepared for mischief.' In response to rumours of further action involving (Black) 'deputations from Salt Spring Island, New Westminster and the American side' that was to occur the following Saturday, the *British Colonist* (8 November 1860) warned Blacks of the potential negative consequences of participating. 'Respectable Negroes, who would never countenance the acts of the ruffians, will suffer alike with the guilty; and very few white people will be found willing to brave public opinion by giving employment to a man of color.'

At this time, Canadians generally believed that Blacks were inherently less intelligent than Whites, and the only widely available intelligence tests administered to Blacks in the 1900s tended to support this belief. White Canadians considered Blacks to be lazy and childlike (Winks, 1968), and, similar to the situation with Asians described in chapter 3, descriptions of Blacks appearing in the popular press promoted negative stereotypical images of members of this group. For instance, an article appearing in *Canadian Magazine* (Delesser, 1900) noted that 'the Negro is a human being, not a machine with which you can experiment. His character is not so very simple as may be supposed.' Providing support for some of the more popular stereotypes in existence during this period, Delesser suggested that 'Negroes are deeply superstitious,' were characterized by 'not keen imaginations,' and 'much like singing.' The article concluded that 'the Negro is intensely emotional, impulsive, polite, given to begging, has no strict regard for the truth, is generally grateful for past kindness, and is cheerful. When enraged, he does not reason, and is ungovernable.'

This brief examination of Blacks' early history in Canada thus suggests that, despite their formal legal equality, several informal restrictions were imposed on them by a racially conscious society that was influenced by stereotypical depictions of Blacks. In the limited number of commentaries on Blacks that began to appear in Canadian popular and academic literature in the 1900s, however, authors commonly drew attention to the fact that, in comparison with the situation in the United States, Canada was far more benevolent in its treatment of Blacks.

The U.S. Influence

Canada's attitude toward the Negro race has on the whole been characterized by sympathy, justice, and generosity. Probably no other country can show as favourable a record in this respect. (Edmonds, 1929)

The colour question is of little importance in Canada because, though at one time there was a considerable African population, still it gave Canada no trouble. In recent years it has declined relatively, if not absolutely. (*Globe*, 1923, as quoted in Sher, 1983: 30)

As Winks (1968: 299) asserts, historically, Canadians have seen Blacks through 'an American lens refracted by Canadian institutions.' From portrayals of Blacks in American popular media and literature, and later in films and television, Canadians developed an impression of what Blacks were like, what their alleged capacities and incapacities were, how they should behave, and what place they should occupy in society. As Walker (1980: 79) notes, 'the smiles, the banjos, the watermelons, entered the white Canadian image of Blacks, however preposterous that was in the Canadian context.'

An important factor contributing to the drawing of colour lines in both Canadian and American society, and the subsequent discrimination against Blacks, was the emergence during the later part of the nineteenth and the early twentieth-century of scientific theories that purported to prove the inferiority of the Black race on a number of diverse dimensions. Although these early twentieth century theories superseded earlier and even more ludicrous notions that the blood, brains, skull, and semen of Negroes were Black (Smedley, 1993), natural and physical scientists amassed evidence of racial differences in cranial capacity, anatomy, intelligence, and other physical and behavioural characteristics to document the supposed innate inferiority of Blacks, with these differences commonly being relayed to the general public.[3] It was not difficult for socially and politically powerful Whites to utilize such 'evidence' to justify discriminatory policies against Blacks in the areas of immigration, employment, housing, and services.

In addition, scientific racism also raised Whites' general consciousness of another and ultimately more important potential threat from the Black population. This was the concern that interracial reproduction would lead to contamination of the superior White gene pool. Although in Canada this ideology never reached the levels achieved in the American South, where 'virtually every aspect of social life, when it concerned Blacks, was ultimately considered in relation to its potential to promote sexual contact between the races' (Tolnay and Beck, 1992: 35), it was an important determinant of the reactions to Blacks in Canadian law and social policy. Interracial unions, especially those that were initiated by what were believed to be aggressive Black males, became a major concern of many commentators throughout the late nineteenth and early twentieth centuries, especially as these related to the commission of sexual crimes, as is documented in chapter 7.

Although certainly far less recognized in popular and academic literature then, the patterns of discrimination practised against Blacks in Canada over the past 150 years do not differ significantly from patterns characteristic of the northern United States. Canadian commentators have tended to examine domestic racial problems in contrast to the situation in the United States 'with a clear assumption of moral superiority' (Winks, 1968: 288), and have tended to applaud the virtues of the supposedly more egalitarian Canadian society. At the same time, there has been a decided inclination to attribute these domestic problems to American influence, and to suggest that the emergence of such problems would be prevented by restricting Black immigration to the country.

The theme of the non-existence of racial problems in Canada and the notion that the country was more even-handed than the United States in its treatment of

Blacks were common in much of the Canadian popular literature dealing with racial issues in the early to middle twentieth century. For instance, the *Ottawa Journal* (29 February 1924), reporting on the trip of a local judge to New Orleans, asserted that the judge was 'amazed at the ostracism to which Negroes are subjected [in that jurisdiction].' In an article appearing in the *Dalhousie Review*, McKenzie (1940: 198) suggested that 'Negroes comprise only a fraction of a percentage of Canada's total population ... this means that there is no Canadian Negro problem.' However, the same article asserted that the prejudice that did exist in Canadian society is 'undoubtedly due, in part at least, to American influence.' Similarly, an editorial appearing in *Saturday Night* magazine (1 August 1936) while correctly identifying the existence of discrimination in Canada in access to hotel accommodation, placed the blame for this situation squarely on the shoulders of Americans:

We doubt if Canadians are aware that the situation in Canada in regard to coloured persons in public hostelries is little if at all better than it is in that country, the explanation being, of course, that Americans constitute a large proportion of the patronage of Canadian hotels and are therefore able to dictate their policies.

In a somewhat different context, Hewitt (1947) attributed the restriction of access to labour unions by Blacks in Canada to the influence of White union members in the Southern United States.

In assessing the evidence regarding discrimination towards Blacks in Canada presented below and in later chapters of this book, it is thus necessary to place it in the context of patterns in the United States.

Racist sentiments in Canada became even more prominent in the early 1900s, primarily in response to large numbers of Blacks from the United States who were attempting to immigrate to Western Canada. As a result of the threat posed by such immigration, informal restrictions on such migration were imposed by the Canadian federal government.

Immigration

At no time has the immigration of Negroes been encouraged by the Canadian government. (William Duncan Scott, Superintendent of Immigration, 1914, as quoted in Troper 1972: 272)

The people of Canada do not wish, as a result of mass immigration, to make a fundamental alteration in the character of our population. (Mackenzie King, Prime Minister of Canada, 1947, as quoted in Hill, 1960: 66)

The number of Blacks in Canada decreased from an estimated 50,000 in 1860 to approximately 17,000 in 1911, owing to the fact that many Blacks returned to the United States from Canada after the Civil War. From the years 1904[4] to 1910, inclusive, there was a total of only 444 black immigrants to Canada. However, even the *Toronto Daily Star*, the most liberal of the Toronto daily newspapers (Levitt and Shaffir, 1987), expressed opposition to Black immigration in its editorial policies. When a movement for the annexation of the West Indies developed in Canada in 1905, the *Star* was opposed on the grounds that it would result in the immigration of Blacks to Canada. 'To hold up the ideal of a white Canada is not to foster race prejudice or to condone injustice to men and nations of other races ... A nation has a right to determine the quality of its citizenship ... Canada must consult her own interests' (as quoted in Harkness, 1963: 93).

In the 1910s, reports of a possible wave of Black immigrants to Western Canada prompted concerns that Blacks were being systematically sent to Canada by unscrupulous Americans.

This is a very beautiful dream you say, but stop. It is not a dream but actual fact. The movement has started. Today a trainload of southern beauties passed through Melville, a town on the Grand Trunk Railroad, en route to the Tramp Lake District ... where the free land awaits them. Seventy *curly-haired pickanninies* were in the party, showing the financier in the movement has an eye to business as they can be brought in much cheaper. It was a wonderful sight to the people in the west to see this *chocolate colony*, as many had never seen a darky, and few indeed had seen a carload, to say nothing of a trainload. Anyone who has ever lived or visited the south knows that southern darkies as a whole have not one dollar to rub against another, let alone enough to emigrate. Will the west have a black peril to face, as well as a yellow? A Negro or Chinaman may say 'Your God Shall be my God,' but they cannot say 'your people shall be my people.' (Fisher, 1911: 2; emphasis added)

This alleged influx of Black immigrants from the state of Oklahoma was at least in part precipitated by the Canadian government's offer of free land to immigrants that inadvertently appeared in the Black press in that state. The xenophobic reaction to this reported migration of Blacks on the part of the press and Canadian government officials reached its height when a southwestern Ontario member of Parliament suggested that 17,000 Blacks had entered Canada during 1910. As Winks (1971: 309) notes, however, this was 'an absurd confusion with the census total for 1901.'[5] Whether this member of Parliament's incorrect citing of the number of Black immigrants was inadvertent or not, it signalled a renewed attention to issue of Black migration to Canada.

In reaction to this migration, at some point in April or May 1911, federal government authorities sent agents to Oklahoma in an attempt to 'stem the tide' (Shepard, 1991). Included among these agents was a Black clergyman who was hired by the government to travel the state, preaching against Black migration to Canada.

Blacks who persisted in their attempt to immigrate were sometimes turned back at the border, and medical inspectors at border points were given direct instructions to declare all Black immigrants medically unfit for life in Canada (Walker, 1980). The Commissioner of Immigration even offered a medical inspector in Emerson, Manitoba, a fee for every Black rejected (Winks, 1971). In the federal House of Commons, William Thoburn, a Conservative member of Parliament for the Ontario riding of Lanark North, asked the minister responsible for immigration, Mr Oliver, whether the government was prepared to place restrictions on, or 'stop altogether,' Black immigration from the southern United States.

We find by the newspaper reports that these people are coming over into Canada by the hundreds; later on they will come by the thousands, and so long as we give them free homesteads in the Canadian northwest they will come by the tens of thousands. I would like to ask the government if they think it in the interests of Canada that we should have Negro colonization in the Canadian northwest? Would it not be preferable to preserve for Canada the lands they propose to give to Niggers? (Canada, *House of Commons Debates*, 1910–11: 6524)

In response to questions from a southwestern Ontario member of Parliament regarding whether the federal government was considering placing a head tax of $500 on Black immigrants as they had done with Asians, Minister of the Interior Oliver essentially left the specific question unanswered, but stated, 'so far as my information goes there is a very strong sentiment on the part of a great many people in this country against the admission of Negroes' (Canada, *House of Commons Debates*, 1910–11: 5942).

Federal politicians were also influenced by their constituents in their reactions to Black immigration. In 1911, Arthur Fortin, a lawyer from the province of Quebec, wrote a letter to Minister of the Interior Oliver, in which he suggested that the government should 'control the immigration of Darkies in the Dominion, just as it does for the Chinies [*sic*] the Hindoes [*sic*] and the Japs ... I only wish you to know that at least from this part of the province the people would favour a Government measure controlling effectively the immigration of that special element – the worst of all' (as quoted in Bertley, 1977: 128).

A letter sent to the Department of Immigration signed by twelve individuals from the province of Alberta expressed concern that 'Negro immigration' would discourage White settlement and depreciate the value of land in areas of Alberta where Blacks settled. This letter also referred to the sexual threat posed to White women by Black immigrants, noting that 'we do not wish that the fair fame of Western Canada should be sullied with the shadow of Lynch Law but we have no guarantee that our women will be safer in their scattered home- steads than white women in other countries with a Negro population' (as quoted in Bertley, 1977: 128). Letters expressing similar sentiments, and calling for the segregation of Blacks into particular districts of the province, were forwarded to the Department of Immigration by the Board of Trade of Athabasca Landing, and the municipal council of the city of Edmonton. The *Edmonton Bulletin*, a newspaper which was owned by Minister of the Interior Frank Oliver, warned that 'increased Negro immigration could serve potentially as an incitement to racial violence as yet unknown in Canada' (as quoted in Troper, 1972: 280).

Restrictions on Black immigration were also supported by the Toronto media. An editorial appearing in the *Toronto Mail and Empire* (27 April 1911) once again emphasized the differences between Canada and the United States and drew attention to the threat posed by increased Black immigration.

If negroes and white people cannot live in accord in the South, they cannot live in accord in the North. Our western population is being recruited largely by white people from the United States. If we freely admit black people from that country, we shall soon have race troubles that are the blot on the civilization of our neighbours. Canada cannot be accused of narrowness if she refuses to open up her west to waves of Negro immigrants from the United States. The negro question is of the United States' own making and Canada should not allow any part of her territory to be used as a relief colony on that account.

This is not to suggest that there was complete consensus among Canadians on the threats posed by Black immigration or with respect to proposals to restrict such immigration. One member of Parliament from the South Essex riding of southwestern Ontario, whose riding contained a substantial number of Blacks, was critical of the fact that the government had taken steps to prevent 'the entrance of these people on account of their colour ... Coloured people in my experience have been amongst the most loyal citizens of this country' (Can- ada, *House of Commons Debates*, 1910–11: 5911). Similarly, the member from West Kent, another southwestern Ontario riding, noted 'in my section of the country there are a good many coloured farmers who are amongst the most industrious and successful citizens of the Dominion' (ibid., 5913).

Those calling for restrictions on Black immigration ultimately won out, how- ever, and the federal cabinet passed an order on 12 August 1911, which effectively banned 'Negro immigration, which is deemed unsuitable to the climate[6] and requirements of Canada' (Shepard, 1991: 30). This order was never formally implemented, however, being repealed on 5 October of the same year on the pretext that the minister of the interior had not been present when it was passed. Troper (1972) argues that the real reason the bill was not passed was because it was vetoed by Prime Minister Laurier, who was concerned with the possibility that it would raise diplomatic problems in the United States, and upset Black voters in the province of Nova Scotia and in southwestern Ontario. Although this bill did not become formal legislation, as Shepard (1991: 3) argues, 'the fact that the original was passed at all indicates the depth of Canadian feeling on the black immigration issue.' In fact, given the informal exclusionary program adopted by the Immigration Branch, which simply adapted the standard medical and character examination at entry points to reinforce a White-only admission policy, formal legislation was not necessary, and the use of such informal practices was certainly politically safer. Apparently, these informal measures were sufficient, as they effectively stopped any further large-scale immigration to Canada by Blacks for a number of years (Grow, 1974; Thompson, 1979).

Following these early concerns surrounding Black immigration during the 1910s, media commentary and legislative action waned, primarily because the Black population in Canada remained relatively numerically stable during this period. None the less, the threat posed by Black immigration to Canada was intensified through assertions that, within the existing population, 'the number of colored people [was] increasing out of proportion to the increase in whites' (*Canadian Forum*, 1925), not just in Canada, but globally. In his presidential address to the Canadian Geography Association, Professor Gregory emphasized the seriousness of this problem.

The position at present is that one-third of the inhabitants of the world rule eight-ninths of it, or the colored people who constitute two-thirds of the population rule only one-ninth of it ... Thus, the number of colored people is increasing out of proportion to the increase in whites, the colored people are beginning to discern the principles on which the white man's success has rested. Education has levelled up races of all colours, and race sentiment is growing in regions where internal strife has been allayed largely by the white man's rule.

Between 1911 and 1951, the total number of Blacks in Canada increased by fewer than 2,000 (Anderson and Frideres, 1981) from a 1911 figure of 16,994 to 18,020 in 1951. Thousand of Blacks, convinced that the situation south of the border had improved, decided to leave Canada and pursue opportunities in the

United States, resulting in a fairly large outflow of Blacks. However, increased Black immigration from the West Indies in the 1950s, especially to the large cities of Toronto and Montreal, led to a resurfacing of anti-immigration sentiments during this period.

Provisions of Canada's 1952 Immigration Act gave the minister power to prohibit entry of immigrants on the basis of their nationality, citizenship, ethnic group, occupation, class, or geographical area of origin. In addition, restrictions could be applied on the basis of 'peculiar customs, habits, modes of life or methods of holding property, and unsuitability having regard to the climatic, economic, social industrial, educational, labour, health or other conditions' (Canada, *Statutes of Canada*, 1952).

In a justification of his government's restrictive immigration policy that focused on the necessity of maintaining a homogeneous (presumably White) population, on 24 November 1954, minister of immigration, J.W. Pickersgill, stated that 'Canadian immigration policies are discriminatory and the government intends to keep them that way. We don't want immigration to change the character of our population.' However, less than one year later, in a speech delivered in Victoria, British Columbia, Pickersgill claimed that 'there is no racial discrimination in Canada's immigration policy, despite some public feeling to the contrary' (*The Canadian Negro*,[7] December 1955).

In 1954, the Negro Citizenship Association of Toronto presented a brief to the federal minister of citizenship and immigration, protesting the discrimination against Negroes in Canada's immigration policy. Noting that one of the official reasons given for refusing West Indians as immigrants was that people from tropical areas supposedly experienced difficulty adjusting to the cold Canadian climate, the association pointed out that the government itself had no statistics available to support this claim (*Canadian Unionist*, May 1954). *The Canadian Negro* (July–August 1953) pointed somewhat sarcastically to a further glaring inconsistency in Canada's climate-unsuitability clause, noting that no restrictive measures had been adopted by the Canadian Immigration department to protect Whites against the climate of the West Indies or Africa. The editorial noted that Canadian Whites were free to migrate to such countries regardless of what the climate did to their health, and suggested that 'the government is apparently interested only in the health of West Indians who may wish to settle in Canada.' A later editorial (*The Canadian Negro*, May 1954) correctly asserted that 'there has been no proof, scientific or otherwise, that the Canadian climate has any adverse effects on persons from tropical areas.'

The disjuncture between official rhetoric and actual immigration policy is further revealed in a situation documented by Daniel Hill in his 1960 PhD thesis (Hill, 1960: 64). In response to a letter sent by a member of Parliament regarding a Black constituent who wanted to bring his granddaughter to Canada from the West Indies in the early 1950s, Walter Harris, the minister of citizenship and immigration, wrote:

One of the conditions for admittance to Canada is that immigrants should be able readily to become adapted and integrated into the life of the community. In the light of experience it would be unrealistic to say that immigrants who have spent the greater part of their life in tropical or sub-tropical countries become readily adapted to the Canadian mode of life which, to no small extent is determined by climatic conditions ... They are more apt to break down in health [and] ... persons from tropical or sub-tropical countries find it more difficult to succeed in the highly competitive Canadian economy.

Several Canadian newspapers defended the necessity of blocking Black immigration, not from prejudice, they of course asserted, but to prevent Canada from developing a racial problem of its own. The *Globe and Mail* (16 February 1955) argued that Canada could help solve the 'racial question' by extending financial aid to the West Indies so that there would be enough jobs in that country to keep West Indians home. In an editorial urging Blacks not to agitate regarding their subordinate position in Canadian society, the *Globe* asserted:

This newspaper urges coloured people here, however strongly they may feel they have grievances, not to introduce the poison of race hatred into Canada. Whatever they have to say will have much more force if said dispassionately. As to the specific question, we do not believe that massive immigration from the British West Indies to Canada would be advantageous to either party ... To put it another way, there is no point in creating a colour problem where none exists.

The *Globe*'s sentiments were echoed at a press conference in Madison, Wisconsin, in May 1960 by Ellen Fairclough, Canada's minister of immigration: 'Canada has no racial problem, nor has Canada a racial policy. And that's the way it's going to stay' (as quoted in Winks, 1968: 295). As Winks (1968) suggests, 'in other words, the "American virus" could be kept out by keeping the black man out as well.'[8] Although the existence of racial problems in Canada was frequently denied by government and media officials, as later sections of this book demonstrate, there is little doubt that racial discrimination was prominent and pervasive in the country.

Access to Housing, Employment, and Services

Race prejudice is practised in Toronto, in Ontario, in the Dominion of Canada, and

Negroes imbued with race consciousness very readily determine its presence in the housing situation, in the procurement of jobs, and too, in the quest for food and refreshments, that they have been rudely discriminated against. (Petgrave, 1944: 1)

In addition to proposals to restrict the number of Black immigrants to Canada in the 1900s, there were also several practices in the contexts of access to housing and property, employment, and services for those already resident in the country that resulted in Blacks' inability to fully participate as equal citizens in Canadian society. While many of these discriminatory practices were informal, a consideration of media commentary surrounding these issues and judicial interpretations of discriminatory laws and social conventions reveals an unwillingness to recognize, let alone effectively address, problems of racial bias in Canadian society.

Housing/Property

One of the most prominent and important contexts of discrimination against Canadian Blacks relates to housing and accommodation. From the time of their arrival in the country, Blacks have been forced into segregated districts, which were, not surprisingly, usually the least desirable ones. The Ontario cities of Hamilton, Windsor (Walker, 1980), and Toronto (Hill, 1960) developed neighbourhoods where Black residence was accepted, and others where it was not, resulting in considerable residential segregation of this group. The constraints on the residential mobility of Blacks and other minority groups were, and still are, primarily informal and therefore difficult to track in a systematic, empirical fashion. However, one method of identifying the existence of such constraints is to examine judicial decisions from the mid-1900s that upheld the legality of restrictive land-sale covenants in the province of Ontario. Although most of the cases addressed in law reports involved challenges to covenants launched by more politically and economically powerful individuals such as Jews, the restrictions included in these covenants, and the judicial reactions to challenges of them, provide valuable insights into an underresearched area of Canadian law. These laws worked to the detriment of various minority groups in Canada, restricting their ability to purchase land and resulting in their geographical segregation, and further contributing to their disadvantaged status in Canadian society.

For example, a covenant in the city of Hamilton prevented the sale of the land in question to 'Negroes or Asiatics, Bulgarians, Austrians, Russians, Serbs, Roumanians, Turks, Armenians, whether British subjects or not, [and] foreign-born Italians, Greeks or Jews' (Re Byers and Morris, 1931). The purchaser in this case was a 'foreign-born Jew,' and the legitimacy of the covenant was upheld by the Ontario Supreme Court.

In *Essex Real Estate Company Limited* v *Holmes* (1930), a southwestern Ontario case, a restrictive land-covenant clause stated that 'the lands shall not be sold to or occupied by persons not of the Caucasian race nor to Europeans except such as are of English-speaking countries and the French and people of French descent.' The plaintiff company in this case contended that the proposed purchaser of the land, a Syrian, was within the provisions of the restrictions and was not entitled to purchase it. In its decision allowing the appellant to purchase the land, the court noted that he was a Syrian, 'Syria being a country or district in Asia, but he is, it is admitted, of the Caucasian race.' Unwilling to challenge the racist nature of the covenant itself, the court noted that 'a fair interpretation of what was really intended would be to say that a proposed purchaser of the lands must be by colour white.'

A 1945 case, Re McDougall and Waddell (1945), involved a covenant indicating that the land in question was not to be 'sold to, let to, or occupied by, any person or persons other than Gentiles of European, British, Irish, or Scottish racial origin.' Although the racial affiliation of the proposed purchaser of the land in this Toronto case is not clear, he objected to the covenant on the basis that the clause violated Ontario's 1944 Racial Discrimination Act (see discussion below). In his decision, Justice Chevrier of the Ontario Supreme Court noted that, 'with the present scarcity of housing, the rapid development of the city in all available directions, and the increasing desire to do away with all slum quarters and generally improve living conditions, [these] restrictions took on a new significance.' In the final analysis, however, the Court upheld the restriction, deciding that the discrimination contained in the covenant in question was not covered by the Racial Discrimination Act.

In another 1945 case, Re Drummond Wren (1945), the Ontario Supreme Court chose to invalidate a restrictive covenant stating that the land was 'not to be sold to Jews or persons of objectionable nationality.' Justice McKay, in allowing the purchase of the land in question by a person of Jewish faith, argued thus: 'In my opinion, nothing could be more calculated to create or deepen divisions existing between religions and ethnic groups in this province ... It appears to me to be a moral duty, at least, to lend aid to all forces of cohesion, and similarly to repel all fissiparous tendencies which would imperil national unity.' McKay concluded that the covenant was void because it was 'offensive to the public policy of this jurisdiction.'

The Ontario Supreme Court's decision in *Drummond Wren*, and a Supreme Court of Canada decision in the case of *Noble and Wolf* v *Alley et al.* (1950), which also invalidated a racially restrictive covenant, were seen by some as milestones in the fight against this type of discrimination (Saalheimer, 1952). In *Noble and Wolf* v *Alley et al.*, a provision drawn in 1933 stipulated that the lands in question should 'never be sold to any person of the Jewish, Hebrew, Semitic, Negro, or Colored Race or blood,' and that the restriction should remain in force until 1962. In this case, Mr Wolf, a Jew, attempted to purchase land in a summer-resort development on Lake Huron. The defendants in the case, thirty-five members of the 'Beach O' Pines protective association,' argued that the sale would 'change the character of the community, with the result that the desirability of the locality as a summer residence for the present owners would be lessened and the value of the lands depreciated.' In its decision, the Canadian Supreme Court noted that, if literally construed, the covenant would prohibit any person possessing the slightest degree of race or blood specified from purchasing land in the area. Although the decision disallowed the restrictive covenant, the Court chose not to address the much more important issue of whether such covenants were considered to be contrary to public policy.

In response to the mounting concerns over the discriminatory impact of such laws, in March 1950 the Ontario legislature amended the Conveyancing and Law of Property Act to remove restrictions on the sale, ownership, occupation, or use of land because of the race, creed, colour, nationality, or place of origin of the proposed purchaser. While it is difficult to empirically assess the effectiveness of this change in eliminating discriminatory practices, it is notable that a 1959 study conducted by the Toronto and District Labour Committee for Human Rights found evidence of considerable racial discrimination in access to Metropolitan Toronto apartment buildings. Of the twenty-six buildings selected for the survey, eleven would accept Negroes, nine would refuse them, and six were in the 'doubtful' category. Hill (1960: 403) notes that a similar study conducted in 1957 revealed that 50 per cent of the apartment buildings did not allow Blacks to rent.

The existence of racially restrictive covenants governing sales of land, combined with informal practices which prevented minorities from obtaining housing, constitutes an important component of racism in this period of Ontario's history.

Employment

Negroes are restricted largely to a few remunerative and servile types of employment, they are not always served at the best restaurants, nor admitted to high class hotels. They are restricted in cities to the poorer residential districts, and are not accepted socially – intermarriage with whites is not approved. (McKenzie, 1940: 200)

Since Canada passed through longer and often more chronic stages of depression, and because Canadian Blacks faced constant competition from proportionately larger groups of immigrants, Canada moved much more slowly than the United States in recognizing the need for legislation which would assure equality of access to employment (Winks, 1968).

There is little doubt, however, that discrimination against Blacks in access to employment existed in the early to mid-1900s,[9] and that it still exists today. Unfortunately, the historical record with respect to Blacks' difficulties in securing employment and promotions is rather sketchy, owing to the fact that detailed quantitative data on unemployment and occupational distributions was not collected on the basis of race/ethnicity by the Canadian government. In addition, Blacks did not possess the social and political power to challenge what they may have deemed to be discriminatory decisions by employers or potential employers. The discussion of this topic is thus by necessity restricted to the limited qualitative evidence that was uncovered in a search of popular and academic literature and case law. However, this qualitative evidence reveals that discrimination on the basis of racial characteristics was commonly practised by employers in virtually all sectors of the Canadian economy. This discrimination was commonly justified through attributions of blame to other workers, who ostensibly would not feel comfortable working with Blacks, and the general public, who were apparently reluctant to patronize businesses employing Black workers.

Walker (1980) indicates that, in the early 1900s, Blacks were concentrated in road and railway construction, and filled a large proportion of the jobs in domestic and hotel service in Canada, mainly because the serving of Whites was considered to be appropriate work for them. One result of this concentration of Blacks in low-level service occupations was that it contributed to a perpetuation of Whites' notions of Blacks as servile, which to a certain extent were the cause of this occupational segregation in the first place. As Walker (1980: 100) notes, 'Whenever a White saw a Black, it was with a pick and shovel or with pots and pans.' This service labour role for Blacks, and their apparent satisfaction with it, reinforced and perpetuated the categorization and exploitation of them, and never required the support of formal legal sanction.

Several examples from the federal civil service illustrate the difficulties Blacks experienced in securing employment, and in obtaining promotions once employment had been attained. In 1911, at the same time that concerns were being expressed regarding Black immigration, it was noted in the House of Commons Debates (1910–11) that a 'young coloured man, who passed first on the list for a certain position in the naval service,' was denied the position, presumably on the basis of his race. In the same year, a 'coloured gentleman who was at the head of the examination list for the census department was given an inferior position by the Minister of Agriculture, looking after the black Minorca hens on the farm' (ibid.). In 1932, White civil servants objected to the hiring of a Black university graduate, and when the individual came up for promotion he was refused as a result of threats of White resignations. It is also notable that the Canadian National Railway, a crown corporation, refused to hire Black conductors until at least the 1950s (Hill, 1960).

Another interesting manifestation of employment discrimination is revealed in the situation of racial-minority groups in the Canadian army. During the first two years of the First World War, Blacks, aboriginals, and other racial minorities were rejected for military service (Henry et al., 1995) and, although eventually accepted, such individuals were subsequently placed in separate military units. As one battalion commander explained after rejecting nineteen Black volunteers, 'I have been fortunate to have secured a very fine class of recruits, and I did not think it fair to these men that they should have to mingle with Negroes' (as quoted in Walker, 1980: 95). Another commander wrote, 'Neither my men nor myself would care to sleep alongside Negroes, or to eat with them, especially in warm weather' (ibid.).

When the Second World War began, attitudes towards Blacks serving in the Canadian military had not altered significantly, and, once again, Black volunteers were rejected. Although the army eventually accepted them, and although there were no segregated Black units, Walker (1980: 96) reports that Blacks in regular units were often placed into service jobs as 'cooks, orderlies, and batmen, or found themselves with extended latrine and kitchen duties.'

During the period of the Second World War, and despite labour shortages in the Canadian economy caused by the war, the National Selective Service, the federal government agency responsible for assisting the unemployed in securing jobs, formally accepted requests for racial restrictions from employers. A card used for registering the needs of employers referred to 'requirements as to skill, age, and race' (MacLennan, 1943). If employers indicated that they did not want a Jew or Negro to be employed in their establishment, this request was noted, and Selective Service workers generally heeded the employers' wishes. Not surprisingly, such attitudes and practices resulted in restricted access to employment for Blacks, and in response to the revelations of the Selective Service's discriminatory practices, a group of concerned Blacks told the *Globe and Mail* (28 October 1943) that 'some of us, even those of us who have university educations, are finding doors closed on us, even in war time.'

MacLennan's (1943) survey of employers in the city of Toronto confirmed the existence of widespread discrimination in employment practices. One industry was willing to employ Blacks 'if necessary,' another would insist on a separate department for them, several claimed that White workers would object to the employment of Blacks, while others actually 'boasted' that they employed only people of a certain colour.

While such discriminatory practices on the part of employers are problematic enough, evidence also suggests that Blacks were additionally denied access to certain educational opportunities. The *Globe and Mail* (26 February 1947) reported on the situation of a Black woman who attempted to enrol at a hair-dressing school in Ontario and was told that, because she was coloured, she would not be accepted. The manager of the school, reflecting the common prac-tice of denying personal responsibility for discrimination, attributed the refusal to admit the woman to the 'natural objection of the [other] students.' This woman was eventually accepted at another hairdressing school, but after gradu-ating and applying for jobs at more than twenty-five beauty parlours, was unsuccessful in securing employment.

During this period, the Canadian popular media and certain activist groups became more cognizant of the problem of employment discrimination, and accounts of the extent of the problem began to surface in some sources. For instance, another survey of 158 businesses and industrial firms in Toronto, con-ducted by the Home Service Association of Toronto, and partially reported in the *Globe and Mail* (26 February 1947), uncovered that the majority of employ-ers attributed their reluctance to hire Blacks to the general public, who, it was claimed, would not patronize businesses with Black employees. A department store representative told the *Globe*, 'It isn't that I have any personal objection, but the feelings of the staff must be taken into consideration, and, of course, the public with whom we do business may object.' The superintendent of the Toronto Western Hospital invoked a somewhat different, although still self-exculpatory, justification in explaining that institution's rejection of Black female nursing students. 'We want girls who will be most suitable and happiest, and we have to think of that when considering a coloured girl. My personal opinion is that coloured girls would be happiest taking a course at a school in the United States where they will be among their own race.'

Overall, the justifications for not hiring Blacks revealed in the responses to this survey exhibit a combination of stereotypical notions of Blacks' inability to perform in certain types of jobs, and attributions of blame to the general public. Companies in the survey who reported never hiring Blacks offered the follow-ing reasons: (1) none qualified had ever applied; (2) other employees would object; (3) the public would object; (4) Negroes are emotionally and intellectu-ally immature and incapable of performing satisfactory work;[10] (5) Negroes are unclean, unhealthy, and would endanger the lives of other workers; (6) Negroes have bad morals and bad manners; (7) Negroes are lazy and irresponsible; (8) Negroes are overly-aggressive and do not respect the rights of others; (9) Negroes would seek social equality and cause unrest in the firm; (10) Negroes only adapt to hot, heavy work; (11) Negroes would not be happy in this type of work (Hill, 1960: 128).

The National Employment Service, which had responded to allegations of its discriminatory practices in 1943 by asserting that 'no official of selective service shall do anything to encourage or facilitate any such discrimination ... and no official shall take into consideration any other factor other than the applicant's ability satisfactorily to fill the vacancy' (MacLennan, 1943: 165), later defended its policies by arguing that it was only protecting Blacks:

It does irreparable harm to race relations to send a Negro, unannounced, to a waiting employer. The shock generally is too much for the employer, and does not give us a chance to gradually educate such people. I won't send a Negro to a firm where he is not wanted, for it does no good; but I will work to get them where I think they have the slightest chance of being accepted. (as quoted in Hill, 1960: 132)

Despite the diverse rationalizations offered for the existence of restrictive hiring policies, the Ontario Government was finally forced to deal with the mounting concerns in the early 1950s, with the Ontario Fair Employment Practices Act coming into effect on 4 June 1951. Under this act, which applied only to employers of more than five people, employers were forbidden to refuse to employ, to discharge, or to discriminate against any person because of race, creed, colour, nationality, ancestry, or place or origin (Ontario, *Statutes of Ontario*, 1951). However, the effectiveness of this act as a deterrent to discriminatory practices on the part of employers is called into question when we consider that the penalties for violations amounted to only $50 for individuals, and $100 for a corporation. In addition, there is no indication that violations of the provisions of the act were pursued by government authorities. Such symbolic measures apparently accomplished little in improving the situation of racial-minority groups with respect to access to employment.

Perhaps the most significant federal government measure in the area of employment law was a 1952 Order in Council which established a fair-employment-practices policy regarding government contracts. The preamble to this order stated:

It is considered advisable that a clause prohibiting discrimination by the contractor in the employment of labour in respect of race, national origin, colour, or religion should be incorporated in all contracts made by the government of Canada for the remodelling,

repair, or demolition of public buildings or other works, and for the manufacture or supply of equipment, materials, and supplies. (Saalheimer, 1952: 6–7)

Despite these provincial and federal legislative initiatives, many companies
and businesses, including agencies in the public sector, were apparently slow to
change their practices. For instance, the hiring of four Black streetcar operators
in Toronto in 1954 marked the first time Blacks had held such positions. These
individuals were hired following an inquiry into the Toronto Transit Commission's inconsistent and questionable hiring practices by the Black activist newspaper *The Canadian Negro*, which uncovered that, while Blacks held executive
positions within the company, they were not able to secure streetcar-operator
positions. Although the Toronto Transit Commission claimed that the absence
of Blacks in these positions was justified by the fact that few Blacks applied for
them and those that did failed to pass 'rigid' operators' tests, *The Canadian
Negro* (March 1954) asserted that many Blacks who applied were told that 'the
public is not ready for Negro operators.' Similarly, the Metropolitan Toronto
Police force hired a Black in the late 1950s, claiming that he was 'the first
Negro with proper qualifications who had ever applied to the force' (Hill, 1960:
135).

It is thus clear that there was widespread discrimination against Blacks in
their access to employment in Canada throughout the first half of the twentieth
century. There is little indication that legislative enactments which were ostensibly designed to eliminate this discrimination were effective in improving the
social position of Blacks in Canadian society. The disadvantaged social positions that Blacks occupied may at least in part explain their overinvolvement in
crime, as documented in chapters 6 and 7 of this book.

Access to Services

Hell, Niggers? I don't even think about 'em. But I try not to pick them up in my cab.
They smell, you know. (as quoted in Winks, 1968: 300)

Racial discrimination with respect to access to services was also pervasive in
Canadian society, cutting across geographical lines and involving such businesses as theatres, restaurants, and taverns. As was the case for the discussion
of employment discrimination, it is important to realize that, because the evidence presented in this section relies primarily on reported case law where
racial restrictions were challenged, it represents only a sampling, and perhaps
an unrepresentative sampling, of the extent of discrimination that existed. The
majority of these cases involve appeals of decisions by lower courts, and it is

obvious that most Blacks would not have access to the legal and financial resources to launch such appeals. However, a detailed examination of these cases reveals a marked reluctance on the part of the most powerful judicial officials in the country to effectively address issues of racial discrimination.

An editorial appearing in *Saturday Night* magazine (25 August 1888), which referred to an incident in which a Black minister was denied admittance to a Toronto hotel, is representative of the general tone of response to revelations of restrictions on access to services for racial-minority groups. The editor of *Saturday Night*, who supported the hotel's decision, emphasized the difference in the treatment of Blacks in Canada and the United States, and argued that a reluctance to associate with Blacks did not make one racist. Instead, the source of the problem was with Blacks themselves, who, according to the editorial, refused to accept their subordinate position in society.

I am free to admit that I would not care to share my bed and board with the aforesaid missionary. It does not follow that I have any prejudice against the Negro race. Many a kind old colored 'mammy' have I known in the southern states, and recollections of her biscuits and fried chicken, accompanied by the jokes and jollity of Aunt Chloe, endear to my memory the good-natured and generous people who have come up through so much tribulation to a freedom which should always have been theirs. In Canada there is no active prejudice against the coloured race. They meet with sympathy rather than surliness, and none of them are ever affronted on account of their complexion, except when they forget that no well-bred person will endeavour to force himself into a place where he is not wanted.

Denial of services to Blacks was pervasive in Canadian society, and Canadian judicial officials frequently upheld the right of businesses to discriminate. For instance, in a 1919 case heard in the province of Quebec, a Black plaintiff sued a Montreal theatre for the management's policy of not allowing Blacks access to orchestra seats. In its decision on this case, the Quebec Superior Court ruled that racial discrimination was not contrary to public order or morality in Canada (*Loew's Montreal Theatre* v *Reynold*, 1919).

Similarly, in the early 1920s, a light-skinned Black woman purchased a ticket for her son at a skating rink in Toronto. The boy, who was much darker in complexion than his mother, was refused admittance when he appeared at the rink, and his mother sought damages in the divisional court. Although the offending company agreed to pay twenty-five cents, the price of the ticket, the judge dismissed the action with the opinion that no other damages beyond the ticket could be shown (Winks, 1971).

In a 1924 case from the province of Ontario (*Franklin* v *Evans*, 1924) a

Black watchmaker, described by the judge hearing the appeal as a 'thoroughly respectable man,' asked to be served lunch in a London restaurant and was refused by a waitress, who informed him that the restaurant 'did not serve coloured people.' The Black male left the restaurant, consulted with a police officer, and returned to determine whether the attitude of the waitress was shared by the proprietor of the restaurant. As the presiding judge noted in reaching his decision on the case, '[the proprietor] in effect repeated [it], and he certainly was not as humane or considerate as he might have been. If I said that he was unpardonably offensive, the expression may have been too strong, but not much too strong.' Although the judge criticized the 'unnecessarily harsh, humiliating, and offensive attitude of the defendant and his wife towards the plaintiff,' he dismissed the claim, referring to the legal differences between restaurant operators and hotel keepers. Hotel keepers, he asserted, 'in the consideration of the grant of a monopoly or quasi-monopoly, take upon themselves definite obligations, such as supplying accommodation of a certain character, within certain limits, and subject to recognized qualifications, to all who apply.' The position of the restaurant proprietor, however, was legally similar to that of a department-store owner, who was not subject to the same obligations of providing service. Thus, according to the judge's decision, the existing law justified the proprietor's right to refuse service to this Black male.

In *Christie v York Corporation* (1940), a male 'who had a good position as a black chauffeur,' and who had been served in the same establishment on several prior occasions, claimed the sum of $200 for the humiliation he suffered in front of seventy other patrons after being denied service in a Montreal tavern. Although Christie's counsel told the court that he wanted the record to confirm that his client was not 'extraordinarily black,' Justice Rinfret, in the majority opinion of the Supreme Court of Canada, upheld the tavern owner's right to refuse to sell beer to a coloured person solely on the ground of his colour. Rinfret justified this decision through reference to the doctrine of freedom of commerce, noting that the tavern owner was merely protecting his business interests, and that the waiters who refused to serve Mr Christie did so 'quietly, politely, and without causing any scene or commotion whatever. If any notice was attracted to the appellant on the occasion in question, it arose out of the fact that [he] insisted on demanding beer after he had been so refused and went to the length of calling the police, which was entirely unwarranted by the circumstances.'

Justice Davis, dissenting with the majority court opinion, noted that 'there is no suggestion that in this case that there was any conduct of a disorderly nature or any reason to prompt the refusal to serve the beer other than the fact that he was a coloured gentleman.' The editor's note to the Christie case appearing in the *Dominion Law Review* aptly noted that 'this would appear to be the first authoritative decision on a highly contentious question and is the law's confirmation of the socially enforced inferiority of the coloured races.'

Although the Christie case was decided on the basis of Quebec law, and thus should not have been deemed a binding precedent in other provinces, courts across the country, reflecting similar racist attitudes, employed the rationale of the decision in justifying their own verdicts in analogous cases.

A similar case from the province of British Columbia (*Rogers* v *Clarence Hotel Co. Ltd.*, 1940) involved an appeal by a tavern owner from a judgment awarding a Black male damages of $25 for refusing to serve him beer in her premises solely on the basis of his colour. Although the Supreme Court overturned this award and once again upheld the tavern owner's right to refuse service, the dissenting Justice O'Halloran evidenced signs that at least some officials were aware of the racially discriminatory implications of such practices:

All his majesty's subjects being equal under the law, a refusal by a beer parlour operator to serve a subject must be based on reasonable grounds. It is admitted that the respondent was of respectable appearance and in a fit condition to be served in the beer parlour and that the only objection to him was his race and colour. This appeal involves questions of fundamental importance. For if a person may be refused on account of his race and colour, he may be refused also because of racial extraction, religion, political views or upon any ground according to caprice, malice, whim, or humour of the beer parlour operator. It is contrary to the common law to refuse a person solely because of his colour or race. There is no evidence in the appeal book that the respondent's race or colour was obnoxious to other patrons. It is true that the appellant testified that she had 'some trouble' at another beer parlour from serving a coloured man. Even if that were admissable evidence in this case, it proves little. The respondent might have had some unexplained trouble from serving a Scotchman or Irishman in one beer parlour, but that could hardly be accepted as a reasonable ground for refusing to serve all Scotchmen or Irishmen in any other beer parlour she might operate.

In a 1947 case from the province of Nova Scotia involving somewhat different legal principles, but still starkly illustrating the existence of a colour line in access to services in Canada, a Black woman paid for a balcony seat in a New Glasgow theatre which restricted Blacks to that section of the theatre. She offered to pay the extra ten cents that an orchestra seat would cost, this price including one additional cent of provincial tax, but her offer was refused. However, in defiance of the theatre's policy, the woman took an orchestra seat, and the manager of the theatre not only forcibly removed her from the theatre, but also called the police and had her charged with failing to pay the extra cent of tax, resulting in the woman spending a night in jail (Milner, 1947). At her trial, Viola Desmond was found guilty and fined $20, plus $6 in court costs. Her subsequent application to the Nova Scotia Supreme Court to quash the conviction was refused, apparently because too much time had elapsed and also because the court could see no substantial reason for overturning the conviction. Although Justice Hall of the Nova Scotia Supreme Court noted that 'one wonders if the manager of the theatre who laid the complaint was so zealous because of a bona fide belief that there had been an attempt to defraud the province of Nova Scotia of the sum of one cent, or was a surreptitious endeavour to enforce a Jim Crowe rule by misuse of a public statute,' no recourse was available to Viola Desmond.

The existence of such discriminatory practices was certainly not completely ignored by federal and provincial legislators, although resistance to effectively dealing with the situation was pervasive, and remedies were painfully slow to be implemented. One of the first legislative attempts to deal with racial discrimination in access to services in the province of Ontario was a bill proposed in 1933 by Argue Martin, the member of provincial Parliament for Hamilton West. Although this bill was more specifically concerned with addressing discrimination against Jews, as opposed to Blacks, the debate in the Ontario legislature surrounding its passage reveals the reticence of legislators to implement effective solutions to the problem. In the discussions dealing with the proposed legislation, E.F. Singer referred to signs on Toronto beaches stating, 'Jews and Dogs Not Allowed,' and expressed the belief that a community of dogs would perhaps be more charitable towards Jews. Martin's proposed legislation did not require proactive measures to ensure the employment of minority groups and their unrestricted access to services, but only asserted that businesses not 'display to the public that a certain race or creed is unwanted.' Despite its relatively benign nature, the bill was not passed, with Wilfred Heatherington, a Conservative member of the legislature, arguing, 'We cannot legislate people into good manners and sound private judgement. We should depend on the fair play of the people of this province rather than on statutes for this sort of thing.' Even more strikingly, Heatherington concluded 'I wouldn't like to see the house admit that such unfair practices exist by passing this bill' (*Toronto Star*, 14 March 1933).

In response to the continuing problems of discrimination, and the emerging public and media consciousness of the issue, legislative change in the province of Ontario slowly evolved throughout the 1930s and 1940s, and culminated in the passage of the 1944 Racial Discrimination Act and the 1954 Fair Accommodation Practices Act. Prior to the passage of these acts, a series of minor legislative provisions were enacted that addressed discrimination in access to services. These included amendments to the Insurance Act (Ontario, *Revised Statutes of Ontario*, 1937, chapter 256), which provided that 'any licensed insurer which discriminates unfairly between risks within Ontario because of the race or religion of the insured shall be guilty of an offence,' and the Community Halls Act (Ontario, *Revised Statutes of Ontario*, 1937, chapter 284), which indicated that 'no organization shall be denied the use of [the] hall for religious, fraternal, or political reasons.'

The Ontario Racial Discrimination Act, passed in 1944, narrowly confined itself to prohibiting the publishing of signs, notices, and symbols indicating discrimination against any person or class of persons because of race or creed (Saalheimer, 1949), and did not deal directly with issues of access to employment or restrictive land covenants. This legislation was apparently ineffective in altering the attitudes and practices of individuals and businesses in the province, with the Black newspaper *The Dawn of Tomorrow*[11] (18 December 1946) noting that a Black had been refused as a participant in a bridge tournament in Toronto. The paper also suggested that, although hotels in Ontario denied restrictions on Black patrons, in practice they treated Blacks differently from others. Similarly, there were reports of restrictions against Blacks at the Lakeview golf course in Port Credit, Ontario, where members objected to playing alongside Blacks (*The Canadian Negro*, April–May 1954), and indications that several 'social clubs' in the province admitted Black sports and entertainment celebrities, but excluded all other Blacks (*The Canadian Negro*, November 1953). In addition, several barbers in the province refused to cut Blacks' hair – one barber was quoted as telling the *London Free Press* (21 April 1950), 'You bet your life a white barber won't give a Negro a haircut. You can't mix 'em; either you have one kind of customer or the other and you can't have both.' Earlier, a Chatham barber 'won local fame' for declining to cut a Negro's hair because he had no Black soap (Winks, 1971: 294).

The Toronto Civil Liberties Association submitted a brief to the Ontario government in 1949, calling attention to the ineffectiveness of the 1944 legislation. This brief urged the enactment of a Fair Employment Practices Act, and an amendment to the Racial Discrimination Act which would provide that restrictive covenants, excluding members of certain races and religions from buying or renting property should have no legal validity. Finally, the association requested a measure that would prevent municipalities from issuing licences to any hotel keeper, restaurant proprietor, or operator of a public place who practised racial or religious discrimination in the conduct of business[12] (Saalheimer, 1949). Ontario's Fair Accommodation Practices Act repealed the Racial Discrimination Act in 1954, and stated:

No person shall deny to any person or class of persons, the accommodation, services or facilities available in any place to which the public is customarily admitted because of the race, creed, color, nationality, or ancestry or place of origin of such person or class of persons. (Ontario, *Statutes of Ontario*, chapter 28, 1954)

Despite the apparent benevolent intentions of this act, as *The Canadian Negro* (April–May 1954) aptly asserted, the penalty structure of the act, which allowed for fines of $50 for individuals and $100 for corporations who were in violation, did not serve as a sufficient deterrent to the commission of discriminatory practices.

That egalitarian attitudes towards minority groups could not be legislated is perhaps most clearly illustrated in a consideration of a series of incidents in the southwestern Ontario community of Dresden, a community whose chief claim to fame, as Katz (1949) notes, was 'that it served as the terminus of the underground railway in the 1800s.' Although a Dresden drugstore clerk asserted that 'we have no race problem in our town' (as quoted in Winks, 1968: 300), and despite the provisions of the 1944 Racial Discrimination Act, in 1949 the community decided explicitly by ballot to continue its local ban on serving Blacks, by a vote of 517 to 108. Dresden's approximately 300 Black citizens were apparently seen as constituting a serious threat to the 1,400 Whites in the community, as was revealed in interviews recounted in a *Maclean's* article (Katz, 1949). For instance, a Dresden barber who banned Blacks from his establishment pointed to a photograph of his daughter on the wall and stated, 'You know what they're aiming at? They want to marry white women. That's the main reason they're agitating for rights. And that's why I'm against giving way to them.' Similarly, a member of the local legion branch told Katz, 'It's perfectly all right for them to join the branch because, after all, they did fight overseas. But when one of them starts dancing with my wife, that's when I take my coat off.'

Racial discrimination in Dresden became the focus of considerable media attention in the mid-1950s, when two restaurant owners were charged with violations of Ontario's Fair Accommodation Practices Act for refusing to serve Blacks. The resulting three cases were the culmination of attempts on the part of the National Unity Association and the Joint Labour Committee for Human Rights to test the effectiveness of the legislation. In the first two cases, both proprietors were found guilty by a local magistrate, but on appeal the convictions were quashed because of 'insufficient evidence.' The circumstances and resultant controversy surrounding these cases is worth considering in some detail, as they are reflective of the prevailing attitudes towards racial issues in Ontario during this period, and of the ineffectiveness of the legal system and its representatives to adequately address systemic racism in the province.

Regina v *Emerson* (1955) involved an appeal by Mrs Emerson on a conviction under the Fair Accommodation Practices Act resulting from her denial of service to Mrs Bernard Carter because of her colour. Following discussions with Mr Burnett, secretary-treasurer of the National Unity Association, Mrs Carter and her brother had entered Emerson's Dresden restaurant for the express purpose of seeing whether the Fair Accommodation Practices law was being obeyed. Carter first asked to be served soda-pop and was told that there was none available. Seeing a container of milk on a counter in the restaurant, Carter asked to be served milk, but was also denied. Reflecting a decided inability to see the relevant facts of the case, the County Court judge (Grosch), who overturned Emerson's original conviction, apparently was not convinced that the evidence proved that Carter had been denied service. He suggested that, even if there was denial of service, it had to be shown that the food requested was available, and the soda-pop evidently was not, 'and it may be quite possible the milk which Mrs. Carter saw was reserved specifically by some other customer or customers.' Grosch also called attention to the fact that Carter was an 'outsider,' and noted that the community of Dresden was a small one in which people knew one another, and often knew the 'inclinations and expressed opinions of other citizens ... Could there not have been any other logical or rational reason why service might be denied under such circumstances?'

Judge Grosch also presided over the appeal of McKay, another Dresden restaurant proprietor convicted under the Fair Accommodation Practices Act (*Regina* v *McKay* 1955). In this case, Bromley Armstrong, a resident of Toronto, went to Dresden in October 1954 with Mr Blum, executive secretary of the Joint Labour Committee for Human Rights, and Mr Donaldson, a reporter for the *Toronto Telegram*. Armstrong asked to be served coffee 'about three times' and waited approximately twenty minutes, but the waitress in McKay's restaurant did not serve him. Blum and Donaldson, who were White, entered the same restaurant and were served in about five minutes. Once again, Judge Grosch was not convinced that the incident constituted a violation of the Fair Accommodation Practices Act, and concluded that there was no evidence to the effect that McKay, the proprietor of the restaurant, had given instructions to the waitress not to serve Armstrong. As he had in the Emerson case, Grosch asserted that 'there quite possibly could also be reasons other than colour if service was in fact denied' and expressed concern that 'this whole thing was a scheme to try and create a situation [there].'

In the third Dresden case, also involving the restaurant owner McKay (*Regina ex rel. Nutland* v *McKay*, 1956), the previously mentioned Blum went to Dresden with Percy Bruce and Jack Alleyne, two West Indian students from the University of Toronto. The two students, who were 'dressed respectably and acted properly,' placed an order with a waitress, who started to prepare it 'until she received a look from [another] waitress.' Bruce and Alleyne spent approximately twenty-five minutes in the restaurant and were not served during that time, and when they asked McKay if they were going to be served, they received no reply. In addition, McKay apparently went as far as to pull down the blinds and lock the doors to the restaurant, a 'pattern that [McKay] commonly followed' in handling Black customers.

The County Court judge (Lang) hearing McKay's appeal from his original conviction in this case apparently saw things somewhat differently from Judge Grosch. He noted that the evidence demonstrated that all the White people in the restaurant had been served, and indicated that it was not necessary that the waitresses, or McKay, 'say in so many words "I refuse to serve you food" ... All McKay had to do was tell the waitress to serve Bruce and Alleyne, and he refused or refrained from doing so.' Although McKay was ultimately found guilty and fined $25, plus court costs of $226, it is questionable whether such penalties would serve as a sufficient deterrent to others engaging in such discriminatory practices. An editorial in *The Canadian Negro* (1955) aptly observed that the Fair Accommodation Practices Act 'has proven to be as weak as a newborn kitten.' In an interesting denouement to the Dresden cases, Charles Daly, minister of labour for the province of Ontario, attributed the agitation to 'Communist-sponsored troublemakers' (*Maclean's*, 12 May 1956). In the same *Maclean's* article, the editor asserted that Dresden was the *one* town in all of Canada where there had been considerable overt discrimination against Blacks.

The response to the Dresden incidents, both in the popular media and on the part of provincial legislators, provides further evidence of the characteristic denial that racial problems existed in Ontario. The more general reluctance to enact and enforce meaningful legislation to address such problems provides further evidence of the ability of powerful groups to maintain their advantaged positions, and the existence of systemic racism in the province which kept Blacks in positions of subordination.

Miscegenation

It should be positively forbidden. It is not at root a question of social philosophy. It is at root a question of biology. There is abundant proof, alike furnished by the intermarriage of human races and by the interbreeding of animals, that when the varieties mingled diverge beyond a certain slight degree the result is invariably a bad one. If the governments of white peoples have any justifiable function, that function is to prevent race deterioration by miscegenation with coloured races. (Pestle, 1925: 337)

While there is considerable evidence of discrimination in Blacks' access to housing, employment, and services that was at least in part attributable to individual racism on the part of Whites, perhaps the most prominent concerns among Whites in Canadian society surrounded the issue of the intermixing of races. In many quarters, interracial contact between White women and Black men aroused even greater anxiety than immigration itself, with such encounters serving as an effective vehicle for the expression of views about race.[13] In the city of Toronto, for instance, 'dance halls where Negroes and white girls danced together' were closed or 'made to abate the practice' (*Toronto Daily Star*, 29 June 1922). A 1925 *Saturday Night* editorial (15 August) entitled 'Girls Be Careful Who You Marry' asserted that the number of marriages between 'Canadian girls' and 'Chinamen, Hindus, Moslems or African Negroes [had] increased to a disquieting extent' and called for the Canadian government to 'ban such unions.' In his address to the Geography section of the British Association, reprinted in *Canadian Forum*, Professor Gregory (1925) also supported a restriction on interracial marriages, asserting that the White–coloured 'hybrid' children that were the result of such marriages were 'inferior to both parents.'

The issue of interracial mixes led directly to one of the most disturbing racial incidents in Ontario in the early 1930s, involving the Hamilton branch of the Ku Klux Klan.[14] This branch of the Klan was apparently among the most active in Canada, and they held a public parade in Hamilton in the summer of 1929, 'at which time they increased their membership by several hundred' (*Toronto Daily Star*, 1 March 1930). In reaction to the proposed marriage of a Black male[15] and White female in the neighbouring city of Oakville, what was described as a 'mob' of between fifty and seventy-five men, 'disguised with hoods extending from the top of the head to the knees,' appeared at the residence of the woman and asked her to accompany them. After burning a large cross outside of the Black male's home, the men then transported Isabella Jones to the Salvation Army Barracks in Hamilton. Only one individual (Mr Phillips) was charged as a result of this incident, the charge being that he had 'his faced masked or blackened or otherwise disguised, without lawful excuse' (Canada, Criminal Code, Section 464 [c]). The sentencing magistrate found Phillips guilty, and imposed a $50 fine.

Although Robin Winks (1971: 324) suggests that Canadian newspapers 'condemned the Klan's offensive buffoonery,' a closer examination of the historical record suggests otherwise. The official reaction to this incident as documented in media coverage of it is particularly revealing of the prevailing attitudes towards racial issues in Canadian society. The *Toronto Daily Star* (1 March 1930), neglecting to address the issue of the cross-burning, noted that the Klan members, many of whom were 'prominent Hamilton businessmen,' carried out their business 'courteously and quietly' and 'at no time during the evening was violence either offered or received.' The Toronto *Globe* (1 March 1930), while devoting much less attention to the issue than the *Star* did, also noted in their headline that 'No Violence Was Involved.'

The *Star* asserted that the actions of the Klan were justified by the fact that the mother of Isabella Jones had written to the Klan, asking them to assist her in breaking up the match between her daughter and the Black male (1 March 1930). In a later article (*Toronto Daily Star*, 24 March 1930), a spokesman for the Hamilton Klan asserted, 'we did not go down to Oakville specially to get those two to separate. We did not pick on Johnson because he was coloured. We would have done the same thing with anyone who was living immorally with a girl if her mother asked us to.' However, this attitude seems difficult to reconcile with the spokesman's additional comments, quoted in the same article:

Dr. Harold Orme, spokesman for the organization, said they were inspired by knowledge of crime conditions which pointed clearly to a mixture of blood as creating fiery, subnormal peoples to whom most of the violent crimes could be traced. 'If this is allowed to go on here we will have the same condition in Canada. Our main purpose is to preserve racial purity. We take Christ as our criterion of character. Our only interest in race matters is that we want our country kept pure from contamination by mixed marriages.'

The mayor of Oakville, who supported the actions of the Klan, told the *Star* (1 March 1930), 'Personally, I think the Ku Klux Klan acted quite properly in this matter. The feeling in town is generally against such a marriage. Everything was done in an orderly manner. It will be quite an object lesson.'

The *Star* (1 March 1930) also conducted a series of interviews with prominent Southern Ontario Blacks, many of whom expressed opposition to the actions of the Klan in the Oakville affair. Interestingly, however, some of these Black leaders were quoted as indicating they were also opposed to interracial mixes. For instance, Lawrence McNeil, 'Negro clergyman,' suggested, 'I hold no brief for the promiscuous intermingling of the races, but I am unalterably opposed to the substitution of purely authorized law enforcement agencies by such agencies as the Ku Klux Klan. If an illicit relationship existed, the police should have interfered.'

Phillips eventually appealed his conviction and sentence to the Supreme Court of Ontario. Chief Justice Mulock, in his decision to dismiss the appeal and substitute a sentence of three months' imprisonment for the original $50 fine, noted the gravity of the offence, and warned against the further commission of such acts:

The attack of the accused and his companions upon the rights of this girl was an attempt to overthrow the law of the land, and in its place to set up mob law, lynch law ... The greatest calamity that can befall a country is the overthrow of the law ... Mob law, such as is disclosed in this case is a step in that direction, and, like a venomous serpent, whenever its horrid head appears, must be killed, not merely scotched ... This being the first case of this nature that has come before the court, it has dealt with the offence with great leniency, and the sentence here imposed is not to be regarded as a precedent in the event of repetition of such offence. (*Rex* v *Phillips*, 1930)

However, the extended sentence and admonitions of Chief Justice Mulock were apparently not sufficient to deter other members of the Klan from engaging in intimidation against those who were opposed to their activities. Threatening letters were sent to Johnson, warning him not to marry Isabella Jones, and members of the Black community who had spoken out against the Klan's conduct were also the subject of further Klan action. For instance, a prominent Black Toronto lawyer, E. Lionel Cross, received at least three letters from members of the Klan, threatening to burn him and put him out of business unless he ceased his criticism of the Klan (*Toronto Daily Star*, 24 March 1930).

Following the imposition of the extended sentence, Phillips still expressed no remorse for his actions, stating he was 'happy' to serve three months in prison as 'all [Klan] members are willing to sacrifice freedom for Christianity and country' (*Toronto Daily Star*, 17 April 1930). The *Star*'s editorial stance was subtly critical of the Ontario Supreme Court's decision to increase Phillips's sentence, with the paper quoting the former Isabella Jones: 'He [Phillips] thought he was doing me a kindness. I have a letter that he sent me containing good advice. I don't like to think of him having to go to jail.'

Eventually, Johnson and Jones were secretly married at the New Credit Six Nations Indian Reservation, north of Oakville. The *Toronto Daily Star*'s (24 March 1930) description of the marriage quotes the wife of the minister who conducted the marriage, who had 'pleaded with her husband not to take the chance of defying the Klan.'

Concerns surrounding interracial mixes continued into the late 1950s, and religious officials often refused to marry Whites and Blacks, usually citing concern for the children of mixed marriages as the justification for their reluctance. In 1959, for instance, a Toronto Seventh Day Adventist minister refused to marry a West Indian printer and his Canadian (White) bride, and although a United Church minister eventually married the couple, he too expressed reservations. 'I am not in favour of mixed marriages generally speaking, simply because they are often unsuccessful ... These marriages may work out for awhile, but when children enter the picture, that's when the trouble begins. The children are not readily accepted by either the white or coloured society, and it inevitably brings unhappiness and bitterness, even toward their parents' (*Toronto Daily Star*, 7 December 1959). This concern was also shared by others in the society, as Hill's (1960: 266) quote from a Toronto police official demonstrates:

There is a lot of mixing going on [in the area], but for the life of me, I can't see why anyone would want to marry outside of his race. I don't mind and I can understand two races going around together and perhaps even dating, but not marrying. Just look at what happens to the kids. I knew a fine coloured girl, came from mixed parentage, who was a social outcast, and had no friends, because she didn't know which way to associate. I felt sorry for her, but none of us would consider her seriously.

Hill (1960) reports that even Black clergymen were 'especially alarmed' at the increase in mixed marriages that was reportedly occurring in the 1950s. Similarly, Austin Clarke (1963), a prominent member of Toronto's Black community, in an otherwise progressive article, lamented the fact that some Blacks '[take] out their hostility in aggressive social and sexual behaviour. Some marry white women and seek to drown their fears and complexes in their wive's environment. In my opinion they only create another problem – the problem of producing mulatto children who belong neither to the white world nor the Black.' While such comments certainly represent a reasonable assessment of the social reaction to the children of such mixed marriages, they are in many ways self-defeatist and reflective of racist attitudes. And, as chapter 7 will demonstrate, the criminal justice system also demonstrated considerable concern regarding interracial mixes, reserving some of the harshest penalties for Black males who sexually assaulted White females.

The Resistance to Change

In my eight years in Canada I have been treated with prejudice and discrimination by most white people, in large and small ways. In Canada the restaurants, buses, washrooms and other public places do not carry 'white only' and 'coloured only' signs; but every black man can read these signs in the attitudes of white Canadians. (Clarke, 1963)

While genuine change in the social situations and positions of Blacks in Canadian society was not manifest, there is little doubt that there was an emergent consciousness of racial problems in Canadian society in the 1950s. In addition to this increased awareness, isolated discussions of the indefensibility of racial biology and societal conventions surrounding intermarriage began to appear in some segments of the academy and popular media (see Berrill, 1956). For instance, writing in the *Dalhousie Review*, K.A. Baird (1958) went as far as to assert that Blacks were *more* advanced biologically than Whites: 'Consider, for example, that the gorilla and the chimpanzee tend to have lank hair, thin lips, and a profusion of hair on the body. In these respects therefore, the white man stands nearer to the apes than does the Negro.' On the topic of intermarriage, Baird noted, 'I would prefer to see my daughter married to an intelligent and cultured Negro that to some of the "white trash" I have met.'

Such pronouncements should not be taken as indicative of the fact that widespread attitudinal and social change was occurring, however. In fact, there is evidence that, as Blacks in Canada became more socially active and voiced concerns about their disadvantaged position, there was something of a backlash on the part of the Canadian populace, and a renewed emphasis on the notion that, while the situation for Blacks in Canada was perhaps not ideal, it was at least better than what they experienced in the United States.

For instance, in 1956 the Toronto Board of Education, in response to the concerns of a delegation of Black parents who felt the children's book *Little Black Sambo* contained harmful racist passages, voted to discontinue use of the book in its classrooms. In its attempt to trivialize the importance of this issue, the *Globe and Mail* (4 February 1956) included a blatantly disparaging cartoon, depicting a tiger, with the label 'phony racial issues' attached to it, apparently ready to attack a Black child with a 'Toronto Board of Education' label. The caption to the cartoon reads: 'And little Black Sambo said: "Please Mr. Tiger, don't eat me up."' Perhaps even more disturbingly, the *Globe* printed the following editorial, with the blank spaces seemingly intended to underline the hazards associated with using the word 'Black,' given the board's decision:

It was a _____ day for Toronto when some _____ guard smuggled copies of little _____ Sambo into the public schools. But now the _____ mark on our fair city's record has been expunged. By order of the Board of Education, little _____ Sambo is to be removed from all classrooms and school libraries. Any child having or reading it will get _____ looks, he will be considered a _____ sheep, and may eventually be hauled away in the _____ Maria.

Let no Toronto teacher, from now on, advise his students to read _____ Beauty, or the _____ Arrow, or _____ Lamb and Grey Falcon. Let him not refer to the _____ Sea (if he must refer to a sea, let it be the Red Sea. And the redder, the better.) Let him not be found drinking _____ coffee, watching Bad Day at the _____ Rock, or taking up residence in _____ Boulevard.

'Pink is my true love's hair.' 'Mauve as the pit from pole to pole.' 'I am green, but comely.' The teachers will learn. And if some of them think the whole business is rather silly, if some of them think it gives Toronto a _____ eye, well, a city that is stupid enough to elect a school board that is stupid enough to do anything as stupid as this, deserves not one but two of them.

In a letter to the editor of the *Globe* in response to the editorial, which the paper chose not to publish, Elspeth Hall referred to the editorial and cartoon as 'filthy pieces of journalism,' and accused the paper of 'simply upholding the white supremacist attitude that Blacks are too moronic to decide what is good for them' (*The Canadian Negro*, March, 1956).

Equally disturbing and representative of the fact that racism was still pervasive in Canada was a 1956 *Maclean's* article. Reporting on the social conditions in an isolated Black community in New Road, Nova Scotia, Staebler (1956) emphasized the high levels of illegitimacy, illiteracy, poverty, and crime that supposedly characterized the village. New Road is referred to as 'almost as obscure and sinister a village as an African jungle,' and Staebler indicates that the police patrolled the community in pairs and never at night, and truck drivers making deliveries were allowed to carry loaded revolvers. The Black women in the community 'fight and throw rocks at each other ... I was told by a policeman that when [the women] come into town [Halifax], they talked loud and pulled each other's hair, upset the tables at rummage sales, begged for handouts, and sometimes stole clothes for their children – some are wild ones.'

The villagers were alleged to 'practice sorcery' and apparently harboured by 'many queer superstitions.' Reporting on an interview she conducted with a 'big black man,' Staebler resorts to the practice of language discrimination (Mann, 1993) to emphasize the difference between these people and the rest of conventional society. '"I took a few jobs deah, now an' then ... but they always fiahed me foah doin nothin, just thinkin."' A woman is quoted as saying: '"but dis Friday night we was at a weddin out heah, de grandes' weddin' you evah seen ... School's a good place for chillens in wintah. They goes up there and keeps warm and maybe learns readin' and writin. Ah dont mind my kids goin' to school."'

What is perhaps most interesting about Staebler's article is not that she was able to document these deprived social conditions which New Road Blacks experienced, but that she failed to attribute the existence of the problems to larger societal forces, blaming them instead on the personal inadequacies of the Black residents themselves. This is perhaps even more curious when we consider the *Maclean's* (12 May 1956) editor's lead-in to the article, which suggested 'if our reputation for racial tolerance is any better than our neighbours it is simply because we have not generally been faced with the imbalance of colour that exists elsewhere.'

John White, the editor of *The Canadian Negro*, criticized *Maclean's* for publishing the article, claiming that Staebler was a 'southerner who would do anything for a buck' and who was only interested in protecting Canadian womanhood from Black men. Although Winks (1971: 407) suggests that *Maclean's* intention was to draw attention to the need for reform and labelled White's response 'an absurd attack,' there seems little doubt that the presentation of such material would only serve to reinforce the stereotypes of Blacks already extant in Canadian society.

To conclude, the material presented above leaves little doubt that Blacks in Canada experienced considerable discrimination in virtually all aspects of their social and economic lives. While an emerging consciousness of racial issues led to some minor, and ultimately ineffective, legislative change beginning in the 1950s, an undercurrent of racism still prevailed in Canadian society. Although this discrimination against Blacks was systemic and pervasive, it was often manifested at the level of individual prejudice, and it is important to realize that it was not solely attributable to perceptions of economic threats posed by Blacks. The combination of this individual-level and systemic racism rendered it virtually impossible for the majority of Canadian Blacks to escape the disadvantaged social and economic positions to which they had been assigned since their arrival in the country. And while such deprived conditions may in themselves have been criminogenic for Blacks, the racist stereotypes that influenced the reluctance of Canadian legislators to act effectively to improve the situation of Blacks were even more prominently manifested in Blacks' disproportionately severe treatment in the criminal justice system.

5

Criminal Courts and the Racialization of Crime in Ontario

The judge ordered that the bull pen be emptied, and some 50 defendants crowded in front of the bench. After making a few jokes, the judge asked how many were working men. Nearly all hands were raised. So the judge asked, 'Is there anybody here who is not a working man?' One Polish defendant who had not understood the question, raised his hand. His case was dismissed for being an honest man. The clerk began to call the names that the defendants had given when arrested but got no answers. When one man finally responded, he was complimented by the judge for remembering his name and his case was dismissed. The judge asked anyone with a dollar to raise his hand – the implication being that they would be fined a dollar. About half the hands went up. The judge then tried one man and fined him $5, after which he asked 'How many of you men will go to work?' Every hand was raised. The judge warned 'If I catch any of you back here again I'll give you $200 and costs,' and dismissed them. More than 50 cases were disposed of in less than 30 minutes. (Anderson, 1922, as quoted in Haller, 1976: 309–10)

Before presenting the results of quantitative analyses examining the effects of race on criminal-justice outcomes, it is instructive to consider the characteristics of police courts and the key participants in these courts, and the influence these factors exerted on the administration of justice in Ontario during the early to middle part of the twentieth century.

From the late 1800s to approximately 1930, the lower courts in Canada were characterized by a routinization of procedure and an emphasis on 'rough and ready' justice (Friedman, 1993). The lack of attention to procedural and legal issues evidenced in courts during this period, combined with the popular press's and criminal justice system's proclivity to racialize crime, exerted a strong influence on the differential treatment of racial-minority groups revealed in the quantitative analyses presented in chapters 6 and 7.

Beginning in the 1930s, however, there was an increase in attention in the legal community to inequalities in the administration of criminal justice, and the potential negative consequences of such inequalities. Although commentators did not specifically address the issue of racial inequality in the criminal justice system, this chapter briefly discusses the implications of the proposed changes in criminal-sentencing practices in dealing with minority-group offenders.

The Social Contexts of Criminal Sentencing, 1892–1930

Feeley (1979) asserts that, in early American courts, rules were often applied arbitrarily, tending to fall with disproportionate harshness on the masses of poor people and recent immigrants. Similarly, Pound and Frankfurter (1922) observed the 'tendency to perfunctory routine' in Chicago's police courts, and Pound (1930: 175) further asserted:

The bad physical surroundings, the confusion, the want of decorum, the undignified off-hand disposition of cases at high speed, the frequent suggestion of something working behind the scenes, which characterize the petty criminal court in almost all of our cities, create in the minds of observers a general suspicion of the whole process of law enforcement which, no matter how unfounded, gravely prejudices the law.

Similar observations have been offered by Friedman (1993: 240), who, in describing the Oakland police court of the late nineteenth century, notes that it was 'not a place where the ritual and majesty of law hung heavy in the air. The court often did its business in a hurry and with little fuss.'

The Ontario police courts that are the focus of this analysis were apparently little different from those in the United States. These courts constituted the first level of the Ontario court system, with the majority of criminal cases taken no further, and, as immigration contributed to increases in Ontario's population and crime rates during the early 1900s, the courts' business grew commensurately. For example, with the explosive growth of the city of Toronto in the late 1800s and early 1900s, the number of cases heard by the police court in that city grew from approximately 5,000 in 1877 to almost 40,000 in 1913 (Homel, 1981). When Colonel William Denison was appointed to the Toronto police court in 1881, he sat as the lone magistrate and was assisted by only one court clerk. By the 1920s, there were four magistrates and seven clerks serving the Toronto police court, and the growth of Toronto's immigrant population forced the court to expand its number of translators from one to four.[1]

More important to the operation of the court than the additional personnel, however, was the introduction of a separate juvenile court in the 1890s (Hagan and Leon, 1977) and separate trials for women in the early 1900s, which, it was argued, would keep female offenders 'away from the mob' and prevent 'young girl(s) from going astray' (Denison, 1920: 257).

In the late 1800s and early 1900s, the police court in Toronto was characterized by a 'circus-like' atmosphere, and it served as a 'popular public attraction' (Homel, 1981: 173). Police courts were apparently similar in the city of Hamilton, where attendance often increased 'when the weather gets cold' (*Hamilton Spectator*, 30 October 1893). Police-court sittings were generally attended by a large crowd of interested spectators, who 'had its heroes, hissed its villains, and left its seats to clap acquitted comrades on the back ... The crowd's purpose in attending was complex; partly for warmth, partly for comradeship, and in great part, for sheer fun' (Craven, 1983: 272). In several sittings, the demand for seats in the court was so pronounced that people were 'forced to stand in the corridors' (*Toronto Daily Star*, 29 March 1909). Homel (1981: 173) suggests, 'For tourists, a visit to the Queen City [Toronto] without visiting [police court] would be like going to Rome and not seeing the Pope.' The *Toronto Daily Star* (30 October 1901), echoing the observations noted above, but also describing the similarities between the viewers and the viewed in the police court setting, suggested:

Every day the police court is held, the benches back of the dock are filled with a motley of spectators. To many the police court is a daily free show, the court-room the theater in which are enacted for their amusement tragedies and comedies, burlesques and farces, with real clowns and real villains and very infrequent saints as the actors and actresses ... Who can derive pleasure from a daily gloating over the wreckings of lives and character revealed as the cases proceed? It would seem to be an easy step from the seat of the police court steady to the dock and jail.

Given the attendance by predominantly lower-class members of society, decorum in the courts was not a prominent feature, and magistrates constantly had to deal with disruptive elements. There were frequent complaints by court officials about the 'noise nuisance' in the court, and at one particular sitting in Toronto, Magistrate Patterson expressed concern about the level of talking in the courtroom: 'Inspector McKinney gave a demonstration of his usual resource. Picking on several groups of offending women, [he] separated them, placing a man between them on the seats around the body of the court' (*Toronto Daily Star*, 5 June 1923).

This theatrical air was particularly characteristic of Colonel Denison's court, which heard the majority of the Toronto cases during the early period covered in the analyses. Denison was something of an urban legend in Toronto, and his personality and the activities that occurred in his court were the subject of a great deal of commentary in the popular press. For instance, the *Globe* (30 July 1912) noted that, on one day in July 1912, a group of 'fashionably-dressed women' arrived in the court to view the man they had heard so much about. Apparently, Denison's 'witty sayings' were published in the funny columns of a considerable number of U.S. newspapers (Homel, 1981). Denison also commanded the respect of other key actors in the criminal justice system. For example, J.N. Curry (1906), a Toronto crown attorney, claimed in an article that appeared in *Saturday Night* magazine, 'The city of Toronto has been wonderfully blessed, much more than her citizens realize, in having for so many years a magistrate so admirably qualified as Police Magistrate Denison, for the many and onerous duties cast upon him.' Upon Denison's retirement from the bench, Toronto's Chief Constable Dickson suggested, 'As police magistrate he discharged the duties of that office in an able, impartial, and conscientious manner, earning the confidence and respect of all' (Toronto, *Annual Report of the Chief Constable*, 1921).

Similar to other Canadian police-court magistrates of the period who were from upper-class backgrounds, Denison was the member of a wealthy and prominent Toronto family, who was appointed to the Toronto police court in 1877 by his friend Oliver Mowat, the premier of Ontario. Harry Wodson (1917: 27), a long-time police-court reporter for the *Toronto Telegram*, described Denison as follows: 'He was one of the governing class. His mind is more or less remote from the affairs of the rank and file of humanity.' Denison apparently regarded the lower classes' 'street fights, domestic wrangles, and lesser crimes as incidental to the commoner's life.' Wodson (1917: 39) further expounded on Denison's idiosyncrasies:

A swift thinker, a keen student of human nature, the possessor of an incisive tongue, he extinguishes academic lawyers, parries thrusts with the skill of a practised swordsman, confounds the deadly-in-earnest barrister with a witticism, scatters legal intricacies to the winds, will not tolerate the brow-beating of witnesses, cleans off the 'slate' before the bewildered stranger has finished gaping, shuts the book with a bang, orders adjournment of the court, then, stick in hand, strolls off to lunch at the National Club.

While Denison's class background and personality certainly had some impact on his treatment of the offenders who appeared before him, more salient to the operations of his court was the expeditious manner in which he dispensed justice, and his reluctance to allow legal principles to influence his decisions.[2] The British writer John Fraser, who attended a session of Denison's court on his visit to Toronto in 1904, noted, 'the only place I saw hustle was in the police court ... With some acquaintance of the slow formality of the English court, I was a little breathless at the slap-dash manner in which [Denison] disposed of forty cases in exactly forty minutes' (as quoted in *Canadian Law Times*, 1904: 386). Denison noted that he never allowed a point of law to be raised in his court, since his was a 'court of justice, not a court of law ... Not so long ago a young attorney wanted to quote law against my sending his man down for six weeks. He wanted to quote Mathews, I think. "Well," said I, "Mathews may be a great authority on law, but I guess he hasn't got as much authority as I have in this court. Your man goes down for six weeks"' (as quoted in ibid.).

While Denison was certainly a somewhat unconventional individual, evidence suggests that the principles he adhered to and the speed with which he dealt with cases was not unique to his court. In police courts presided over by other Toronto magistrates, and in urban courts throughout the province, there was a decided lack of concern with procedural and legal issues, and a tendency to administer justice promptly. When a judge from Chicago visited the Toronto police court in the early 1930s, he was apparently impressed by the 'swift disposition of the cases ... Whatever other blemishes the police court may possess, procrastination is not one of them' (*Toronto Daily Star*, 6 February 1931). Similarly, research on the Hamilton police courts of the early 1900s indicates that, although the volume of cases heard was lower than in Toronto, at approximately 3,000 per year, 5 to 10 cases were heard per day. This meant that, on average, a case was decided in roughly ten minutes (Weaver, 1995).

While the speed with which trials were conducted in this period is certainly worthy of concern and was at least partially responsible for inequities in the administration of justice, other contributing factors included the political nature of appointments to magisterial positions in the late 1800s and early 1900s (Angus, 1967) and the absence of legal training for magistrates appointed to such positions (Canadian Bar Association, 1916). In addition, Popple (1921) drew attention to the lack of legal representation for many defendants and the insufficiency of records on offenders' prior history to which the court had access. When these factors are considered in combination with the general atmosphere that prevailed in the courts, one would not expect a great deal of attention to issues of procedural justice or equality in dealing with offenders. We would predict that extralegal factors, especially more visible ones such as racial origin, would have a significant impact on the treatment of offenders during this period. Descriptions of criminals appearing in newspaper court reports provide convincing evidence that attention to such factors was a primary concern during this period, and it is to a consideration of the racialization of crime that the discussion now turns.

The Racialization of Crime

One of the most important factors that influenced and shaped the criminal justice system's reaction to minority-group offenders in the United States was the tendency of the popular press to focus on the commission of crime by Blacks, with the almost total neglect of any 'positive' news about Blacks. Sellin (1928: 54) was one of the first researchers to emphasize the importance of the media in presenting accounts of Black crime, suggesting

the colored criminal does not as a rule enjoy the racial anonymity which cloaks the offenses of individuals of the white race. The press is almost certain to brand him, and the more revolting his crime proves to be, the more likely it is that his race will be advertised. In setting the hall-mark of his color upon him, his individuality is in a sense submerged; and instead of a mere thief, robber, or murderer, he becomes a representative of his race, which in its turn is made to suffer for his sins, through mysteries of emotionally conditioned thought processes.

Myrdal (1944) also commented on this tendency of the popular press to publicize Black crimes, noting that a majority of the news about Blacks involved discussion of their deviant activities. Importantly, Myrdal pointed out that, 'when a Catholic or Jew, Swede or Bulgarian, commits a crime that is serious enough to get in the newspapers, it is not usual for his religion or nationality to be mentioned. When a Negro commits a newsworthy crime, on the other hand, only rarely is an indication of his race not prominently displayed' (p. 554). Myrdal asserted that this negative reporting was unfair, not only because of its emphasis on individual cases instead of statistical proportions, but also because all other aspects of Black life were neglected in the White press.

Some early, and rather unsophisticated, 'content analyses' of print media in the United States provided more objective evidence of the popular press's focus on sensational Black crimes. For instance, the Chicago Commission on Race Relations (1922) analysed all articles dealing with Negroes during 1916–17 appearing in the Chicago press and found that, of the 1,338 stories identified, 606 dealt with crime and vice. In another content analysis of twenty-eight Texas newspapers, Bryant (1935) found that 84.4 per cent of all items about Blacks were 'anti-social,' with most consisting of stories about crime. Similarly, in a study of four Philadelphia newspapers for the years 1908, 1913, 1923, 1928, and 1932, Simpson (1936) indicated that the percentage of 'Negro crime news' as a proportion of all news space devoted to Blacks ranged from 51 to 74 per cent.

In a more detailed examination of 60 issues of seventeen 'White' newspapers from various regions of the United States published in 1928 and 1929, Gist (1932) found that 47 per cent of the news space devoted to Blacks was 'anti-social.' Among such news items, one-third involved reporting of Black personal violence against Whites. In addition, Gist noted that crimes of violence committed by Blacks against other Blacks apparently had little news value, amounting to only quarter of the space devoted to crimes committed by Blacks against Whites. One of the most important points Gist (p. 408) made in this study is related to his discussion of the placing and positioning of news about Blacks, which, he asserted, 'undoubtedly for the reader, has considerable psychological import.' Gist noted that approximately one-quarter of the space devoted to news of anti-social events involving Blacks appeared on the front page of newspapers. 'For many, the front page undoubtedly constitutes the sum total of their daily reading matter, it comprises a considerable portion of their "mental" stimuli, and probably forms a background for many of the attitudes they possess.' Gist concluded, 'it is highly plausible that a continuous panorama of Negro crime spread out before the newspaper reader might be a factor in engendering racial antipathies and prejudices, or at least in bolstering up prejudices already existing' (p. 409). Such assertions were further confirmed by the Chicago Commission on Race Relations (1922), which concluded that, by virtue of their misleading presentation of news about minority groups, the city newspapers were at least partially responsible for race conflicts in that city. Similarly, Lukas (1945: 273) noted, 'the role of journalism in perpetuating the myth of Negro crime is not insignificant.'

The importance of such media depictions in terms of their influences on the treatment of minority groups by the criminal justice system should not be underestimated. As Frankfurter (1922: 516) noted in his report on the role of newspapers in criminal justice,

The inference is inescapable that the nature of what is printed, or not printed, its quality and underlying standards, above all, the general atmosphere that is [hereby] generated, must exert a most potent influence upon those who administer justice as well as upon the thought of the community, upon which, in the last analysis, the quality of the administration of justice ultimately rests.

While systematic empirical studies concerning the coverage of racial issues by the Canadian press in the early to middle 1900s were apparently not conducted, the material presented below demonstrates a similar tendency on the part of Canadian newspapers to make reference to the race of offenders in their coverage of crime and criminal-justice issues. This focus on the racial characteristics of offenders served to identify Asians and Blacks as alien and influenced, and to a certain extent seemingly justified, their differential treatment by the criminal justice system.

The Racialization of Crime: Asians

The racialization of crime was prominent in Canadian media sources of the late 1800s and early to middle 1900s, and was evidenced in newspaper headlines and descriptions of offenders from racial-minority groups. As indicated in chapter 3, the alleged moral depravity of Chinese, their use of opium, and their involvement in gambling offences became a prominent theme in descriptions of Chinese lifestyle appearing in popular magazines and newspapers. This was especially true after the implementation of Canada's first narcotic-drug legislation in 1908 (see chapter 6), a law that was directed primarily against Chinese opium users. In describing Chinese opium users and gamblers, Ontario newspapers of this period employed a number of different strategies to distance the reading public from the supposedly degenerate Chinese. The following excerpts from various court reports illustrate the sometimes subtle, but often blatant, racism directed towards these Chinese deviants.

Headlines such as 'Chinese Gambled – These 18 Chinks Were Roped in Last Night by Police Who Raided a Chinese Laundry' (*Toronto Daily Star*, 29 March 1909); 'Chink Joint Was Raided' (*Fort William Daily Times Journal*, 17 May 1909); 'Troubles of Chink' (*Hamilton Spectator*, 22 August 1912); 'Warm Pipe Scorches Chink Opium User' (*Toronto Daily Star*, 3 April 1916); 'Butter, Chink, Pole, Each Play Court Role' (*Toronto Daily Star*, 3 March 1920); and 'Ching Chang Chinaman, Muchee, Muchee Glad' (*Toronto Daily Star*, 15 May 1922) were representative of the focus on the race of offenders in court reports of this period. In addition, the description of the physical characteristics of Asians, juxtaposed with the deleterious effects of opiate drugs, served to provide readers with a decidedly stereotypical view of such individuals. For instance, 'Lee You and Lee Kee visited the spirit world. They didn't use a magic carpet. The trail they hit was the pipe' (*Toronto Daily Star*, 2 March 1920). Similarly, in the case of Joe Woyn and Jung Yue, charged with opium possession, the *Toronto Daily Star* (29 December 1916) noted,

'Not my stuff', protested Joe Woyn as he stood beside Jung Yue, a fellow Celestial, to the charge of having opium in his possession. Plainclothesmen Ward and Scott were equally positive that both of the *almond-eyed* gentlemen had a plentiful supply in their pockets when arrested. They did not have the $100 and costs that the law demanded, so they will be separated from their beloved sleep inducer for ten days. (emphasis added)

A similar focus was revealed in the case of Lee Chong, 'another cadaverous dejected Chinaman,' who was charged with being the keeper of an opium den (*Toronto Daily Star*, 31 October 1921).

Reporters actively ridiculed Chinese opium users who appeared in the courts, and constantly pointed out the differences between these Chinese and the more respectable members of society. In the case of a 'fine opium joint' raided on Elizabeth Street in Toronto, the court reporter commented on the use of a character witness by the Chinese defendant: 'A comical denouement to the case was provided by Lee Sing, one of those found in the opium joint, who produced a letter of good character from his employer, a resident of Rosedale, by whom Lee is employed as a cook' (*Toronto Daily Star*, 16 July 1914).

Descriptions of the notorious opium dens in which the Chinese practised their vice also served as an effective strategy in conveying to the public the moral degeneracy of these individuals. In reference to an opium den in the city of Ottawa, the *Citizen* (14 October 1912) reported:

Horrible scenes were seen in what the Mongolians term their temple. Above a wooden altar is to be found the picture of a hideous idol. The smaller rooms surrounding this sanctuary were small dens where around a coal oil lamp were groups of five and six Chinamen smoking opium. Some were so prostrated that they were entirely dead to the world, others were in a state of semi-consciousness but rubbed their eyes like a man who has been asleep for several days.

A more subtle, but equally effective method of emphasizing the differences between the Chinese and the rest of society was to focus on their principal occupation as laundrymen and restaurant workers. For instance, in one Hamilton case (*Hamilton Spectator*, 5 March 1921), a magistrate was forced to sentence his own laundryman for possession of opium. This 'Chinaman ... had other subjects but the washing of shirts and starching of collars occupying his mind.' In the case of William Quan, found guilty of keeping a disorderly house, the *London Advertiser* (6 May 1924) noted, 'Quan is a Chinese chef by profession and should he decide to take the three months in jail, the prisoners at Dawson Villa may be treated to Chicken a La King, and then again they may not.'

Yet another effective method of stereotyping Chinese offenders was to refer to the difficulties court officials experienced in pronouncing their names.[3] In the case of fourteen Chinese charged with gambling on the Lord's Day in Windsor (*Evening Record*, 26 February 1917), the reporter asserted, 'The names as read by Chief Willis, as usual, sounded like a song with the key to it thrown in the river.' In the Northern Ontario city of Fort William (*Fort William Daily Times Journal*, 17 May 1909), a report on convicted Chinese gamblers noted, 'The players gave the names of Lee Sing, Lee Bow, Lee Suey, Chop Suey, Lee Cow, Lee Chong [etc.] ... It is thought that many of the names are fictitious, as well as facetious.' In another gambling case from the city of Toronto, the *Star* (15 May 1922) reported, 'five Celestials answered to their names read out by Sergeant Childs in a manner that sounded like an Oriental temple chant. For once there was a smile on their bland faces when they learned through the interpreter that it would cost them only $5 each plus $1 costs.'

Court reporters also frequently referred to the difficulties Chinese immigrants experienced with the English language, which, as Mann (1993) notes, serves to further distance members of minority groups from the majority by making them appear less intelligent and less capable than English-speaking Whites – as in these two descriptions of Chinese offenders appearing in the *Toronto Daily Star*:

Although the English vocabulary possessed by Charlie Sing and Young Lung was not particularly extensive, they knew one word at least sufficient to serve the ends of justice. Found wooing the poppy with an elaborate outfit at his home on Darcy Street, Charlie was asked if the pretty paraphernalia belonged to him. 'Sure' he replied. Young Lung in the same monosyllable gave acquiescence to the fact that the fumes he fooled with were also of the naughty narcotic. (*Toronto Star*, 18 August 1916)

Celestials had a field day in Women's Court. Four Chinamen, ably supported by a well-dressed respectable countryman, and chattering among themselves in a *language that can only be written with a brush*, were charged with being in the act of preparing opium for smoking when their laundry establishment was entered by the Constables. (*Toronto Daily Star*, 31 October 1921; emphasis added)

In another example, Lee Wheel, 'an exponent of the wash tub ... for fifteen minutes attempted to tell the magistrate that he could not speak English' (*Hamilton Spectator*, 28 April 1913). Finally, in a particularly vivid description of the language problems experienced by Asians, the *Toronto Daily Star* (13 May 1909) reported:

Judge Morson deeply lamented the fact that he is unacquainted with the Chinese lingo when four Celestials jabbered away at the same time before him this morning. Equally as well try to stem Niagara Falls as close up the agitated sons of dragon. There were 17 Chinese in court and four interpreters, these gave different versions of what witnesses were saying, which made his honour wonder if they understood their own language.

Asians were thus portrayed as being disproportionately involved in drug and public-order crimes, and their distinctive racial eccentricities were prominently and frequently communicated to the reading masses. These court reports thus served to reinforce in the minds of the reading public the physical and intellectual, but, most important, moral, differences between these offenders and others. Evidence presented in chapters 6 and 7 suggests that criminal justice system officials shared these attitudes towards the Chinese, leading to differential treatment of such offenders by the police and judges.

The Racialization of Crime: Blacks

There were unusual doings at Number 2 police station yesterday morning. A stranger in the city passing the building at an early hour would have thought some religious service was going on inside. The music was supplied by the cheerful bunch of colored boys arrested for shooting craps ... With the good humor characteristic of their race, they soon cheered up. They were given newspapers to spread around the floor to keep the splinters out of their anatomy, and to while the time away sang old plantation melodies and southern songs ... It was the strangest combination of crap shooters, coon shouters, and dark brown revivalists that the police have met in many a day. (*Hamilton Spectator*, 28 June 1909)

Similar to the situation with Asians, stereotypes and general fears regarding the criminal proclivities of Blacks were prevalent in media reports of the early 1900s. The descriptions of Black criminals emphasized that, like the Chinese, they were prone to involvement in drug and other public-order offences such as gambling and prostitution. However, of greater concern to the public was the notion that Blacks were violent and likely to be involved in more serious forms of crime than the Chinese, and thus posed a greater threat.

It was quite common in the late 1800s and early 1900s for newspaper accounts to refer to the race of Black offenders in the headlines of police-court reports. In one of the most interesting examples of this form of the racialization of crime,[4] the *Hamilton Spectator* (26 August 1909) headlined the sentence of Adolphus Lewis, a 'one-eyed coloured man, charged with committing an indecent act,' in the following manner: 'No More Chicken Dinners or Watermelon Feeds for Adolphus Lewis; At Least Not for the Next Five Years.' Numerous other headlines made specific reference to the colour and physical characteristics of Black offenders, as in the following examples: 'More Bad Boys – 3 Curly-Headed Coloured Boys were Remanded at the Request of the Crown' (*Hamilton Spectator*, 18 July 1893); 'The Black Burglar' (*Globe*, 20 November 1900); 'Colored Man Given Free Board and Lodging for the Rest of the Season' (*London Free Press*, 17 January 1908); 'Bad Coloured Man Goes Down for Six

Months' (*London Advertiser*, 27 December 1907); 'Mulatto Woman Sent to Mercer' (*London Advertiser*, 17 November 1910); 'Negro Wielded Iron Bar' (*Globe*, 22 November 1910); 'Colored Woman to Mercer' (*Toronto Star*, 20 January 1911); 'Negro Thieves Given Stiff Sentences' (*Windsor Evening Record*, 20 October 1912); 'Negro Resorter is Given 8 Months' (*Windsor Evening Record*, 14 November 1912); 'Boy of 18 and Negro of 20 Severely Sentenced' (*Toronto Daily Star*, 7 January 1915); 'Negro Weeps as He Gets 2 Years on Bigamy Count' (*London Advertiser*, 16 August 1917); and 'Coloured Men, White Girls' (*London Free Press*, 7 September 1937).

The racialization of crime was not limited to headlines; court reporters seemed particularly interested in commenting on the ethnic and racial affiliation of those attending court, and often provided lengthy descriptions of court clientele. The *Spectator* (27 December 1901), referring to police-court proceedings in Hamilton, noted, 'The docket was unusually long, the names of 24 men, young and old, and of all shades and complexions, and from all parts of the city, appearing on it.' In London (*Advertiser*, 9 March 1923), in a court sitting which involved several 'coloured individuals,' it was noted that 'one of the most cosmopolitan arrays of prisoners to grace the cramped quarters of the city police court in some months was paraded before Magistrate Graydon this morning.' In the case of twenty-one 'colored' men charged with gambling in Toronto, the *Toronto Daily Star* (17 April 1916) suggested 'a dark complexion was given to the atmosphere of the police court today.' Similarly, in the Windsor murder trial of Andersen Veney, who was eventually sentenced to be hanged for the killing of his wife, 'the court house was crowded and large numbers were unable to get in. Nearly all the prominent citizens of Amherstburg were present, coloured and white' (*Windsor Evening Record*, 15 April 1893).

Particularly vivid descriptions were provided by newspapers when large numbers of Blacks appeared in court, as in the Windsor case of Sharper Bell, charged with committing seduction. The *Evening Record* (16 April 1901) noted, 'The elite of the Burg's coloured 400 were present in a dazzling array of Easter hats and the very latest cut in gowns.'[5] Similarly, in the case of the Black offender William Thompson, sentenced to five years' imprisonment for killing his father, the court report noted, 'the case was reached at 10 o'clock, by which time the court was jammed, many coloured faces appearing in the rows of spectators' (*Windsor Evening Record*, 25 March 1909).

Evidently of most interest to court reporters, and evoking the most striking descriptions, were court cases involving several different minority groups. In the report on a case prefaced with the headline 'Bizarre Effect Found in Contrasting Hues – Court is Nonplussed by Case of Assault and Giving Liquor to an

Indian,' the *Toronto Daily Star* (28 March 1930) offered the following account of the dialogue surrounding the court's decision:

The case is somewhat peculiar went on Mr. Cross (Defense Counsel), 'here we have a Negro being accused of giving liquor to a noble red Indian.' 'Almost as peculiar as a Scotsman giving somebody a drink' said Mr. Gordon (Crown Attorney). The prisoner, not to be outdone, in cheerfulness, explained that after a social evening, the Indian maid desired to visit Chinatown. 'What club is this where you were entertaining the Indian girl?' (Mr. Gordon) 'Coloured Porters' (accused). 'Not Sons and Daughters of I Will Arise?' ... What card game were you playing?' (Mr. Gordon) ... 'We started (with that), but changed to Coon Can', replied the coloured gentleman, amid loud laughter. Dismissing the case, Magistrate Browne said 'There's a nigger in the fence somewhere.'

In some accounts of cases involving Black offenders, reporters invoked the strategy of referring to their geographical roots in order to distance them from the reading public. For instance, a *Hamilton Spectator* (27 April 1910) article suggested, 'the southern element was very much in evidence ... in police court today.' Peter Williams, a Black male charged with assault, was described by the *Hamilton Spectator* (30 October 1893) as 'a son of Africa.' In addition, newspaper reports often made reference to the physical characteristics of Blacks, in particular their dark complexions and comparatively large body size. Describing the sentencing of a Black drug user, the *Toronto Daily Star* (21 August 1922) noted, 'Today George White, with a dark complexion and according to the police carrying on an even darker business, was fined $200 and costs or two months for selling two decks of cocaine.' An account of another Black offender also focused on his darkness and size in a more sarcastic, but still deprecating, manner: 'Two hundred pounds of Julius Wagstaffe, a jet-black import from North Carolina, threw its shadow yesterday, the officials claimed, over the precincts of the Mimico freight yards. As a result, the railway felt almost forced to adopt the daylight savings plan' (*Toronto Daily Star*, 25 July 1916). In some cases, the physical size of Blacks allegedly rendered them immune to pain, as in the case of a 'savage attack on a Negro.' George Smith, 'coloured,' was 'hit over the head with a whiffletree several times' but 'the coloured man was not even rendered insensible by the blows' (*Globe*, 25 February 1908).

The racialization of crime was also accomplished through the condescension towards Blacks, and a devaluing of their social life. Perhaps most representative of these tendencies was Magistrate Denison's (1920: 49–50) commentaries, appearing in his book *Recollections of a Police Magistrate*. It is worth quoting at length from Denison's description of a disorderly-conduct case involving several Blacks, especially given the fact that Denison was responsible for sentencing the majority of Blacks who appeared in Toronto courts during the period from 1890 to 1920. The racist viewpoints evidenced in his writings undoubtedly influenced his decisions in dealing with such offenders.

In a small street in a humble section of the city there lived a number of Negroes ... One of these, more ambitious than the others, by close saving and hard work, had succeeded in buying a piano. The wife, as well as the husband, was anxious for social distinction, and they decided to give an evening party in order to show off the piano. They invited a colored woman, who, I think, gave lessons in music, to come and try the piano. The colored woman was evidently of a higher social scale than the other guests. She was an ample personage, well dressed, and with an impressive manner.

The party had scarcely begun when the news of it spread through the street among the other colored people who had been formerly on the visiting list of the hostess; and, finding they had not been invited to meet the distinguished musician, a feeling of deep resentment arose, then indignation, and then they gathered in the front of the house and acted in a most disorderly manner. The police heard of it and came and arrested the principal offenders on the charge of disorderly conduct, and they appeared before me the next morning and were fined. It was an interesting and most amusing case, and gave me great insight into the point of view of that particular stratum of society in Toronto life. I did not grudge the time given to investigating it.

In another example of Denison's (1920: 40) view of Blacks, he referred to Richard Lewis, 'a burly Negro, evidently a labourer,' who appeared in court on a charge of assault.

I told him he was charged with assault and asked him his plea. 'I pleads guilty, yo honah, but it was under succumstances of de very gravest provocation.' I turned to the complainant ... he was a small, dandified little Negro, very black, wearing a high white collar and large white cuffs, and the whites of his eyes and teeth seemed to be shining out.

Similarly, Charles Page was described as 'an elderly gentleman of very dark complexion and thick lips, a characteristic Negro' (p. 45). Denison further reports that one of the most 'remarkable characters' who appeared in his court was Mr Sheppard, 'an active, well built man of medium height, of very dark colour, with an immense mouth and large protruding lips ... The lips were so protruding that when he spoke they seemed to wave in the air, and from practice, or unconsciously, he was in the habit in conversation of using them so freely that I always said he gesticulated with his lips' (p. 62).

Similar to Denison's views, there was a tendency in court reports towards frequent trivialization of racial issues and the ridiculing of Black offenders.

For instance, with a headline stating 'Coloured Maid Celebrates Emancipation Day,' the *Border Cities Star* (1 August 1919) elaborated on a narcotics-possession case. 'Madge Wilson, a dusty maid of Detroit, spent Emancipation Day trying to collect the $400 and costs to save her from postponing her celebration of freedom until after having spent six month behind bars at the Mercer Reformatory.' In another example of the mockery of Blacks who appeared in court, the *Windsor Evening Record* (18 January 1901) reported on the case of a male convicted of committing an indecent act:

There is a coloured 'brudder' at Goyeau Street who is evidently affected with the jim-jams or the aftereffects of a sunstroke. Either of these afflictions will furnish the material for his very strange actions. Immediately after reading the weather forecast in an almanac, he at once proceeded to disrobe without the slightest provocation. After he had taken everything off but his collar, which he left on as a safeguard against the grip, he set his belongings on fire. After hitting the air, he found that the prediction in the almanac was about 50 degrees too high.

Although Blacks apparently possessed a better command of the English language than Asians, as in some examples quoted above, an effective method of distancing such individuals from the rest of society was an attempt to provide literal accounts of their court testimony.[6] As a further example, in the case of a 'coloured man' charged with assault and carrying a weapon, a 'coloured restaurant keeper' was reported to have testified, 'Ah was out, and returned at hafpest ait, and grabbed two men, but at the time Ah had me arms full' (*Hamilton Spectator*, 14 November 1910). In the instance of a 'negro' woman charged with assaulting a police officer, the headline read: 'Taylor and Dusky Queen Remanded for Sentence.' In this case, Muriel Baldwin apparently told the court, 'I didn't 'sault the police, I defended meself' (*Hamilton Spectator*, 29 May 1917). Similarly, Lizzie White, charged with 'being involved in indecent acts with white boys ... claimed to be 15 years old, but didn't know "when her buffday wuz" (*Windsor Evening Record*, 19 January 1894). Edward Fountain, sentenced to three years in prison on a theft charge, testified, 'dis am a serious thing you honoh. I am an innocent man. The evidence of dat dere Smith was a pack of lies from beginning to end, he and his baby sister and brother. I still maintain that I aint guilty' (*London Advertiser*, 22 February 1915). Zacariah Shields, a 'cullud pusson,' in describing the incidents that led to his charge of assault, told the court, 'he guv it to me and I guv it to him an' that's all there is to it' (*Hamilton Spectator*, 5 May 1898).

Some court reports also commented on the manner of testimony of Blacks. In the case of Pablo Vaise, 'coloured,' charged with attempted murder, the *Wind-*

sor Evening Record (11 March 1925), describing a female witness, noted, 'The African race is one of actors, as demonstrated by Mrs. Marshall, the landlady of the accused, who, in giving her evidence, used many gesticulations and reminded one of the melodrama. His Lordship suggested that the witness might have done well on the stage.'

Related to their apparent problems with the English language, stereotypes of Blacks also focused on their purported weakness of intellect. In commenting on Andrew Woodward, charged with possession of heroin, the *Toronto Daily Star* (3 October 1924) noted, 'The accused, who showed quick wit and *even clever mentality* endeavoured to prove his innocence by casting the blame on a group of his companions, already convicted' (emphasis added). In the case of Thomas Lawrence, 'a coloured boy known on the racetrack as Yeller,' sentenced to three years for assault, the *Hamilton Spectator* (10 June 1901) asserted, 'the sentence dumbfounded the coloured boy and he hadn't a word to say.' Similarly, in the case of John Bayliss, charged with theft, the *Hamilton Spectator* (5 October 1909) suggested that Bayliss 'appeared to have more than the average education which belongs to his class.'

The above discussion provides extensive evidence of the stereotyping of Asians and Blacks and the racialization of crime in the Canadian media, especially between 1892 and 1930. As chapters 6 and 7 will demonstrate, these stereotypes of minority groups also influenced their treatment in the criminal justice system. However, as was pointed out in chapters 3 and 4, there was a growing awareness of the extent of racial inequality in Canadian society beginning in the 1930s, and some attempts were made to remedy these inequalities. Newspaper editors and journalists were also ostensibly aware of the tendencies to stereotype minority groups and altered their practices in reporting on crime – this is reflected in the fact that the majority of the examples of racial stereotypes documented above are from sources produced in the earlier part of the twentieth century. In addition, there was an emerging concern on the part of criminal-justice system officials and commentators regarding sentencing inequalities in the criminal-justice system itself. Although racial inequality was not a specific issue addressed in debates surrounding the problems in Canada's criminal justice system that began to appear in the 1930s, these discussions signalled a change in criminal justice philosophy that may have exerted an impact on the treatment of minority groups.

The Social Contexts of Criminal Sentencing, 1930–1961

As Canadian courts became increasingly bureaucratized, and as crime rates in Canadian society increased over the 1930-to-1960 period, there emerged concern on the part of several commentators regarding irregularities in sentencing practices. This concern was manifested in a call for a 'referendum on judicial decisions to correct this inequality and standardize sentences' (Adamson, 1933: 681). Not surprisingly, criminal justice system officials, in particular judges, felt that such proposals 'not only strike at the independence of the judiciary but are diametrically opposed to the best juristic thought of today.'

Justice Adamson (1933) of the Manitoba Court of Queen's Bench, in expressing his opposition to change, argued that individual offenders who were dissatisfied with their sentences had the right of appeal, and pointed out that, in his province at least, there was a relatively low rate of appeals. He cited these low appeal rates in support of an argument that the apparent sentencing disparities should not generate undue concern on the part of the public. Although Adamson's conclusions failed to take into account the fact that the majority of defendants who appeared in the criminal courts would not have sufficient monetary resources or awareness of their options to appeal their sentences, his assertions are instructive in relation to their emphasis on individualized justice.

This small number of appeals in some sense is an acceptance of very nearly all sentences as not palpably unreasonable or unjust even by those most concerned. As a matter of fact there are very few appeals against sentence only. If from this it can be taken that almost all of the sentences now imposed are just it means that the work of a new court for the purpose of dealing with sentences would only do work which is now satisfactorily done even in the opinion of prisoners ... As a matter of fact, if justice is to be done, there must be inequality of sentence, because though crimes may be called by the same name, they are always unequal. They are never exactly the same, no matter by what name you call them, any more than two men are ever exactly the same. (Adamson, 1933: 683)

There thus appeared to be a realization on the part of some senior judicial officials, at least, that inequality in the application of the criminal law was inevitable, and in fact desirable. As McRuer (1949: 1003), Chief Justice of the High Court of Ontario, argued in a 1949 *Canadian Bar Review* article:

It is apparent that there is to be a wide difference of opinion between presiding officials, be they judges or magistrates, on the appropriate sentence likely to operate as a deterrent to others in the community and at the same time have a corrective effect on the convicted person. With human agencies there will always be a wide difference of views on the severity with which certain crimes should be punished.

McRuer also noted that the most serious problem in the criminal justice system was not in determining whether a convicted individual should receive a prison sentence or not, but in determining how long that prison sentence should be. According to McRuer, the critics seemed to have the impression that offenders were sentenced according to the human characteristics of the judge. McRuer (pp. 1007–8) lamented the fact that sentencing guidelines for magistrates were not more explicit, and asserted that there were three primary considerations that should be borne in mind in deciding on the length of a sentence: '(1) What punishment for the particular offense committed will serve as a deterrent to others who may be disposed to commit crime, and will at the same time maintain public confidence that the law is being properly enforced in the community? (2) What effect will the punishment have on the offender; will he at the end of it be more or less likely to commit crime? (3) Is the offender one who ought to be segregated from society as a protection to those with whom he might come into contact?' However, McRuer cautioned that, while it was important for sentencing judges to attend to these concerns, a move towards uniformity of sentences would create even more injustice in the system.

Despite the arguments of criminal justice system officials and commentators that sentencing disparities were functional, and hence acceptable, concern over inequalities in sentencing in the Canadian criminal justice system continued throughout the 1940s and 1950s. In 1956, the Canadian Bar Association held a symposium on the topic 'Inequities in the Criminal Law,' with sentencing disparities occupying much of the attention. Future Canadian prime minister John Diefenbaker expressed considerable concern over the issue of sentencing disparities in general, and the often lengthy terms of incarceration that Canadian offenders were sentenced to in particular. Diefenbaker argued that 'putting people into prison and keeping them there beyond a reasonable length of time ceases to make for potentially good citizens' (Canadian Bar Association, 1956: 274). Arthur Martin, a prominent criminal lawyer from Toronto, noted, 'it is inevitable that some magistrates and judges will tend to take a more severe view of certain types of anti-social conduct than others' (ibid.: 275), with sentencing disparities being the inevitable result. In order to correct for these disparities, Martin called for the establishment of a permanent board of review to examine all sentences and make recommendations for remission, if the board found a particular sentence to be excessive.

Although there was no evidence in these discussions of an emerging consensus regarding the functionality of, or necessity for, sentencing disparities in the criminal justice system, it is clear that attitudes towards sentencing in this period were changing.

Developments in other components of the Canadian criminal justice system, particularly with respect to corrections, also signalled a move towards the individualization of justice (Archambault, 1938). Concerns were expressed regarding the placement of young offenders in the same environment as more hardened criminals, and similar importance was attached to the necessity of segregating female offenders. There was thus an emerging realization that it was necessary to take the age of offenders into account in sentencing them, and to treat young offenders more leniently in order to prevent them from adopting a criminal lifestyle. As O'Halloran (1945: 556–8), former Chief Justice of the British Columbia Court of Appeal, argued:

It is hard to escape the feeling that the youthful first offender may have fallen into crime through a combination of circumstances for which he may not be directly to blame ... In the opinion of many who have studied the question, the youthful first offender ought to be treated as an erring or misguided youth and not as a criminal.

This philosophy of the importance of treating younger offenders more leniently was also manifested in some of the case law of the period. For instance, in *R v Gilroy and Patrick* (1949), two offenders had their sentences reduced by the Ontario Court of Appeal because they were seventeen years of age, and neither had any previous criminal record. Similarly, in *R v Shewchuck* (1948), a sentence for motor-vehicle manslaughter was reduced by the Alberta Court of Appeal because the accused was only twenty years old, and of previous good character.

While the above discussion thus indicates an emerging awareness of inequalities in the criminal-justice system and their potentially deleterious consequences, it is notable that racial issues did not become part of the discourse. This is not surprising, given the prevailing beliefs that Canadian society was not characterized by racial conflict and inequality. However, these more general changes in criminal-justice philosophy are important to consider in the analyses of criminal sentencing that appear in chapters 6 and 7, as they may have inadvertently exerted an impact on sentencing for minority-group offenders during the period from 1930 to 1961.

6

Drug and Public-Order Crimes

The Chinese population of Ottawa again received a rude jolt as the result of a little surprise party conducted on a Saturday night by Detective McLaughlin and a number of his stalwart braves. Chinamen, to the extent of 10, spent Sunday in the Nicholas Street Apartments ... the point of the attack was 541 Sussex Street, a villa occupied by Charlie Lung, washee man. (*Ottawa Citizen*, 22 January 1912)

A wagon-load of officers made an unexpected raid on the home of Sarah Grant, a colored woman. The dusky Sarah was escorted to the King William Street retreat on a charge of keeping a house of ill-fame. Eliza Brooks, a somewhat flashy looking white woman, was held as an inmate, and William Adams and John Gains, both colored, were charged with being frequenters. (*Hamilton Spectator*, 31 July 1911)

The literature reviewed in chapter 2 indicated that racial discrimination is more likely to occur in the earlier stages of the criminal justice system than in the later stages. Specifically, it is more likely to occur in the context of decisions by police officers than in decisions by prosecutors and judges. The most fruitful context in which to examine such biases is the category of drug and public-order crimes – offences seldom brought to the attention of the police through public complaints, with most arrests being made through police-initiated activity. Some researchers have argued that the overrepresentation of minority-group offenders in the criminal justice system is at least in part the result of 'overpolicing' – the tendency of police to exercise their discretion to focus on surveillance of particular communities (Henry et al., 1995), searching for particular types of crime. Thus, if bias exists in the criminal justice system, it is most likely to manifest itself at the level of police activity with respect to drug and public-order crimes.

In this chapter, I separate public-order offences into drug-related and general

public-order offences, and begin by examining the racial basis of Canada's initial drug legislation. I then address the issue of enforcement of these drug laws
and sentencing for drug offenders, first analysing the decision to imprison such
offenders, then undertaking multiple-regression analyses of the length of sentence they received. A similar format is used for a detailed consideration of the
same issues for public-order offences. The analyses reveal that minority-group
drug and public-order offenders were subject to disproportional police attention
and differential treatment in Ontario's criminal courts.

Drug Legislation and Enforcement

Myths about drugs and the effects of these substances on their users have influenced, and consequently determined, society's definition of minority drug use
as a social problem, both historically and in more contemporary contexts (see
Blumstein, 1993). As Musto (1987) points out in his discussion of the history of
drug legislation in the United States, certain drugs were labelled as dangerous
because they had the potential to undermine important social restrictions which
kept minority groups under control. Concerns that opium smoking facilitated
sexual contact between Chinese and White women was a factor in its total prohibition, just as the belief that cocaine led to sexual assault and superhuman
strength on the part of Blacks influenced the criminalization of that substance.[1]

The situation in Canada was no different, and there is a plethora of literature
on the implementation of narcotic-drug laws in Canada (Boyd, 1984; Chapman,
1979; Comack, 1985; Cook, 1969; Giffen, Endicott, and Lambert, 1991;
Solomon and Madison, 1976–7; Trasov, 1962) which has emphasized that certain powerful groups in the country were influential in generating legislation
that was directed primarily against Canada's immigrant Chinese population.
While this literature has generally done an admirable job of explaining the role
of social conflict in the passage of narcotics laws in Canada, it has rather uncritically accepted the notion that the legislation was implemented to control the
immigrant Chinese. While there is indeed considerable evidence to support the
claim that these laws were enacted primarily in response to the use of opium by
the Chinese on Canada's west coast, most of the extant studies have asserted
that the legislation was racist in its origin but have not provided sufficient
empirical evidence to substantiate such claims. A limited number of studies
(Boyd, 1984; Giffen, Endicott, and Lambert, 1991; Green, 1979) point to arrest
data as proof that, in the early periods of the legislation, Asians were more
likely to be charged for narcotics violations. However, these studies generally
do not go beyond noting the overrepresentation of Chinese in these arrest statistics, and have generally failed to address how narcotics statutes were inter-

preted by those responsible for enforcing them, and the vigour with which narcotics offenders were pursued by law-enforcement agencies.

These studies have also focused exclusively on the Chinese in their discussions of the racial basis of narcotics legislation, neglecting the fact that Blacks as a group were also susceptible in the enforcement of drug legislation.

Finally, the extant studies have neglected the equally important issue of the punishment of drug offenders at the sentencing stage of the criminal justice system. If the Canadian legal system was primarily concerned with controlling minority drug use in the passage and strengthening of narcotics legislation, as most of the literature has presumed, we would expect that these concerns would also manifest themselves in more severe sentences for minority-group drug offenders.

The discussion in this chapter attempts to remedy these shortcomings in the extant literature through an examination of several issues surrounding Canadian drug legislation. I first deal with the racist foundations of Canadian narcotics legislation, focusing on the racial stereotypes offered by parliamentarians in their passage of the initial legislation, and the racist sentiments of Edmonton judge Emily Murphy, who was extremely influential in the effecting of changes in Canada's narcotics laws in the 1920s. I also discuss the tendency of Royal Canadian Mounted Police officials to focus on Chinese, and to a lesser extent Blacks, in their enforcement of drug legislation. Finally, I present a detailed analysis of the enforcement of these laws and sentencing decisions in narcotics cases in Ontario cities. While the discussion emphasizes that race was indeed an important factor in the passage of narcotics legislation and in the enforcement of these laws, the analysis reveals that racial bias was tempered to some extent at the level of sentencing.

Canada's Narcotics Legislation

Opiate drugs were freely prescribed, readily available without a prescription, and widely used throughout the late nineteenth and early twentieth centuries in Canada (Green, 1979). For most of the nineteenth century, drug addicts were not publicly labelled as a deviant social group, but were seen simply as individuals guilty of a specific, and relatively non-threatening, moral transgression. In the late 1800s, opium eating was viewed as a vice that was more prevalent among the upper than the lower classes (Brecher, 1972), and many homes of the North American élite were equipped with boudoirs for the purposes of smoking opium (Calkins, 1871). By 1876, the chewing of opium was reported to be on the increase in both North America (Terry and Pellens, 1970) and the British Isles, where the substance could be purchased in pubs (Berridge and Edwards,

1987). Preparations containing cocaine were sold as soft drinks and alcoholic beverages, and the substance was also promoted for its supposed medicinal value (Murray, 1987). It has been estimated that between 200,000 and 2 million Americans were addicted to opiate drugs at the turn of the century (Duster, 1970), and, while no comparable statistics are available, it is probable that levels of opiate addiction were also high in Canada during this period.

While some Canadian provinces introduced minor controls on the marketing of narcotics during the 1870s, the federal government was unwilling to act to criminalize the use of drugs at this time, primarily because of the middle-class origins of most users (Green, 1979). In addition to this apparent widespread middle-class use of narcotic drugs in the late 1800s, however, there was also a significant amount of opium use associated with the socially disadvantaged immigrant Chinese population, a fact that was frequently mentioned in media descriptions of Chinese lifestyle.

The perceived threat posed by higher levels of Chinese and Japanese immigration in the late 1800s and early 1900s led to the intensification of anti-Asian sentiments in Canada, particularly on the west coast, where the racial tension culminated in a riot in the city of Vancouver in 1907 (see chapter 3). In response to claims for property-damage losses incurred in Vancouver's Chinese and Japanese districts as a result of this riot, Prime Minister Laurier sent his deputy minister of labour, Mackenzie King, to the west coast. Among other submissions, King received claims from two opium manufacturers, whom he discovered had combined gross receipts of over $300,000 for the year 1907 (MacFarlane, 1979). Somewhat astonished by the extent of the opium industry,[2] King carried on further investigations and submitted a brief to the House of Commons entitled *Report on the Need for Suppression of the Opium Traffic in Canada* (Canada, 1908).

This report suggested that opium smoking was increasing among young White men and women, and that considerable profits were being made by Chinese opium merchants. King's initial reaction to the situation was to call for the licensing of Chinese druggists, but when affluent and powerful Chinese spoke out regarding the dangers associated with opium smokers in their community, he decided to legislate against the substance. 'The support of these Chinese then elevated King to the status of "moral entrepreneur," he moved swiftly and decisively against the use of opium' (Boyd, 1984: 116–17).

King's report on opium and recommendations to the House of Commons were dated 26 June 1908. By 13 July the House had passed the Opium Act, prohibiting the sale and importation of opium for non-medical reasons. The fact that the legislation was passed within three weeks of the initial proposal clearly illustrates how little public or political debate took place over its passage. It must be remembered that, at this time, there was little evidence to suggest that opium smoking affected the health or social functioning of the users of the drug. In fact, many argued that opium was safer than alcohol and that opium smokers were altogether a better class of people than drinkers (Smart, 1983). However, the racist and moralistic foundations of the 1908 legislation are apparent when it is compared with other drug-related bills proposed in the House of Commons in the same year (Green, 1979). For instance, a private member's bill to prohibit the importation and manufacture of cigarettes generated considerable discussion regarding the adverse moral, medical, and intellectual consequences of tobacco smoking on youth. However, at least in part because tobacco use was not associated with socially marginal groups such as the Chinese, this bill was defeated.

The Opium Act of 1908 prohibited only trafficking and possession for sale of the substance, not simple possession itself. Possession for sale and trafficking in opium both carried a $50 minimum and $1,000 maximum fine, with an option of up to three years in jail for importation and manufacture of the substance (Canada, *Statutes of Canada*, 1907–8).

The early history of enforcement of narcotics legislation was surrounded by controversy, however. In 1910, the Conservative opposition contended that the Liberal government was aware of customs officials on the Canadian west coast who sold opium after its seizure, and subsequently appropriated the funds (Giffen, Endicott, and Lambert, 1991). In response to this controversy, and additionally to address the continued concern with Asian immigration, the Liberal government appointed Mr Justice Murphy to head a royal commission into alleged Chinese frauds and opium smoking on the west coast (Canada, 1911). The commission found no substance to the allegations regarding the improprieties of customs officers. However, the commission concluded that, in order to control the use of opium, it was necessary to create criminal offences for opium smoking and the possession of opium for non-medical purposes.

In part as a result of the recommendations of the Murphy Commission, but also because of his personal moral beliefs, Mackenzie King, who at this time was serving as the minister of labour in the federal government, introduced an expanded Opium and Drug Act in 1911 (Canada, *Statutes of Canada*, 1911). The changes encompassed in this act included penalties for the smoking of opium (maximum of a $50 fine or three months in jail); for being found in an opium den; and for the possession of opium, cocaine, morphine, and eucaine.

In order to justify the passage of the revised and more stringent legislation, King cited several alarmist statements concerning the extent of drug abuse in Canada. For instance, the Dominion parole officer had apparently informed

King that 12 to 15 per cent of young prisoners he came into contact with attributed their downfall to drugs (Canada, *House of Commons Debates*, 1911:
2523). There was also reference to a probation officer from Montreal who
spoke of 'little girls taken out of cocaine dens and of young boys whose future
had been ruined' (ibid.: 2526). King claimed support for the legislation from
the Royal College of Dental Surgeons, the Young Men's Christian Association, the University Settlement of Montreal, various clergymen and religious
leaders from across Canada, and 429 Montrealers, 'including many prominent
citizens.'

The most debated aspect of the 1911 narcotics bill was section 14, which
would have provided for the governor in council to, 'from time to time, add to
the schedule of this Act any substance, the addition of which is deemed necessary in the public interest' (Canada, *Statutes of Canada*, 1911). Several members of the House expressed concern over such a provision, one pointing out
that certain substances in vogue, especially among the middle and upper
classes, might be subject to criminalization:

It seems to me that this legislation gives absolute power to the Governor in Council to
say that tobacco is a drug, and ought to be treated in the same way as these here mentioned. That would create a situation which it is not intended to create, because every
tobacco smoker would become a criminal. I presume alcohol might be treated in the
same way. (Canada, *House of Commons Debates*, 1911: 2550)

King finally succumbed to the opposition to section 14, and amended it by
inserting the words 'Alkaloids, derivatives and preparations of the drugs named
in the schedule hereto' in lieu of the word 'substance.'

Cook (1969: 38) suggests that the passage of narcotics legislation provides
clear evidence of the importance of power differentials in Canadian society,
despite the 'political passivity of those defined as deviant.' She maintains that
the medical profession was probably just as much responsible for opiate addiction as the Chinese opium pedlars, yet no legislation was enacted to deal with
this problem. Senator J.H. Wilson was the only member of Parliament to
express concern that the Chinese were being singled out as the offenders, rather
than the medical profession. Wilson pointed out that the use of opium was a
'deleterious habit' associated primarily with the Chinese, but questioned
whether its use should be criminalized:

Have we the right to make criminals of people, because they have learned the habit in
their younger days and now desire to continue it? Much of the habit of using opiates,
morphine, or cocaine has been brought about by its indiscriminate use as authorized by

physicians. ... Why not punish the physicians? (Canada, *House of Commons Debates*, 1911: 399)

It is thus evident from the above discussion that the initial Canadian narcotics legislation was enacted primarily for purpose of controlling Chinese opiate use. The amendments to the legislation that followed in the 1920s were similarly focused on these Chinese users, with changes allowing for the deportation of Chinese narcotics offenders and a general strengthening of the penalty provisions of the act.

The 1920s

As issues arising from the First World War occupied the attention of the Canadian House of Commons from 1914 to 1918, no significant changes to narcotics legislation were introduced until 1920, when the government proposed to 'put into legislative form the conclusions embodied in the International Opium Convention signed at the Hague in 1912' (Canada, *House of Commons Debates*, 1920: 557). The 1920s saw a great strengthening of Canada's drug laws, and, by 1929, a total of twenty-eight separate offences were covered by the legislation. In a provision specifically directed at the immigrant Chinese, the legislation was amended in 1922 to allow for the deportation of convicted aliens. In the same year, the maximum penalty for trafficking was increased to seven years, and sanctions for selling drugs to minors included whipping and a minimum of six months' imprisonment. The right to search premises for illegal drugs without a warrant was introduced in 1923, and cannabis was added to the list of controlled drugs in the same year (Canada, *Statutes of Canada*, 1923). In addition, persons found to be in a building containing a narcotic drug were deemed to be found in possession of the drug, unless it was there without their knowledge, another provision that was specifically designed to control the Chinese (see the discussion of enforcement, below).

The House of Commons debates and media commentary surrounding the drug issue in the 1920s reveal more of the moralistic and racist attitudes that initially appeared some years earlier with the passage of the first legislation. One parliamentarian suggested that it would be useful to allow for the deportation of aliens convicted under the Opium and Narcotic Drug Act, as it would facilitate the removal of Chinese from the country:

In view of the fact that of 835 convictions [under the Opium and Narcotic Drug Act] last year, 635 were of Chinese, would it not be advisable that all Orientals found trafficking in drugs be deported? This would help to solve to some extent the Oriental question in this country. (Canada, *House of Commons Debates*, 1921: 2894)

After the deportation provisions of the act were passed in 1922, the minister of health indicated that they were being utilized extensively by the government: 'We are deporting Chinamen as fast as we can' (ibid.: 1923: 699).

An extremely influential figure in the increasing severity of Canada's drug laws in the 1920s was Mrs Emily Murphy, a police magistrate and judge of the Juvenile Court in Edmonton, Alberta. Murphy was commissioned to write a series of articles on the drug problem for *Maclean's* magazine in the early 1920s (Murphy, 1922b; 1922c) and from these articles she published a book on the subject, *The Black Candle*.[3] Although, as Solomon and Madison (1976–7: 255) note, 'both the articles and the book were a blend of statistics, moral anecdotes, popular racial bias, and sensationalism,' Murphy's book received very favourable reviews in the Canadian popular media. For instance, the *Toronto Mail and Empire* asserted, 'If we had more crusaders against the use of narcotics of the calibre of Mrs. Murphy, the drug ring would not be the great source of danger ... that it is today' (as quoted in Chapman, 1979: 102).

Murphy informed her readers that drug pushers were almost exclusively non-White and non-Christian, and behind them was an international conspiracy of Yellow and Black drug pushers whose ultimate goal was the domination of the 'bright browed races of the world' (Murphy, 1922a: 88). Murphy had little sympathy for these drug traffickers, suggesting at one point, 'All honest men and orderly persons should rightly know that there are men and women who fatten on the agony of the unfortunate drug addict – palmerworms and human caterpillars who should be trodden underfoot like the despicable grubs that they are' (p. 7). Murphy's blatant racial bias was most prominently illustrated in *The Black Candle*, where she provided a picture of a young White woman lying on a bed beside a Black man, with opium-smoking paraphernalia between them. The caption accompanying the picture stated, 'When she acquires the habit, she does not know what lies before her; later, she does not care' (p. 30).

Facilitated by influential figures such as Murphy, the public identification of opium smoking with the socially disadvantaged Chinese population allowed for the passage of legislation which was initially directed at them, and vigorously enforced against them. While the material presented above has outlined the impact of legislators, interested bureaucracies, and individuals on the legal response to narcotic drugs and drug users in Canada in the early 1900s, it does not specify how these legislative enactments were translated into police enforcement activities and the treatment of drug offenders by the criminal courts.

The Policing of Narcotics Offences

The mere existence of narcotic-drug legislation does not specify its punitive content nor the energy with which it will be enforced by the police, and the manner in which it will be interpreted by the judiciary. In order to understand the enforcement of early narcotics laws in Canada, it is initially important to consider the activities of the Royal Canadian Mounted Police. The former North-West Mounted Police officially became the RCMP in 1919, and this body had as one of their primary responsibilities the enforcement of federal narcotics legislation. The annual reports of the RCMP for the 1920s and 1930s devoted substantial attention to drug-enforcement activities in each Canadian province, and served as a major source of public information on the drug trade (Solomon and Madison, 1976–77). The following statement from the 1922 report is reflective of the racial stereotypes promoted by the RCMP, and suggests that, although the popular conception was that the Chinese only used opium, they were enticing White addicts to their opium dens by offering supplies of other dangerous substances.

It has been observed that Chinese addicts to this vice continue to be devoted to opium, and to be little inclined to the use of the other drugs; but further that cocaine and the other noxious drugs usually are to be obtained in the Chinese opium dens, so that White addicts repair to these plague spots.

The difficulties of repression are exceedingly great, for several reasons. One is the ease with which these drugs, which are small in bulk, can be imported ... Yet another obstacle is the repulsive nature of the work of repression, entailing as it does contact with particularly loathsome dregs of humanity; our men greatly dislike it, and it is undertaken only in accordance with duty, and because of the knowledge that while unpleasant, it is a service to humanity. (Canada, *Annual Report of the RCMP*, 1922: 16–17)

These annual RCMP reports also provided evidence that, in their drug-law enforcement activities, the police focused primarily on racial minority groups. In 1926, for instance, the superintendent of the Manitoba RCMP emphasized that most of the arrests under the Opium and Narcotic Drug Act in that province were of Chinese, and also suggested that Blacks were responsible for spreading the drug habit to other racial groups: 'Some dozen Chinese men were convicted during the year, most of them for minor infractions. One Negro was convicted for the illegal possession of drugs, and it is known that his dive had been a particularly vicious resort for male and female addicts of all races (Canada, *Annual Report of the RCMP*, 1926: 34). Similarly, in 1930, the Alberta superintendent wrote, 'In southern Alberta, a series of convictions of Chinese extending over

Table 6.1: Race of Offenders Arrested under the Opium and Narcotic Drug Act by the RCMP, 1924–1936

| Year | Race | | | |
	White	Chinese	Coloured	Total
1924	117(40.5)	158(54.7)	14(4.8)	289
1925	168(37.3)	280(62.2)	2(4.4)	450
1926	175(47.2)	187(50.4)	9(2.4)	371
1927	88(35.5)	160(64.5)	0(0.0)	248
1928	77(41.2)	107(57.2)	3(1.6)	187
1929	45(14.9)	255(84.4)	2(0.7)	302
1930	59(23.4)	190(75.4)	3(1.2)	252
1931	92(41.3)	127(57.0)	4(1.8)	223
1932	NOT AVAILABLE			
1933	104(36.1)	184(63.9)	0(0.0)	288
1934	86(43.9)	108(55.1)	2(1.0)	196
1935	74(61.2)	47(38.8)	0(0.0)	121
1936	115(68.0)	50(29.6)	4(2.4)	169
Total	1,200(38.8)	1,853(60.0)	43(1.4)	3,096

Source: Annual Reports of the RCMP

several months broke up a traffic which had existed among these people and some degraded whites in Lethbridge' (Canada, *Annual Report of the RCMP*, 1930: 21).

While it is not possible to acquire information on differential rates of drug use among racial groups in the early 1900s, it is clear that federal enforcement efforts were directed at the Chinese and, to a lesser extent, Blacks. Table 6.1 demonstrates that Chinese comprised 60 per cent of the narcotics arrests made by the RCMP over the 1924-to-1936 period. It is also notable that, after 1936, the RCMP reports no longer contain information on the race of those arrested under provisions of the act. Interestingly, this is precisely the period when Whites began to overtake the Chinese in the number of arrests.

This enforcement focus on Chinese offenders was also shared by municipal police officers in Ontario, as is revealed in the statistics contained in table 6.2, which shows that 49 per cent of all drug offenders in the sample for the 1908–30 period were of Chinese origin.

Qualitative data from annual police reports and media sources provide further evidence of this enforcement focus on Chinese drug users. For instance, in 1913, the annual report of Toronto's chief constable notes, 'The sale of opium

Table 6.2: Descriptive Data: Drug Offences, 1908–1930 (Means)

Variable	Overall	Blacks	Chinese	White
Black	0.06			
Chinese	0.49			
White	0.45			
Imprisonment	0.87	0.85	0.85	0.89
Sentence length	5.36	6.44	2.08	8.77
Female	0.07	0.22	0.01	0.13
Single	0.39	0.37	0.30	0.46
Age	35.08	33.78	37.82	32.23
Age 16–24	0.05	0.02	0.04	0.06
Age 25–34	0.38	0.39	0.30	0.46
Age 35–44	0.36	0.39	0.37	0.34
Age 45–54	0.14	0.15	0.18	0.09
Age 55+	0.06	0.04	0.09	0.04
No occupation	0.03	0.06	0.01	0.05
Working class	0.61	0.80	0.57	0.63
Middle class	0.08	0.05	0.01	0.17
Upper class	0.03	0.01	0.02	0.04
Second offence	0.05	0.05	0.02	0.08
Previous offence	0.06	0.09	0.01	0.12
Trafficking	0.08	0.05	0.06	0.10
Hamilton	0.07	0.16	0.04	0.09
Windsor	0.05	0.00	0.06	0.03
London	0.04	0.07	0.03	0.04
Ottawa	0.01	0.00	0.00	0.02
Thunder Bay	0.00	0.00	0.00	0.00
Toronto	0.83	0.76	0.86	0.81
N of cases	1,954	110	965	897

has received close attention, resulting in seizures that involved the imposition of fines amounting to over $3400.00. The traffic is chiefly among the Chinese' (Toronto, *Annual Report of the Chief Constable*, 1913: 5).

The techniques of the police in securing convictions under the Opium and Narcotic Drug Act were strikingly similar to those employed by morality and narcotics squads today. Narcotics use was essentially a victimless crime, in the sense that there were seldom victims present to request police action with respect to such offences, and police activity in the area of narcotics-law enforcement was primarily proactive[4] (Skolnick, 1975) in nature. Furthermore, the fact that most drug users were of Chinese descent made it even more difficult for police officers to penetrate drug networks and secure arrests. As a result of these obstacles, the police relied on two related tactics in their vigorous pursuit of minority-group drug offenders: the use of informants and frequent raids on Chinese opium dens.

In their use of informants, the police were assisted by the formal legal provision that individuals providing evidence against drug users would receive half the amount of the fine imposed by the court (Canada, *Statutes of Canada*, 1911). Given this monetary incentive, at least some individuals would be motivated to assist the police by providing information on narcotics offenders. There was also the informal provision, similar to plea-bargaining situations in contemporary court settings, that providing information on drug offences committed by others could result in a less severe sentence for an accused. For instance, in the case of Sam Bartello, charged with selling cocaine, the accused supplied 'certain information' regarding other alleged drug offenders to the police. The sentencing judge noted that the accused had done so, and accordingly sentenced Bartello to eighteen months in jail plus $200 or six months, 'rather than facing the prospect of a seven-year sentence' (*Toronto Daily Star*, 29 April 1925).

The tactics that informants would engage in, undoubtedly with the full support of the police, would probably be legally regarded as entrapment today. However, they were deemed acceptable by the courts in pursuit of the 'treacherous opiate' (*Toronto Daily Star*, 4 August 1916) and its 'Celestial' users. For instance, in the case of Lee Jim, the Toronto 'Opium King,' who had been convicted several times between 1908 and 1913 for selling opium, 'a white woman who drove up in an automobile gave him a letter, in which it was stated that her husband was an opium fiend. She begged him for the drug and Lee Jim sold her $6 worth. The woman was sent by the police' (*Toronto Daily Star*, 9 December 1913). Although some court officials, in particular counsel for accused persons, regarded the unbridled use of informers by police with some derision,[5] the practice continued unabated.

Raids on opium dens were also a common strategy employed by the police to secure drug arrests during this period. Police officers generally knew the location of such dens, and could seemingly raid them at will. In the city of Hamilton, for instance, there is reference to 'the regular weekly visit of Constables William, Curtis, Pasel and Gent to 51 King William Street ... a suspected opium den' (*Hamilton Spectator*, 13 January 1919). In a raid conducted on another Chinese residence in Hamilton (*Spectator*, 21 December 1923) in 1923, which reveals the vigour with which drug offenders were pursued, Constables Buscombe and Roughead 'obtained a ladder, climbed on the kitchen roof adjoining the house, jumped to the other roof and forced open a window. The floor and baseboard beside the kitchen sink had been cut to form a lid for a little box [containing opium] under the seam of the floor.'

Specific areas where Chinese resided were also subject to increased police surveillance in the Northern Ontario city of Fort William. In reference to Lee Tang, a 'Celestial' resident of that city charged with opium possession, the *Fort William Daily Times Journal* (3 June 1916) noted that 'the joint raided was situated at 340 Simpson Street, at the rear of one of the Chinese laundries.'

Not surprisingly, this proactive police work in the pursuit of drug offenders led to defensive reactions on the part of Chinese opium-den keepers, who engaged in an array of practices in order to protect their premises from police raids and conceal the opium contained therein. For instance, an opium den at 10 Elm Street in Toronto was 'protected by four locked and bolted doors with heavy oaken beams laid across them as bars. Each door was provided with peepholes at which sentries kept watch'[6] (*Toronto Daily Star*, 22 March 1915). In Hamilton, a particular opium den was described as follows: 'The floor occupied by the Chinamen contains a maze of small rooms and twisting passages. The front door was reinforced with a heavy plank and bolts and it is doubtful whether an axe in the hands of policemen could make an impression on the door before the occupants could escape (*Hamilton Spectator*, 21 December 1923).

In reaction to these defences, the police initiated the practice of employing Chinese informants to secure the arrests of opium-den keepers. The usual procedure for making such arrests was for police officers to provide Chinese informants with a few marked dollar bills with which to purchase opium, and send the informants into the opium den (*Rex v Yok Yuen*, 1929). When the informants exited the opium den, the officers would search them for opium, with the discovery of the substance and the subsequent recovery of the marked bills resulting in the arrest of the keeper and frequenters of the establishment.

In some cases, the police would discover opium dens in the course of routine investigations connected with other public-order offences. In the investigation of an alleged Ontario Temperance Act violation, for instance, Constables Roughead and Buscombe of the Hamilton police visited the home of Tom Watkins,

in search of fire water. They found only about sufficient of the spirit to fill a thimble but when they mosied around the house they detected a scent which arose from something more illegal than moonshine. The cellar was searched and a quantity of opium was found. Three Chinamen rented a portion of the basement and when they re-entered Watkins called the police and the three Celestials were arrested. (*Hamilton Spectator*, 13 December 1923)

What is perhaps most interesting about these various tactics is the seeming reluctance of the courts to place any restrictions on what were clearly legally questionable police activities. Given the negative portrayals of Chinese drug users in the media and other sources, however, it is perhaps not surprising to see the exercise of these relatively unbridled police powers. However, research reviewed in chapter 2 would lead to expectations that the exercise of discretion at the level of the criminal court may have been somewhat less likely to result in discrimination against minority groups. I thus now turn to an examination of the processing and sentencing of narcotics offenders in the criminal courts, with a specific focus on Chinese offenders.

Sentencing

The police court looked like a fully equipped opium joint, with two sets of apparatus for smoking opium. There was the thick bamboo pipe, the curiously shaped spirit lamp over which the opium is cooked, the raw opium in an ordinary tin can, and a playing card or two, the backs of which were spattered over with the half-used drug. (*Toronto Daily Star*, 28 July 1909)

The passage quoted above describes the first charges to be heard in Toronto courts under the 1908 Opium and Drug Act. Although the two keepers of this opium den were fined $100 in order to 'give others the chance to cease the practice,' Magistrate Kingsford warned that the next offenders who appeared before him on similar charges would be imprisoned. The ten found-ins had the charges against them dismissed because 'the keeper is most to blame, getting those poor wretches into his place to smoke that stuff.' Portending a concern that soon manifested itself in the sentencing of Asian drug offenders, the *Toronto Daily Star* (28 July 1909) expressed alarm that 'White people were also found in the den.'

Table 6.2 presents descriptive data on the sample of drug offenders appearing in courts in six Ontario cities for the 1908–30 period. Unlike the other quantitative analyses of sentencing contained in this chapter and chapter 7, the analyses for drug offences are restricted to the 1908-to-1930 period. I limit the analyses to this period because Chinese comprised a decreasing proportion of all drug offenders after 1930, primarily as a result of restrictions on Chinese immigration from 1923 to 1947, which reduced the potential pool of such offenders (see Mosher and Hagan, 1994). Table 6.2 indicates that almost 50 per cent of those charged with drug offences in these six Ontario cities in the period were of Chinese origin, while another 6 per cent were Black, providing further evidence of a disproportional police focus on minority-group drug offenders.

Table 6.3: Logistic Regression on Imprisonment Decision: Drug Offences, 1908–1930

Variable	All Offenders		Chinese Offenders		Comparison	
	Coefficient	Odds ratio	Coefficient	Odds ratio	Diff.	T-ratio
Black	−0.68*	0.50				
Chinese	−0.56**	0.57				
Female	−0.79**	0.45				
Single	0.31	1.37	0.12	0.88	0.19	0.40
Age 16–24	−0.19	0.83	0.63	1.87	−0.82	1.22
Age 25–34	−0.31	0.74	−0.47*	0.62	0.16	0.37
Age 45–54	0.09	1.10	0.01	1.01	0.08	0.16
Age 55+	0.32	1.38	0.70	2.02	−0.38	0.62
No occupation	1.25**	3.51	0.47	1.60	0.78	0.93
Working class	0.99**	2.68	1.37	3.92	−0.38	0.86
Second offence	−0.47	0.63	−0.99	0.37	0.52	0.63
Previous offence	0.46	1.58	3.53	34.25	−3.07	1.66
Trafficking	0.41	1.50	0.13	1.13	0.28	0.45
Hamilton	1.81**	6.08	1.68	5.40	0.13	0.15
Windsor	0.53	1.70	0.00	1.00	0.53	0.75
London	−1.78**	0.17	−2.74**	0.06	0.96	1.68
Sentence year	−0.07**	0.93	−0.12**	0.88	0.05	0.33
2 Log Likelihood	1,379.3		704.3			
Chi-square	168.2		118.9			
Goodness of Fit	1,999.4		968.5			
N of Cases	1,954		965			

*p < 0.05   ** p < 0.01

Table 6.3 presents the results of a logistic regression[7] of the decision to imprison drug offenders for the years 1908–30. This analysis is based on 1,954 drug offenders, 87 per cent of whom were imprisoned. The first two columns of the table show that female drug offenders[8] and offenders sentenced in the city of London were less likely to be imprisoned for the commission of drug crimes. In addition, the variable year of sentence exerts a significant negative effect on imprisonment, suggesting that, in the later years of the 1908–30 period, judges were less likely to convict and imprison offenders for the commission of drug crimes. This finding seems to be primarily attributable to evidentiary considerations that began to emerge in the latter part of this period, when astute defence lawyers began to demand more stringent chemical examinations of the substances which their clients were charged with possessing. In some of these cases, laboratory analyses revealed that the substances were not narcotics (see

Mosher, 1992), and judges accordingly determined that narcotics laws had not been violated.

Table 6.3 also indicates that offenders reporting no occupation and those in working-class occupations were significantly more likely to be convicted, an issue that I will return to in discussions of the sentence-length regressions. Drug offenders sentenced in Hamilton were more likely to be imprisoned than those from other cities. However, most important for our considerations here are the negative effects on imprisonment for Black and Chinese drug offenders, which are counter to the predictions of conflict theory in general, and the literature on Canadian drug legislation in particular. The seemingly more lenient treatment of Black and Chinese drug offenders is addressed in more detail below.

Columns 3 and 4 of table 6.3 show the results of the imprisonment-decision regression for Chinese drug offenders only, and indicate similar effects to those obtained for the overall sample of drug offenders. The only exception is that the negative coefficient for offenders in the 25–34 age group in the overall sample is statistically significant in the Chinese subsample;[9] however, the comparison of coefficients between the two samples in columns 5 and 6 indicates that this difference is not significant.

Sentence Length

Table 6.4 presents the results of an ordinary least-squares regression of sentence length for drug offenders for the years 1908–30. Columns 1 and 2 of this table show the results with only racial variables entered, and indicate that Black and Chinese offenders received significantly shorter sentences than Whites. When the additional extralegal, legal, and structural variables are entered in the second model (columns 3 and 4), however, the effect for Black offenders, while still negative, is no longer statistically significant. Similarly, the coefficient for Chinese offenders, while still significant, is not as strongly negative as it was without controls for the additional variables. Females and offenders whose cases were heard in London were sentenced to significantly shorter terms of imprisonment, while those in the working class and those having a prior criminal record were sentenced to significantly longer terms, as were offenders convicted of trafficking in narcotics. The variable sentence year exerts a significant positive effect on sentence length, indicating that, as the penalty structure of narcotics legislation became more severe through the 1920s, magistrates took advantage of the more stringent penalties available to them, and sentenced drug offenders to lengthier prison terms.

Although it is not a specific focus of this analysis, it is important to consider briefly the significant positive effects of the occupational variables on both the

Table 6.4: Regression on Sentence Length: Drug Offences, 1908–1930

Variable	All Offenders Block 1		All Offenders Block 2		Chinese Offenders		Comparison	
	B	Beta	B	Beta	B	Beta	Diff.	T-ratio
Black	-2.16	-0.06**	-0.72	-0.02	-0.09	0.00		
Chinese	-6.53	-0.39**	-4.47	-0.27**				
Female			-2.71	-0.08**				
Single			0.58	0.03	-0.09	0.00	0.67	1.10
Age 16–24			-1.09	-0.03	0.89	0.04	-1.98	2.25*
Age 25–34			-0.18	-0.01	0.00	0.00	-0.18	0.30
Age 45–54			0.14	0.00	0.42	0.04	-0.28	0.41
Age 55+			-0.05	0.00	0.57	0.04	-0.62	0.78
No occupation			1.91	0.04	3.19	0.07*	-1.28	1.14
Working class			1.73	0.10**	1.59	0.18**	0.14	0.23
Second offence			1.27	0.03	-0.21	0.00	1.48	1.63
Previous offence			2.12	0.06**	3.45	0.06*	-1.33	1.25
Trafficking			2.27	0.07*	3.68	0.19**	-1.41	2.03*
Hamilton			-0.14	0.00	-1.16	-0.05	1.02	1.24
Windsor			-0.83	-0.02	-1.03	-0.06*	0.20	0.24
London			-1.85	-0.04*	-2.56	-0.10**	0.71	0.79
Sentence year			0.62	0.31**	0.28	0.27**	0.34	0.64
r2	0.14		0.27		0.15			
Adjusted r2	0.14		0.26		0.14			
Standard error	7.76		7.21		4.06			
F	164.2		41.4		12.3			
N of cases	1954		1954		965			

*p < 0.05   **p < 0.01

imprisonment and the sentence-length decisions and their relevance to conflict theory. Owing to the relatively low number of upper- and middle-class offenders in the sample, the analyses do not include dummy variables for these occupational groups. However, separate analyses suggest that the lengthier sentences meted out to unemployed and working-class offenders may be attributable in part to the relative leniency accorded middle- and upper-class drug offenders, particularly medical professionals who were involved in such crimes. It is also clear that the criminal justice system viewed such offenders and the evidence they presented in court in an altogether different light than they did cases involving racial-minority groups and the lower occupational classes.

In discussions of Canada's narcotics problems during the 1910s and 1920s, there was considerable concern expressed that unscrupulous doctors and druggists were dispensing drugs to addicts. While arrest statistics suggest that police officers were willing to apprehend such individuals for violations of narcotics law, the courts seemed reluctant to convict, and the cases against medical professionals were frequently dismissed. A number of cases from the 1908–30 period are instructive in outlining the disproportionately lenient treatment of these middle- and upper-class offenders.

In a 1924 case, Joseph Ross, proprietor of the Elm Drug Store in Toronto, was charged on two counts of selling morphine to a woman who had not provided him with a prescription. Ross's counsel, R.H. Greer, questioned the testimony of the woman, and asserted that she had told Mr Ross that she was making the purchase for her doctor, who apparently would administer the dose. In promoting his client's positive characteristics, Greer also argued that Ross was entitled to considerable credit for putting himself through college for a doctor's degree. This task, Greer urged, was almost completed, and a conviction for a drug offence would erase many years of 'painstaking labour.' The sentencing magistrate accepted counsel's rather questionable explanation of the drug-selling incident, and, presumably accepting his counsel's representation of Greer's character, granted a dismissal (*Toronto Daily Star*, 27 February 1924).

This willingness to assess evidence to the benefit of upper-class offenders was also revealed in the case of Thomas Cruttenden, a Toronto druggist who was charged with trafficking in morphine. Cruttenden's case was dismissed because the prosecution was unable to prove that he had sold morphine personally: 'He is not liable for the actions of his clerks' (*Toronto Daily Star*, 13 October 1916). Similarly, Dr Louis Goldberg, of Toronto, was acquitted on all twenty-six charges of selling narcotics by Magistrate Jones, apparently owing to the insufficiency of the prosecution's evidence against him (*Toronto Daily Star*, 18 October 1927).

Even in the relatively rare instances where these medical professionals were convicted, advantages occurred at the sentencing stage. In 1928, Drs James Harrington and E. Hill of Hamilton were sentenced by Judge Gould to three months in prison for selling narcotics (*Hamilton Spectator*, 12 August 1928), significantly less than the average sentence length of twelve months for narcotics traffickers in the 1920s. In 1925, Dr Ezra Adams, of Toronto (*Toronto Daily Star*, 5 August 1925), was convicted of fifteen counts of selling drugs, but was sentenced to only $50 or 10 days plus six months' incarceration.

At least part of the advantage these medical professionals enjoyed in the criminal justice system was attributable to their stature in the community, and the fact that they quite literally represented an altogether different class of offender. The *Toronto Daily Star* (5 August 1925), after referring to the fact that Dr Adams had relied on the testimony of Russell Nesbitt, a member of the Ontario provincial legislature, drew attention to the difference between Adams and 'regular' police court attendees: 'The doctor spoke clearly and emphatically, answering his counsel's questions without hesitation.'

In the case of Dr D.W. Shier, who was fined $500 or six months plus six months on two counts of selling morphine, Magistrate Jones of Toronto placed responsibility for the crime on lack of information doctors received with respect to narcotics laws:

The accused is a physician of high standing who has practised in Toronto for many years, and it is difficult to understand how he should have been ignorant or have disregarded the important change in the law. One would think the College of Physicians and Surgeons or some other society to which the accused no doubt belongs would have taken the trouble to draw the attention of their members to the provision which makes it no longer right or lawful to do what the accused has done in this case. (*Toronto Daily Star*, 25 October 1927)

In other cases involving medical professionals, some magistrates expressed their regret at having to sentence them at all. For instance, in the conviction of Dr Paul Marier for drug trafficking in Ottawa, the sentencing magistrate stated, 'It is very painful for me to have to pass sentence on an old member of an honourable profession. But, if any man in the community should know the damning results of the drug traffic it is a medical man; for it is he who has the knowledge of the deadly effects of these drugs' (*Ottawa Citizen*, 29 December 1925). In short, it is clear that narcotics legislation was applied much differently to medical professionals, a finding which provides at least partial support for the predictions of conflict theory, and which assists in an explanation of the social-class effects revealed in the imprisonment and sentence-length decisions.

Most important for the purposes of examining the impact of race on criminal justice, tables 6.3 and 6.4 indicate that Black and Chinese drug offenders were both less likely to be imprisoned, and, when imprisoned, were sentenced to shorter periods of incarceration. The data presented in table 6.2 indicate that the mean sentence length for White drug offenders was 8.77 months, for Blacks 6.44 months, and for Chinese 2.08 months.

Although the qualitative data do not allow for explanations of the more lenient treatment of Black drug offenders, a considerable amount of data suggest that the less severe sentences meted out to Chinese are primarily attributable to two factors. The first involves the rather questionable arrest practices of the police with respect to Chinese offenders discussed above, which exerted an impact on important strength-of-evidence variables that magistrates would consider in their sentencing decisions. The second factor involves a form of 'white paternalism' (Mosher and Hagan, 1994) which was apparently operational in the sentencing of these offenders.

Although the Chinese community was certainly not politically influential in Ontario cities in the early 1900s, the Toronto Board of Police Commissioners received several complaints on behalf of the Chinese which alleged that the 'police had been unduly harsh in their treatment of foreignors [sic] when raiding their premises for gambling or opium'[10] (Toronto, *Minutes of the Board of Police Commissioners*, 1915). Similarly, some defence lawyers were often critical of the fact that the police seemed to focus on Chinese sections of the city in their enforcement of morality laws: 'Chinese are raided for gambling and other things and Irishmen are not' (*Hamilton Spectator*, 1 December 1921). It is thus likely that sentencing judges would have been aware of the discriminatory police practices in enforcing drug laws, and may have attempted to compensate for this discrimination in their sentencing decisions.

The second factor accounting for this lenient treatment of Chinese drug offenders involves a form of 'white paternalism' towards the Chinese that was evident in the Ontario police courts of this period. This paternalism was often revealed in court reports on cases involving Chinese as victims of property and violent offences. For instance, responding to a 'rash' of assaults against Chinese in the city of Toronto in December 1919 (*Toronto Daily Star*, 15 December 1919), a newspaper headline stated, 'Hands Off the Chinese – Don't Knock 'Em About – Quietest of People.' The article went on to quote Inspector McKinney of the Toronto police force, who noted, 'John Chinaman is far from home, but apart from an occasional breeze at fan tan and a stray whiff from the opium pipe, he's not a troublesome person.' Magistrate Kingsford apparently agreed and 'announced that Chinamen were not to be knocked about in any irregular way.' Similarly, in the case of Leonard Leeds, charged with 'breaking down a Chinaman's door,' it was noted that, 'even if an occasional Chinaman "hits" the opium pipe or plays fan tan, there are worse men than the imported laundrymen' (*Toronto Daily Star*, 26 January 1920). In the southwestern Ontario city of London (*Advertiser*, 26 February 1910), Sidney Lawrie was sentenced to three months' imprisonment for 'brutally attacking' Lee Sing, a Chinese laundryman. In dealing with Lawrie, Magistrate Love noted, 'A Chinaman has just as much right to be here as you have, and will be protected.'

These same principles of severity towards offenders who victimized Chinese applied to property offences. In 1926, 'a Chinaman' was held up at his place of business and robbed of $40. The three perpetrators in this case were sentenced to prison for four years, and received ten lashes each (Toronto, *Annual Report of the Chief Constable*, 1927: 12). Similarly, in 1928, Ing Tai, a 'Chinese laundryman,' was held up by two men using a 'nickel plated revolver.' These men were sentenced to three years in prison and five 'straps' each (ibid., 1929: 8).

It is also clear that some court officials in the early 1900s were cognizant of the difficulties the Chinese experienced in overcoming their addiction to opium, and, in some instances, the recognition of these problems led to less severe sentences. In the case of How Dock, defence counsel J.N. Curry stressed the nature of Chinese addiction to opium: 'This drug was formerly forced upon them and now they are being fined for having it' (*Toronto Daily Star*, 20 March 1911). In an Ottawa case (*Citizen*, 18 September 1922) in which three Chinese were charged with opium possession, their counsel, J.C. Grant, asserted that his clients were

many thousand miles from home and in a strange land where strange customs hold sway ... Like a man who is accustomed to his drink of whiskey, they are used to having a smoke of opium. They know it is against the law and have tried to stop the use of it; but it is well known that the opium habit was not one of easy discontinuance.

Similar arguments were made by Coolidge (1929: 452) who, in describing patterns of opium use among Asians in the United States, indicated that the Chinese were not wholly responsible for their use of opium. 'It has already been shown that opium taking in moderation as ordinarily practised by [them] ... is no more disastrous than the use of tobacco among Americans, and that when carried to excess, its effects are scarcely more disastrous to society than the excessive use of liquor drinking which is the characteristic Caucasian vice.'

This belief in the inability of the Chinese to control their addiction was sometimes buttressed by reference to their alleged reduced mental capacity, which, it was argued, made them less responsible for their actions. For instance, the lawyer for Lee Ben, a 'Chinese laundryman' from Windsor, argued that there was 'some excuse' for his client's use of opium since he 'had small mentality and undeveloped intelligence' (*Border Cities Star*, 27 October 1920). This sympathy for Chinese drug users was also shared by at least some judges, with Magistrate Jelfs of Hamilton (*Spectator*, 1 December 1921) suggesting in a 1921 case, 'Look at the poor specimens of humanity that appear in the dock here. That is the result of drugs, and it seems to me that it is inhuman to keep these poor Chinese without their opium.'

Thus, it appears as though a form of White paternalism, which has also been documented in contemporary studies examining the sentences of Black offenders in certain jurisdictions of the United States (Myers and Talarico, 1986), was occurring with respect to Chinese opium users in the early 1900s in Ontario.

Columns four and five of table 6.4 present the results of sentence-length regressions for Chinese offenders, while columns 5 and 6 present coefficient comparisons between the overall sample and the Chinese subsample. The results in the two samples are quite similar, although it is notable that the non-significant but positive relationship for the 'no occupation' variable is statistically significant in the Chinese subsample. Most important is the significant difference between the two samples with respect to the 'trafficking' variable, which suggests that Chinese who trafficked in drugs were treated particularly severely by the courts. Thus, while the apparent goal of the criminal justice system to contain and not severely punish Chinese drug use was reflected in their disproportionately lenient sentences, this focus on containment appears to have held only as long as the Chinese kept their drug-taking habits to themselves.

Although I was unable to obtain comprehensive information on the race of individuals who were the recipients of Chinese drug sales, it is apparent from the qualitative data that, if Chinese were apprehended selling narcotics to Whites, they were treated much more severely by sentencing magistrates. Concerns regarding the spread of the drug problem to the White population had been noted in Emily Murphy's (1922a) book *The Black Candle*. Murphy attributed this diffusion to unscrupulous drug dealers, most of whom she asserted were Chinese or Black. Similar concerns were revealed in various official government documents, such as the 1927–8 federal Department of Health's annual report (Canada, 1927–8: 16–17):

It will be noted from the details of a number of cases (included in this survey) that the connection of members of that race [Chinese] with the narcotic situation is by no means limited to operating or frequenting of opium joints, but extends to trafficking not only in opium, but in three drugs, morphine, heroin, and cocaine, which are more commonly the drugs of addiction for Occidentals.

In a specific case involving the sale of drugs by a Chinese offender to a

White, the *Toronto Daily Star* (22 July 1921) prefaced the fate of G. Sing this way: 'Chinaman Fined $1000 – $500 in Drugs Found – G. Sing Did Not Restrict Sales to His Own Countrymen.' In sentencing this individual, Magistrate Jones of Toronto stressed the gravity of the offence, in that Sing 'had not confined the debauchery to his own people but had sold a quantity of morphine to a white woman.' Interestingly, the same principles of severity did not apply to Chinese charged with selling narcotics to Blacks. Ching Sing, a Windsor offender convicted of selling drugs to a Black male, was sentenced to the comparatively lenient penalty of $200 or six months by Magistrate Gundy (*Border Cities Star*, 4 October 1922).

This finding that Chinese traffickers who sold to White drug-takers received comparatively harsh treatment has parallels in more recent times. Peterson and Hagan (1984) argue that, in the changing context of symbolic 'villains' and 'victims' of drugs, minority drug users may receive more lenient sanctions than Whites, while minority drug dealers may be sentenced particularly harshly because they prey on an already victimized population. Similarly, Myers (1989) found more severe treatment of Black as opposed to White drug traffickers sentenced in the state of Georgia between 1977 and 1985.

Although most other studies that have examined such issues have tended to focus on interpersonal crimes, it is useful to conceptualize White drug users in this particular historical context as the 'victims' of supposedly aggressive Chinese traffickers. Kleck's (1981) finding that Blacks who commit predominantly intraracial crimes, with Black victims, are considered to be less serious offenders by the criminal justice system is relevant here. His argument is that such offences represent less of a threat to the community than do crimes with White victims. Similarly, Myers and Talarico (1986) found that there was greater leniency for Blacks convicted of victimizing Blacks compared with White/White and Black/White dyads.

This analysis of the sentencing of drug offenders for the 1908–30 period thus suggests that the courts adopted a paternalistic attitude to Chinese drug users, who were both less likely to be convicted and, when convicted, likely to receive shorter sentences. However, when Chinese were involved in the trafficking of drugs, particularly to Whites, these principles of disproportional lenience did not apply.

Public-Order Offences

A dark complexion was given to the atmosphere of the police court today when the results of a Sunday morning raid on a gambling house at 253 Queen Street West were

Table 6.5: Descriptive Data: Public-Order Offences, 1892–1961 (Means)

Variable	Overall	Blacks	Chinese	Native	White
Black	0.12				
Chinese	0.02				
Native	0.11				
White	0.76				
Imprisonment	0.90	0.93	0.86	0.96	0.88
Sentence length	1.32	2.35	1.97	1.30	1.15
Female	0.23	0.28	0.01	0.27	0.22
Single	0.61	0.52	0.26	0.55	0.64
Age	37.89	34.93	34.51	35.30	38.80
Age 16–24	0.09	0.11	0.08	0.09	0.08
Age 25–34	0.26	0.34	0.41	0.35	0.23
Age 35–44	0.25	0.25	0.23	0.26	0.25
Age 45–54	0.21	0.16	0.17	0.16	0.22
Age 55+	0.19	0.14	0.11	0.14	0.20
No occupation	0.08	0.08	0.03	0.05	0.09
Working class	0.83	0.79	0.52	0.94	0.83
Middle class	0.06	0.03	0.04	0.01	0.08
Upper class	0.00	0.00	0.02	0.00	0.00
Second offence	0.01	0.01	0.00	0.01	0.02
Previous offence	0.46	0.39	0.05	0.60	0.46
Offence seriousness	0.54	0.62	0.62	0.48	0.54
Hamilton	0.17	0.18	0.10	0.36	0.15
Windsor	0.08	0.20	0.08	0.03	0.07
London	0.15	0.16	0.02	0.37	0.12
Ottawa	0.10	0.00	0.05	0.00	0.14
Thunder Bay	0.12	0.04	0.03	0.23	0.12
Toronto	0.37	0.43	0.73	0.00	0.41
1892–1909	0.12	0.22	0.22	0.10	0.11
1910–19	0.12	0.18	0.30	0.11	0.11
1920–9	0.13	0.19	0.20	0.11	0.12
1930–9	0.15	0.15	0.17	0.15	0.15
1940–9	0.21	0.15	0.10	0.21	0.22
1950–61	0.27	0.11	0.02	0.33	0.29
N of cases	11,818	1,372	198	1,314	8,934

ushered in. No less than 21 colored gentlemen were present, with three white men on the outskirts of the crowd. (*Toronto Daily Star*, 17 April 1916)

Similar to the situation with respect to violations of drug legislation, arrests for public-order crimes almost exclusively involve proactive police work and the exercise of considerable discretion on the part of police in terms of who they arrest for the commission of such crimes. Table 6.5 presents descriptive data on the sample of public-order offenders, and indicates that 12 per cent of all of them from the six cities were Black, 11 per cent Native, and 2 per cent Chinese.

Within this general category of public-order offences, however, arrests for some types of crimes, such as gambling and prostitution, required more vigorous police work and were more likely to involve an enforcement focus on minority-group offenders. In order to control such activities, law enforcement officials usually relied on sections of the criminal code dealing with disorderly and bawdy houses – these provisions allowed for both the keepers and the frequenters of such establishments to be charged. Thus, when the sample of public-order offences is broken down into the more specific categories of liquor offences and disorderly-house offences,[11] we find that, while the latter comprised only 4.3 per cent of all White public-order offences, they comprised 36.9 per cent of Chinese offences, and 13.7 per cent of Black offences, in this category. These statistics suggest that police activity was particularly vigorous with respect to disorderly-house offences committed by Blacks and Chinese, a factor that influenced their more severe treatment in the courts.

Table 6.6 presents the results of the logistic regression of the decision to imprison public-order offenders, with the first two columns displaying the results for the overall sample.[12] The table reveals that Black and Native offenders, those having no occupation, those in the working class, individuals arrested for a second offence, those with a prior record, those sentenced in the cities of Hamilton and London, and those sentenced in the 1930–9 period were more likely to be imprisoned. Female offenders, those in the 16–24 and 25–34 age groups, those sentenced in Windsor, and those sentenced in the 1910–19 and 1950–61 periods were less likely to be imprisoned for the commission of public-order offences. The variable offence seriousness shows a significant negative effect, which suggests that more stringent standards of evidence were applied in determining guilt with respect to cases involving more serious public-order offences.

Columns 3 and 4 of table 6.6 present the results of the imprisonment-decision logistic regression for Black offenders only, while columns 5 and 6 compare the coefficients from the two samples. The most important differences between the two samples revealed in the comparison are that Black offenders with no occupation, and those in the working class, were even more likely to be imprisoned than non-Black offenders from these two occupational categories. This suggests that lower-class Blacks were treated particularly severely by the courts when convicted of public-order offences. The comparison of coefficients also suggests that Blacks were less likely than non-Blacks to be imprisoned when sentenced in Hamilton, Windsor, and London, which implies that such offenders

Table 6.6: Logistic Regression on Imprisonment Decision: Public-Order Offences 1892–1961

Variable	All Offenders		Black offenders		Comparison	
	Coefficient	Odds ratio	Coefficient	Odds ratio	Diff.	T-ratio
Black	0.86**	2.37				
Chinese	0.27	1.22				
Native	0.79**	2.21				
Female	−0.34	0.71	−0.15	0.86	−0.19	0.61
Single	0.09	1.09	0.32	1.38	−0.23	0.77
Age 16–24	−0.92**	0.40	−0.11	0.90	−0.81	0.80
Age 25–34	−0.20*	0.82	0.13	1.14	−0.33	1.00
Age 45–54	0.00	1.00	0.52	1.69	−0.52	1.44
Age 55+	−0.09	0.92	0.11	1.12	−0.20	0.56
No occupation	0.35*	1.42	2.48**	12.00	−2.13	4.95**
Working class	0.28**	1.33	2.59**	13.36	−2.31	6.42**
Second offence	1.87**	6.54	3.79	44.38	−1.92	1.57
Previous offence	0.66**	1.93	0.62*	1.86	0.04	0.12
Offence seriousness	−1.39**	0.25	−1.48**	0.23	−0.09	0.20
Hamilton	0.45**	1.57	−0.56	0.30	1.01	2.66**
Windsor	−0.23*	0.80	−2.61**	0.07	2.38	6.61**
London	0.83**	2.29	−1.58**	0.21	2.41	5.88**
1910–19	−0.43**	0.65	0.85**	2.34	−1.28	3.76**
1930–9	0.27**	1.31	−0.17	0.85	0.44	1.19
1950–61	−0.56**	0.57	−0.15	0.86	−0.41	1.21
2 Log Likelihood	7,195.8		559.3			
Chi-square	706.1		131.3			
Goodness of Fit	11,529.3		1,082.1			
N of Cases	11,818		1,372			

*p < 0.05   **p < 0.01

were treated more severely when sentenced in Toronto. In addition, while the coefficient for the 1910–19 period is significantly negative in the overall sample, the coefficient for Blacks is significantly positive, suggesting that Black public-order offenders were disproportionally likely to be imprisoned in that decade. In short, these results provide strong indications that Black public-order offenders were subject to disproportionally severe treatment in the criminal courts.

The significant difference in coefficients between the overall sample and the Black subsample for the cities of Hamilton, Windsor, and London, indicating that Blacks sentenced in these cities were less likely to be convicted and imprisoned, deserves some explanation. It is apparent that at least some judges in these cities were more interested in ensuring that Black offenders from the United States were returned to that country than in increasing the population of Ontario jails with such offenders. These results thus appear to be due to the rather peculiar, and legally questionable, practice of 'informal deportation' practised by judges in these cities when dealing with Black public-order offenders.[13] In a 1920 Hamilton case (*Hamilton Spectator*, 2 July 1920), for instance, two Black Americans employed by the carnival were found with a quantity of morphine and informed the sentencing magistrate, 'We didn't know about the law here. If you let us go we'll go back to the States.' The two offenders were deported without sentence. In Windsor, Magistrate Miers warned three Black drug users from Detroit to stay away from the city, stating: 'Lately, we've had a number of drug addicts up here from the other side. If you drug addicts do not stay away from here, I'll send you to the prison farm. You just come back here and you'll find out how undesirable you are' (*Border Cities Star*, 1 August 1919). Another 'confessed (Black) drug addict' in Windsor, charged with vagrancy, was 'ordered out of the city within two hours' (*Border Cities Star*, 12 October 1920), but was not convicted of an offence. Similarly, in the case of William Leroy, 'colored,' charged with 'bringing three girls from Montreal for immoral purposes,' the accused was 'deported to the United States and warned not to enter Canada again' (*Border Cities Star*, 14 November 1929). Thus, while Blacks were less likely to be imprisoned for the commission of public-order offences in the cities of Windsor, Hamilton, and London, the tendency of judges to deport them is also reflective of disproportionately severe treatment.

Table 6.5 showed that the mean sentence length for Chinese public-order offenders was 1.97 months, for Blacks 2.35 months, and for Whites 1.15 months. Table 6.7 presents the results of the sentence-length regressions for public-order offences and further confirms this disproportionally severe treatment of minority-group offenders. The first two columns of the table indicate that Blacks and Chinese were sentenced to longer sentences, and, although these coefficients are reduced when other extralegal, legal, and structural variables are controlled in columns 3 and 4, they are still statistically significant. In addition, when these additional variables are taken into account, the positive coefficient for Natives becomes statistically significant. The social-class variables which exerted a significant effect on the imprisonment decision have no effect on sentence length for the overall sample.

Table 6.7 also indicates that female public-order offenders, those in the 16–24 age group, those who committed a second offence, those sentenced in the cities of Hamilton and Windsor, and those sentenced in the 1930–9 period received longer terms of imprisonment. All three legal variables show positive and significant effects on sentence length, with the effect for offence serious-

Table 6.7: Regression on Sentence Length: Public-Order Offences, 1892–1961

	All Offenders				Black Offenders		Comparison	
	Block 1		Block 2					
Variable	B	Beta	B	Beta	B	Beta	Diff.	T-ratio
Black	1.20	0.12**	0.67	0.06**				
Chinese	0.82	0.03**	0.64	0.02**				
Native	0.15	0.01	0.35	0.03**				
Female			0.65	0.08**	1.26	0.12**	-0.61	2.02*
Single			-0.01	-0.01	0.03	0.00	-0.04	0.14
Age 16–24			0.35	0.03**	1.47	0.10**	-1.12	2.87**
Age 25–34			-0.06	-0.01	-0.06	-0.01	0.00	0.00
Age 45–54			0.06	0.09	0.28	0.02	-0.22	0.63
Age 55+			0.13	0.02	0.36	0.03	-0.23	0.66
No occupation			-0.07	0.00	0.62	0.04	-0.69	1.57
Working class			0.08	0.01	1.11	0.10**	-1.03	2.71**
Second offence			1.34	0.05**	2.28	0.05*	-0.94	1.59
Previous offence			0.32	0.05**	0.42	0.04	-0.03	0.10
Offence seriousness			4.75	0.28**	6.69	0.28**	-1.94	4.22**
Hamilton			0.39	0.05**	0.15	0.01	0.24	0.73
Windsor			0.39	0.03**	0.15	0.01	0.24	0.65
London			-0.09	-0.01	-0.26	-0.02	0.17	0.50
1910–19			-0.01	0.00	0.21	0.02	0.22	0.65
1930–9			0.22	0.02**	0.58	0.04	-0.36	1.06
1950–61			-0.49	-0.07**	-0.69	-0.05*	0.20	0.61
r2	0.01		0.11		0.14			
Adjusted r2	0.01		0.11		0.12			
Standard error	3.27		3.11		4.39			
F	56.3		74.8		12.5			
N of cases	11,818				1,372			

*p < 0.05   **p < 0.01

ness being particularly strong. While the 'offence seriousness' variable exerted a negative effect on the imprisonment decision, it is clear that, once imprisonment had been chosen as the sentencing option, those guilty of committing more serious public-order offences were imprisoned for comparatively longer periods.

Columns 5 and 6 of table 6.7 present the results of the sentence-length regression for Black public offenders only, while columns 7 and 8 compare the coefficients for this subsample with the overall sample. Significant differences are revealed for females, those in the 16–24 age group, and those in the working class, suggesting that Blacks from these categories were treated even more severely by sentencing magistrates. Additionally, the strong and significant positive coefficient for offence seriousness in the overall sample is even stronger in the Black subsample, indicating that offence seriousness was accorded even more importance by magistrates in sentencing Black public-order offenders.

These data thus indicate that Chinese and Black public-order offenders were subject to considerable disadvantage in the criminal courts, compared with non-minority-group offenders. But in order to adequately understand the more severe treatment of such offenders by sentencing magistrates, it is necessary to consider the findings from the qualitative data on the enforcement of public-morals legislation. I begin with a discussion of the disproportional police focus on Chinese gamblers and gambling establishments, then go on to examine police attention to Blacks involved in disorderly-house offences.

Chinese and Gambling

Like the use of opium, gambling was a vice that was particularly likely to be associated with the Chinese in many Canadian communities. This association between Chinese and gambling offences provided an additional opportunity for the popular media to negatively stereotype the Chinese on the basis of their questionable morality. Although some early commentators suggested that gambling was more of a recreational pursuit for the Chinese than an attempt to derive wealth (Johnston, 1921; *Saturday Night*, 23 December 1905), Levine (1975, as cited in Thompson, 1989: 89) maintains that gambling among the Chinese in the early 1900s was so lucrative that it was directly responsible for the fact that only 50 Chinese out of a total population of 2,000 in Toronto applied for government relief during the Depression era.

Whether this gambling resulted in profits for those involved, or whether it was only a social diversion for the Chinese, there is little evidence to suggest that there was extensive involvement of organized Chinese gangs, or tongs, in Ontario, which were allegedly prominent in running gambling operations in several U.S. cities (Reynolds, 1934–5) in the early to middle 1900s. Although referring to the situation in Vancouver's Chinatown, Hayner (1937–8: 915) asserts that the area was 'not troubled with Chinese tongs,' a fact that he attributed to the 'Chinese (here) being more sensitive to the attitudes of the dominant group.' Similarly, rumours of 'tong wars' connected to drug trafficking and gambling in Toronto's Chinatown in 1930 were explicitly denied by Police Inspector William Johnston, who stated that he 'had never been able to find any evidence of the hatchet-men being imported from the outside' (*Toronto Daily Star*, 27 March 1930). Regardless of the apparent lack of involvement of organized-crime groups in Chinese gambling, however, the qualitative data reveal that law-enforcement agencies in Ontario cities deemed gambling in Chinese communities to be worthy of considerable attention.

The Chinese gambling problem in Toronto was first mentioned in the 1896 *Annual Report of the Chief Constable* (Toronto, 1896), where it was noted that 'some Chinese were playing fan-tan.' Although in this early report the chief constable did not display great concern over the need to stem this form of vice among the Chinese, as Chinese communities in Ontario cities grew in size police efforts at controlling Asian gambling establishments intensified.

Subsequent annual police reports from both Toronto and Hamilton made frequent reference to the Chinese gambling problem, and, while acknowledging that the individuals involved often considered gambling 'more of a pass-time than a vice' (Hamilton, *Annual Police Report*, 1911) officials stressed the importance of vigorously enforcing the existing gambling laws against the Chinese. In some cities, the enforcement of gambling laws was at least partially justified by concerns emanating from the Chinese community itself. For example, a petition 'signed by a number of Chinese' was presented to the Toronto Board of Police Commissioners (Toronto, 1908), which noted that 'gambling [is] very prevalent among their countrymen, especially in business places.' At the same time, police reports emphasized the difficulties encountered in the enforcement of gambling laws and conviction of the violators: 'The commissioners were of the opinion that in view of the unreliability of evidence forthcoming from the frequenters of the places where Chinese play fan tan among themselves, the police can only succeed in convicting when evidence is forthcoming from the police or other reliable sources' (ibid.).

In the 1909 Toronto report of the chief constable, it is noted that 'raids upon the Chinese who gamble among themselves, that being their chief, if not only form of amusement, have not proved very successful owing to conflicting evidence. Clubs operated under a charter are the latest move of the Chinamen to escape molestation while engaging in their national past-time.' Similarly, in

1910, the Toronto police chief claimed that 'gambling continues to flourish among the Chinese, and all efforts to stop them have been futile, reliable evidence being unobtainable. Admission to play in these Chinese resorts is denied to the public, except in a few places where opium is smoked' (Toronto, *Annual Report of the Chief Constable*, 1910). The Chinese gambling problem in Toronto had apparently not been solved by 1911, when it was noted that 'gambling still goes on in Chinese resorts, and [was] the subject of police prosecution, but the conflict of evidence and doubtful validity of search warrants rendered the action taken void.'

Although Toronto police officials often expressed their frustration in securing arrests and convictions of Chinese gamblers, media reports suggest that at least some of their efforts came to fruition. In an article headlined 'City Collects $1550 from Chinese Gamblers,' the *Toronto Daily Star* (8 March 1907) described the results of a successful police raid on a gambling establishment in that city:

Magistrate Denison was again the mighty mighty emperor of China when 121 Chinamen were scooped up in a raid of the premises at 101 Queen Street West. The magistrate went over the list and separated 74 of them from the multitude ... Those fined were in the cellar when the game was in progress. Each was asked 'will you pay?' – 'me no pay' said some, 'oh yes' said others. 'I am sorry to have to fine these foreignors [*sic*], but the law allows me no alternative.'

In another Toronto case involving Chinese gamblers, the *Toronto Daily Star* (12 January 1920) noted, 'It could not have been a Chinese Sunday school class that lined up before Magistrate Kingsford in police court, because the charge was that of gambling on the Lord's day. But the 16 penitents paid $2 and costs and went back to their laundries.'

An enforcement focus on Chinese violators of gambling laws was also evidenced in Hamilton, where the 1912 annual police report noted, 'the police have been very active in the suppression of the practice, but it is still carried on by the Chinese with more or less frequency, and efforts to stop it have been to little avail' (Hamilton, 1912). Similarly, in the 1913 report of the Hamilton police department, the arrest of ninety-five persons for gambling offences is mentioned, but 'the Chinese continue to gamble and it is difficult to obtain reliable evidence to convict. All efforts to stop them have been unavailing' (Hamilton, 1913).

Police concern about Chinese gambling, and their proclivity for employing gambling laws as a measure to control the Chinese population, were not restricted to the cities of Toronto and Hamilton, however. For example, in the case of a raid on a Chinese gambling establishment in Fort William, the *Daily Times Journal* (17 May 1904) reported:

Twenty Chinamen paid $400 for the pleasure of enacting a scene Saturday before an audience of two – Chief Dods and Sergeant Watkins. The scene was one of wild confusion. Bets were offered and called with as much interest as if vast fortunes were at stake. After being caught like rats in a trap and being escorted to the police court, the proprietors, Chin Chan and Chee Foo, professional Chinese gamblers, were fined $25 and costs while the players escaped with the minimum fine under the law, $20 and costs.

Similarly, in a 'raid' on a Chinese gambling establishment in the city of Ottawa (*Ottawa Journal*, 22 February 1904) which was 'made (last night) under the personal direction of the Chief,' the 'Celestials were caught red-handed.' In this case, the keepers of the establishment were sentenced to three months in jail with hard labour, while the ten 'players' were fined $20 and $2 costs or two months in jail. In another raid on a Chinese gambling den from Ottawa which provides further evidence of the effort police exerted in apprehending such offenders, the court report notes that the raid was 'marked by some interesting details ... In order to make sure of their ground, members of the police force first secreted themselves in a cellar next door to the place they suspected ... It is stated that the police heard the sounds of playing in a cellar next door and they got ready for business. A detail including Sergeant Joliat and morality officer McGlaughlin was decided upon as the attacking party, while four members of the force were stationed outside to watch exits and prevent the possibility of escape.'

The police focus on alleged Chinese gambling establishments continued into the middle part of the twentieth century. As the Chinese reacted to police raids on their establishments by obtaining provincial charters to form legitimate social clubs, police officials contended that these were only fronts for gambling. In his 1944 annual report, Toronto's Chief Constable Draper claimed 'several well known operators of gaming houses obtained provincial charters during 1943 and 1944 and opened so-called charter clubs in Toronto. In reality, these places proved to be kept solely as common gaming houses. Police attention given these "operators" has resulted in eleven such establishments being closed' (Toronto, *Annual Report of the Chief Constable*, 1944).

The question of whether the main activity occurring in such clubs was gambling was often left for the higher courts to decide, and in a number of cases in the late 1940s and early 1950s court decisions often favoured the Chinese. For instance, in 1949, the manager and secretary of the Mow Chong Club in Toronto were convicted in a lower court of keeping a common gaming-house.

However, the conviction was overturned on appeal, with the Ontario Supreme Court noting that the premises in question were occupied by a 'bona fide social club' (*Rex* v *Wong and Seto*, 1950), and that the police raid had resulted in the seizure of only a small amount of money.

Although this decision suggests that police activities with respect to the apprehension of Chinese gamblers were tempered to a certain extent in the middle part of the century, the qualitative data suggest that over the course of most of the 1892-to-1950 period, considerable police effort was devoted to the pursuit of such individuals. These police efforts, combined with the more general media commentary surrounding the evils of gambling, undoubtedly contributed to the more severe treatment of Chinese public-order offenders in the criminal courts that was revealed in table 6.7.

Blacks and Public-Order Crime

Righteous indignation fairly oozed from the oily and impassioned harangue of Gustavansh Binyon, 72-year-old barber, and convicted keeper of a house of ill-fame, as he valiantly but vainly tried to impress upon the court the not very apparent fact that he was a pure and much maligned citizen persecuted by the police. The police reported that the house was one of the worst resorts in the city. The barber shop was run in connection with the dive at the back and the officers gave a mass of unsavory evidence, gathered in the course of the last five months. Lillian Desiocher, the French-Canadian chief attraction at the house, who was taken into custody, admitted that she obtained $2 from the men who frequented the place, 50 cents of which went to Binyon. Binyon was found guilty and sentenced to six months in jail. The woman will be examined and if found all right will be allowed to go. (*Hamilton Spectator*, 16 October, 1918)

The qualitative data reveal that police in these Ontario cities also had a tendency, in their pursuit of public-order crimes, to focus on Blacks, and disorderly-house and other public-morals laws were widely used by the police to control the Black population. Like Chinese, Blacks also apparently had a proclivity to be involved in gambling offences, with the *Hamilton Spectator* (5 October 1910) noting, 'these people [Blacks] played crap as naturally as trees bloom, and [they] denied it as naturally.' The police also directed attention to Black social clubs where gambling allegedly occurred. In 1915, for instance, Chief Constable Dickson of the Toronto police reported that the proprietors of the Excelsior Club ('colored'), had been arrested and convicted for keeping a disorderly house as a result of infractions related to gambling laws. 'As the reports of this club had been equally bad in other locations,' the Toronto Board of Police Commissioners directed that the chief constable's report be forwarded to the provincial secretary, 'with a view to cancellation of the Club's license' (Toronto, *Minutes of the Board of Police Commissioners*, 1915). However, even more common than the law-enforcement focus on Black residences and establishments where gambling was alleged to occur was an inclination for police to pursue Blacks for violations of bawdy- and disorderly-house provisions.

Several examples from the city of Hamilton demonstrate this police focus on Black morals offenders. Hamilton police officers 'scouted [particular] neighbourhoods looking for evidence that would warrant raid(s)' (*Hamilton Spectator*, 25 January 1909), engaged in frequent 'crusades against questionable resorts' (ibid., 3 August 1914), and conducted 'spring house cleanings' (ibid., 15 March 1915). The qualitative data suggest that, in several instances, this proactive police work resulted in the arrest of Blacks.

For example, in the case of Frank and Fanny Bayliss, who were convicted at least five times for keeping a disorderly house in Hamilton between 1908 and 1914, the *Hamilton Spectator* (25 January 1909) noted:

Constable Duffy had been detailed to watch their house and while doing so heard a lot of 'unparliamentary language' and a number of men and women went in and out on the second night ... The prisoner Bayliss, who is a colored man, was then called. He said a game of wist and some drinking was occurring at the time of the raid. The audience laughed and had to be brought to order. Magistrate Jelfs stated that *the police did not choose the house randomly* and that the constables would not perjure themselves. The woman was the greatest sinner. (emphasis added)

When the police once again raided the Baylisses' residence in 1914, the *Hamilton Spectator* (14 February 1914) reported that they found 'two other Negroes and a white woman in the house. Policemen who have been watching the house for some time told of men making visits there oftener than the tax collector would call. And there were women visitors too.' The same house was the subject of police attention less than three months later, when 'the southern element was very much in evidence when Fannie and Frank Bayliss were charged with keeping a disorderly house ... Mrs. Bayliss attempted to do the Romeo and Juliet act on the roof of the rear kitchen, but was captured by police before she could get any further' (*Hamilton Spectator*, 27 April 1914). In another Hamilton case (*Spectator*, 19 January 1920),

John Stevens, a gentleman of dusky hue, must spend the next three months as the guest of Governor Ogilvie. Stevens was found guilty of keeping a disorderly house. *The house has been under surveillance for weeks*. Stevens was found in the front room alone but

when a door leading into a small apartment at the side was opened, a dusky damsel
(Emma Johnson) was revealed entertaining a male visitor. Emma informed the court that
she had picked men up on the street, brought them to the house and had requested a $2
donation from them, half of which she turned over to Stevens. (emphasis added)

The immoral activities that allegedly occurred in such establishments were
invoked by law-enforcement officials as justification for dealing harshly with
such offenders. For instance, testifying in a Hamilton case involving the female
('colored') keeper of a disorderly house, Constable Brown of Hamilton told the
court that 'the conduct and language of the people who visited [the house] was
something disgraceful' (*Hamilton Spectator*, 29 May 1911).

While the police focus on such establishments would thus exert a considerable impact on who appeared in court, and thus which offenders magistrates
would have the opportunity to convict and imprison, there is also evidence to
suggest that a further disadvantage faced by Blacks in court was a tendency for
magistrates to be particularly sceptical regarding the credibility of their testimony. For instance, in a case involving two 'colored gentlemen' appearing in a
Toronto court on charges of keeping liquor, Magistrate Jones had difficulty in
accepting the accuseds' explanation of why they were found in possession of
almost forty gallons of beer. Although the men claimed that they had been
given a permit by another individual and were only delivering the beer to that
person when apprehended by police, Magistrate Jones was not convinced.
'Obviously a liar ... I find on the evidence that I can't believe a word they say'
(*Toronto Daily Star*, 16 September 1931). Similarly, in London (*Evening
Advertiser*, 9 March 1923), 'the plea of Ernest Smith, colored, that dozens of
people who have visited his rented home in the past month were prompted only
by friendship alone was swallowed in a powerful array of police testimony and
he was fined $50 and costs or one month in jail for keeping a disorderly house.'

Questions regarding the validity of evidence also apparently exerted an
impact on the imprisonment decision when Chinese offenders were involved.[14]
In a Hamilton case (*Spectator*, 10 September 1920) in which Gong Why faced a
charge of keeping a disorderly house, Constables McBride and Bizely searched
the accused's café, and in two upper rooms found two men and two women,
'one pair of which were not fully clothed.' The two men testified that they had
had dinner at Why's restaurant, and afterwards had made their way to an upper
room for a smoke. Why asserted that he was not the proprietor of the café but
was serving as manager while the owner was absent, a fact that was corrobo-
rated in testimony by the proprietor of the café, who also testified that he had
not used the premises for immoral purposes. Despite his counsel's contention
that the police had arrested the wrong man and that there was insufficient evi-

dence to convict Why, the Hamilton magistrate hearing the case found him guilty and sentenced him to three months in jail.

In addition to revealing a disproportional police focus on Black public-order offenders and a tendency for judges to disbelieve the testimony of minority-group offenders, the qualitative data provide further evidence regarding the differential treatment of Black and White offenders by sentencing magistrates presented in table 6.7. Particularly informative here are public-order cases in which White and Black offenders were jointly charged and sentenced in the same court. For example, in the case of Sadie and Lewis Bennett, two Blacks charged with keeping a disorderly house and sentenced to six months in jail, the 'police rounded up eight Negroes and one white girl, Gladys Cage ... The charge of being an inmate preferred against the Cage girl was dismissed, she said she just dropped around the house to tickle the piano' (*Hamilton Spectator*, 12 January 1915). Similarly, Walter Price, 'colored,' was sentenced to six months at hard labour and a fine of $50 or an additional two months in default for keeping a disorderly house. 'In sentencing the man, Magistrate Leggatt said he deserved no sympathy from the court and he was only sorry that he could not make the penalty more severe. Maggie Leguie, the white girl who was also found in the house, and was held as an inmate, pleaded guilty and was let off on a suspended sentence' (*Windsor Evening Record*, 30 October 1912). In another disorderly-house case involving the previously mentioned Frank and Fanny Bayliss, which further reveals the differential credibility attached to the testimony of Blacks and Whites, a Hamilton judge sentenced the Baylisses to six months' imprisonment each. Two Black found-ins were fined $10, and a 'white man named French was allowed to go,' as he claimed that it was the only time he had been in the house (*Hamilton Spectator*, 27 April 1910).

Table 6.7 also revealed that Black females convicted of public-order offences were particularly likely to be treated harshly – this was especially the case in prostitution-related offences. The stereotyping of such women in newspaper police-court reports included references to them as 'negresses' (*Toronto Daily Star*, 6 April 1915) or 'the dusky Sarah' (*Hamilton Spectator*, 31 July 1911). Elizabeth Lee, a sixteen-year-old 'buxom colored maid,' was informed by a Windsor magistrate that she was 'badly in need of correction' (*Border Cities Star*, 7 September 1939). Even more blatantly, a *Hamilton Spectator* (22 May 1919) report on Black prostitutes in that city, appearing with the headline 'Dark Girls at it Again,' noted, 'Four big wenches, of various shades of Blackness, cast quite a gloom over the police court this morning. They were the damsels who have been operating in the alleys around town.'

Black female vagrants, many of whom were apparently involved in prostitution offences, were treated quite severely by sentencing magistrates, and were similarly subject to negative stereotyping in newspaper reports. For instance, the *Hamilton Spectator* (9 September 1912) described the case of two female Black vagrants as follows:

When dusky Mary White and Minnie Stewart bid farewell to the attendants at the Barton Street Institute, straw hats and summer breezes will have given way to ear-muffs and snow shovels. The bewitching damsels were booked on the circuit today until New Year's Day. Vagrancy was the charge preferred against the pair by Constables Kay and Campaign, who blushingly swore the girls were acting decidedly unlike Sabbath school graduates in the yard of the City Dairy last night. When the Magistrate slipped over the six months jolt, Mary and Minnie collapsed and their shrieks could be heard all over the building.

Similarly, Fanny Young, sentenced to twenty-three months on a charge of vagrancy in London (*Free Press*, 6 June 1892), was referred to as 'a poor mis-shapen colored woman, [who] has lived like a wild beast on the outskirts of the city.' In the vagrancy case of Mary Randolph, 'an ebony queen who flirted with Constable Dick Elliott' and who '[will] take a dishwashing course at the castle,' the sentencing judge noted, 'I'm going to break up these colored games. You're sentenced to four months in jail' (*Hamilton Spectator*, 5 August 1914).

To conclude, the evidence presented in this chapter indicates that minority-group drug offenders were subjected to selective police attention to their activities. While Chinese drug offenders who appeared in the courts were not consistently more likely to be incarcerated or sentenced to lengthier terms of imprisonment, the unofficial policy of containment of Chinese drug use did not apply when they were deemed to be involved in spreading their drug-taking habits to Whites. In addition, Blacks and Chinese involved in questionable moral activities such as gambling and prostitution were similarly the target of proactive police work, and were sentenced to lengthier terms of incarceration when found guilty of committing such crimes. These findings hold when legal variables such as prior record and offence seriousness are controlled for, and suggest evidence of systemic racism against minority-group offenders at all levels of the criminal justice system in Ontario in the period from 1892 to 1961. Chapter 7 examines whether similar discriminatory principles applied to the treatment of minority-group property and violent offenders.

7

Property and Violent Crimes

In ten years, probably three theft charges have been laid against Chinamen in the Toronto police court. The Chinese here woo chance, frequently mischance, at the altar of Fan Tan and they're fond of flowers, particularly the poppy, but the Toronto Chinaman is not a criminal. (*Toronto Star*, 4 March 1920)

Ten Lashes for Assaulter of Girl: 13-Year Old Girl Victim of Negro.
If (John) Butler had committed his crime in the southern states, he would not likely be here to stand trial. It is fortunate for him that he is under the British flag, where he can get a fair trial in a fair manner and is not subject to the punishment of the masses. (sentencing magistrate) 'Crimes of this kind (if they continue) would break down the social system and the whole religious training of children.' (*London Free Press*, 3 October 1931)

Property and violent offences present a different set of issues in examining the treatment of minority groups in the criminal justice system. The exercise of discretion on the part of police officers that influenced the numbers of minority-group offenders charged with drug and public-order offences, and the sentencing of such offenders, was not as prominent in the context of property and violent crimes, which were commonly brought to the attention of the police through citizen complaints. Thus, in examining criminal justice system processing and sentencing for property and violent offences, judicial discretion becomes a more important consideration.

This chapter will demonstrate that Asians were far less likely to be charged for committing property and violent offences than they were for drug and public-order offences, and were sentenced comparatively leniently when so charged. In fact, popular media and criminal justice system officials often commented that, despite their overinvolvement in drug and public-order crimes, the Chinese were relatively less often involved in more serious forms of crimes.

On the other hand, Blacks frequently appeared in the courts to answer to property-crime charges, and were sentenced to longer terms of imprisonment when convicted of such crimes. Blacks were also subject to disproportionally higher rates of imprisonment when involved in violent crimes, but quantitative analyses of sentence length for violent offenders indicates that Blacks were not subject to longer periods of incarceration than others. This finding is further analysed using qualitative data, which suggests that the race of the victim is important to consider in explaining sentences for Black violent offenders. In short, Blacks who victimized other Blacks were treated quite leniently by the courts, while those who victimized Whites were treated far more severely.

Property Offences

Table 7.1 presents descriptive data on property offences derived from the jail records for the six Ontario cities, and shows that, of a total of 4,467 property offenders in the sample, there were only 66 Chinese, or slightly more than 1 per cent of the entire sample.

Although national data on the number of Asians involved in property and violent crimes over the 1892–1961 period in Canada are not available, Beach's (1932) study of Oriental crime in California suggests that Asian residents of that state were underrepresented in serious-crime categories. Beach notes that, out of a total of almost 65,000 offences committed by the Chinese in California in 1920, only 1 per cent were offences against the person, and less than 1 per cent involved offences against property. Hayner (1937–8) similarly notes that a 1936 study of inmates in British Columbia's Oakalla Prison found that 24 of the 105 Chinese inmates had been incarcerated for lotteries and gambling violations, while another 31 were convicted under provision of the Opium and Narcotic Drug Act.[1] As was the case in Ontario, then, the most common Chinese offences in California and British Columbia in the early 1900s involved violations of narcotics and public-order laws.

While earlier portions of this book documented the popular media's preoccupation with the alleged moral shortcomings of Chinese, it is notable that there was comparatively little media or academic concern about their involvement in other, more serious forms of crime. Even some of the more xenophobic writers referenced in chapter 3 were willing to concede that the Chinese were not particularly prone to engage in serious crime. For instance, Nelson (1921b) asserted that the Chinese were 'honest' and that 'the Oriental [was] as law-abiding as his white neighbour.'

The limited number of Canadian academic studies on Oriental crime and

Table 7.1: Descriptive Data: Property Offences, 1892–1961 (Means)

Variable	Overall	Blacks	Chinese	Native	White
Black	0.19				
Chinese	0.01				
Native	0.07				
White	0.72				
Imprisonment	0.77	0.84	0.83	0.78	0.75
Sentence length	6.48	10.51	8.07	8.33	6.26
Female	0.13	0.11	0.02	0.11	0.14
Single	0.64	0.61	0.48	0.74	0.64
Age	28.47	27.92	32.00	26.75	28.72
Age 16–24	0.29	0.31	0.17	0.35	0.29
Age 25–34	0.37	0.38	0.36	0.38	0.36
Age 35–44	0.19	0.20	0.24	0.17	0.19
Age 45–54	0.09	0.07	0.20	0.07	0.10
Age 55+	0.05	0.05	0.03	0.03	0.06
No occupation	0.07	0.08	0.05	0.05	0.07
Working class	0.80	0.83	0.80	0.94	0.78
Middle class	0.11	0.02	0.02	0.00	0.14
Upper class	0.00	0.00	0.00	0.00	0.01
Second offence	0.12	0.05	0.02	0.10	0.14
Previous offence	0.36	0.40	0.14	0.52	0.34
Offence seriousness	1.38	1.38	1.31	1.49	1.37
Hamilton	0.18	0.15	0.14	0.30	0.17
Windsor	0.13	0.32	0.08	0.04	0.09
London	0.14	0.10	0.08	0.46	0.12
Ottawa	0.13	0.00	0.03	0.00	0.17
Thunder Bay	0.07	0.01	0.03	0.20	0.07
Toronto	0.36	0.42	0.65	0.00	0.37
1892–1909	0.16	0.23	0.12	0.13	0.14
1910–19	0.11	0.12	0.14	0.08	0.11
1920–9	0.12	0.16	0.47	0.12	0.10
1930–9	0.17	0.20	0.17	0.14	0.16
1940–9	0.20	0.16	0.09	0.19	0.21
1950–61	0.25	0.14	0.02	0.34	0.28
N of cases	4,467	829	66	334	3,238

delinquency similarly emphasized the law-abiding nature of the Chinese. For example, in an unpublished study titled 'The Oriental Delinquent in Court' (cited in Hayner, 1937–8), Judge Helen Gregory MacGill of the Vancouver juvenile court found that, during the ten-year period from 1926 to 1935, the rate for White juvenile delinquency in Vancouver was thirteen times as great as that for Orientals. Although not focusing directly on crime and delinquency, Woollacott (1930: 53) reported that principals and teachers in Vancouver were 'decidedly of the opinion that [Chinese and Japanese] children were not a detriment. As a matter of fact, every teacher who has had to deal with them is outspoken in praise of their superiority as pupils to other children. They give no trouble, are easily taught, they are industrious and honourable, they are free from objectionable habits, they are in short ideal pupils.' As these sources indicate, then, Chinese were generally not seen as presenting problems in Canadian society with respect to their involvement in serious crime.

In specific cases of Chinese charged with property crimes, court reporters often made note of the fact that such cases were something of anomaly among members of this minority group. For instance, in the case of John Mond, a Chinese male charged with stealing handkerchiefs from the T. Eaton Company, a *Hamilton Spectator* (13 June 1928) headline noted, 'One of the Rarest of Cases – A Chinaman Charged with Theft.' In another case from the city of Toronto involving a Chinese burglar who was sentenced to five years in prison for his offence, the crown attorney commented, 'this man has quite a record,' and the sentencing magistrate replied, 'quite unusual for a Chinese' (*Toronto Daily Star*, 22 July 1904). Similarly, in a Windsor case (*Border Cities Star*, 23 April 1921), Magistrate Gundy, in sentencing a Chinese offender charged with theft to an indefinite term of two years, informed him, 'One asset you Chinamen have in this country is that you are honest, and if a Chinaman isn't honest he hasn't very much good in him.' In the case of an Asian male charged with fraud in which there was some dispute regarding his place of birth, Magistrate Judd of London 'said that it was rare to see a Chinaman who has emigrated to Canada [in] court for a criminal offence. He doubted that there was a more honest race, declaring Wing must have adopted the ways of some men in the country where he had been educated [Canada]' (*London Free Press*, 28 October 1931).

While it is certainly possible that Chinese property offenders went undetected because they may have been disproportionately likely to commit their crimes against other Chinese, who chose not to report them to the police, the above evidence indicates that commentators in the popular press and criminal justice system officials did not view property crime as representing a serious problem among the Chinese. However, table 7.1 also indicates that property crimes were relatively more common among Blacks, with such offenders representing 19 per cent of the total sample of property offenders. As the analysis presented below indicates, Blacks were more likely to be convicted in the courts when charged with property offences, and were sentenced to lengthier terms of imprisonment.

Table 7.2 presents the results of a logistic regression of the decision to imprison property offenders. This table shows that female property offenders, those in the 16–24 age group, offenders from the city of Windsor, and those

Table 7.2: Logistic Regression on Imprisonment Decision: Property Offences, 1892–1961

Variable	All Offenders		Black offenders		Comparison	
	Coefficient	Odds ratio	Coefficient	Odds ratio	Diff.	T-ratio
Black	0.73**	2.08				
Chinese	0.38	1.46				
Native	0.11	1.11				
Female	−0.45**	0.64	−0.14	0.87	−0.31	0.82
Single	0.13	1.14	0.17	1.18	−0.04	0.12
Age 16–24	−0.64**	0.53	0.13	1.14	−0.77	2.02*
Age 25–34	0.02	1.02	0.96**	2.62	−0.94	2.47*
Age 45–54	0.15	1.17	−0.11	0.90	0.26	0.58
Age 55+	0.44*	1.56	0.29	1.34	0.15	0.29
No occupation	0.03	1.03	1.74**	5.75	1.71	3.56**
Working class	0.43**	1.53	2.38**	10.85	−1.95	4.88**
Second offence	1.82**	6.18	3.05**	21.11	−1.23	0.87
Previous offence	0.85**	2.34	1.21**	3.35	−0.36	0.82
Offence seriousness	−0.08	0.92	0.22	1.25	−0.30	1.00
Hamilton	−0.08	0.92	−2.18**	0.11	2.10	5.25**
Windsor	−0.72**	0.49	−2.94**	0.05	2.22	5.55**
London	0.04	1.04	−1.14**	0.32	1.10	2.50**
1910–19	0.04	1.04	0.32	0.73	0.36	0.90
1930–9	−0.01	0.99	−0.99**	0.37	0.98	2.65**
1950–61	−1.03**	0.36	−1.53**	0.22	0.50	1.35
2 Log Likelihood	4249.5		540.1			
Chi-square	579.5		180.0			
Goodness of Fit	4492.3		726.9			
N of Cases	4,467		829			

*p < 0.05 **p < 0.01

sentenced in the 1950–61 period were significantly less likely to be imprisoned. Offenders in the 55+ age group, those charged with a second offence, those having a previous criminal record, those in working-class occupations, and Blacks were significantly more likely to be imprisoned for the commission of property offences.

While it is certainly true that there were cases in which non–minority group offenders were convicted of, and imprisoned for property offences on the basis of rather questionable evidence, the qualitative data reveal a particular tendency on the part of sentencing judges to regard the testimony of Black offenders as unreliable, which at least in part explains the greater likelihood of imprisonment for these individuals. In addition, principles of 'methodic suspicion'

(Matza, 1967) operated in the police apprehension of Black property offenders – Blacks who happened to be in the general area in which property crimes were committed were often identified as suspects, and the courts often found them guilty on the basis of such limited evidence. For example, in a case involving possession of stolen property in which the offender claimed the goods belonged to another individual, 'Charles Morgan, colored,' was convicted and sentenced to six months' imprisonment 'when he could not produce a mysterious Mr. Williams' (*Hamilton Spectator*, 6 September 1932). Similarly, in another case in which a cash box containing $100 was stolen from the Division Court Office in Windsor (*Evening Record*, 26 February 1917), a Black male was charged with theft, seemingly only because of the fact that he had been seen in the office by a clerk. 'Miss Lea Deziel, deputy division court clerk, stepped out of the office for a few moments and encountered a Negro standing in the hallway. He asked her to direct him to another office in the building. On her return she missed the cash box. She was able to give the police a good description of the suspect.' Perhaps not surprisingly, the Black male was convicted for the commission of this offence.

In a similar fashion, four teenagers, three of them 'Negroes,' were charged with and convicted of breaking and entering, despite the claims of one of the accused that he was not even in the area in question at the time the crime was committed. As the *London Free Press* (10 July 1941) reported, 'Brown, the only member of the quartet who asked to give evidence, denied he had been at the place and said he was on his way to Windsor "lookin for a boxin bout" when he met the other three. The four were arrested by police as they slept on a lawn in the village.'

The same practice of rather questionable evidence being used to convict Black male property offenders also applied to women, as in the case of Viola Dulouse, 'a pretty mulatto from Toronto' charged with theft of $100 from Charles Gentle. The *Hamilton Spectator* (6 March 1917) noted that the only evidence against this woman was given by the complainant, 'but he was positive that she was the damsel that accosted him near his store on a dark night ... He was sure also that the girl was the one who did the trick of black art – that she substituted the worthless roll [blank paper] for the valuable one, but could not just tell how the wizard worked and he saw no magic wand. Viola denied the charge and had her employer as a character witness, but to no avail.' Similarly, Violet Taylor, 'colored,' was charged with theft of $65 from Henry Newman, 'a white man.' The accused claimed she 'never saw him ... [but] she goes to the Mercer for three months' (*Toronto Daily Star*, 30 January 1911).

Columns 3 and 4 of table 7.2 present the logistic regression of the imprisonment decision for Black offenders only, while columns 5 and 6 compare the results of the regression for all offenders with those for Blacks, revealing several important differences. First, while in the analysis for all offenders, those in the 16–24 age group were significantly less likely to be imprisoned, Black property-offenders in the same age group were more likely to be imprisoned – the difference between the coefficients for this variable between the entire property offender sample and the Black subample is statistically significant. Similarly, although property offenders in the 25–34 age group were slightly more likely to be imprisoned than others in the overall sample, the coefficient for this variable in the Black subsample is significant, as is the difference between the two coefficients. These differences suggest that, while magistrates were willing to use their discretion to acquit some young property offenders or to sentence them to terms of probation, these principles of leniency did not apply to younger Blacks, who were apparently more in need of correction.

Table 7.2 also reveals significant differences between the coefficients in the overall sample and Black subsample for those reporting no occupation, and those in working-class occupations. Blacks from the two lower occupational categories were significantly more likely to be imprisoned for the commission of property offences compared with non-Blacks, suggesting that disproportionally severe treatment was meted out to the most disadvantaged Blacks. On the other hand, Black property offenders from the cities of Hamilton, Windsor, and London were significantly less likely to be imprisoned.

Table 7.1 revealed that the mean sentence length for Black property offenders was 10.51 months, and for Natives 8.33 months, compared with 6.26 months for Whites. Table 7.3 presents the results of the sentence-length regressions for property offenders, and shows that, when only racial variables are entered into the equation in model one (columns 1 and 2), Blacks and Natives were sentenced to longer terms of imprisonment. When other extralegal, legal, and structural variables are controlled for in columns 2 and 3, the coefficient for Natives is no longer statistically significant, but the coefficient for Blacks, although slightly reduced, remains significant.

The severe sentences meted out to Blacks for what we might consider to be relatively minor crimes was evident in several property-offence cases. For instance, William Rawlins, 'a colored porter,' was sentenced to three years in the penitentiary for *attempting* to steal a purse containing $75 from a train passenger (*Fort William Daily Times Journal*, 13 December 1917). At least part of the reason for this harsh sentence was that Rawlins attempted to steal the money from a White woman.

Columns 3 and 4 of table 7.3 also reveal that female offenders, and those whose cases were processed in the 1910–19 and 1950–61 period, were sentenced more leniently.

Table 7.3: Regression on Sentence Length: Property Offences, 1892–1961

Variable	All Offenders				Black Offenders		Comparison	
	Block 1		Block 2					
	B	Beta	B	Beta	B	Beta	Diff.	T-ratio
Black	4.25	0.14**	4.11	0.14**				
Chinese	1.80	0.02	2.44	0.03				
Native	2.06	0.05**	0.82	0.02				
Female			-1.35	-0.04**	-1.72	-0.04	0.37	0.44
Single			0.41	0.02	-0.20	-0.01	0.61	0.87
Age 16–24			1.24	0.05*	3.72	0.11*	-2.48	3.02**
Age 25–34			2.12	0.09**	3.60	0.12**	-1.48	1.90
Age 45–54			0.28	0.01	0.23	0.00	0.05	0.05
Age 55+			-0.35	-0.01	0.60	0.01	-0.95	0.92
No occupation			-0.60	-0.01	-3.25	-0.06	2.65	2.52*
Working class			-0.84	-0.03	-0.90	-0.02	0.06	0.07
Second offence			4.74	0.13**	2.43	0.04	2.31	2.60**
Previous offence			0.96	0.04**	1.84	0.06	-0.88	1.28
Offence seriousness			4.16	0.21**	7.11	0.29**	-2.95	4.83**
Hamilton			-0.13	0.00	-2.26	-0.05	2.16	2.77**
Windsor			0.84	0.02	-0.90	-0.03	1.74	2.20*
London			2.44	0.07**	1.19	0.02	1.25	1.49
1910–19			-2.77	-0.07**	-3.55	-0.08*	0.78	0.92
1930–9			-0.11	0.00	0.41	0.01	-0.51	0.66
1950–61			-2.37	-0.09**	-4.40	-0.10**	2.03	2.60**
r2	0.02		0.12		0.13			
Adjusted r2	0.02		0.12		0.11			
Standard error	11.40		10.82		14.02			
F	31.8		30.5		7.2			
N of cases	4,467				829			

*p < 0.05   **p < 0.01

The three legal variables – being charged with a second offence, having a prior criminal record, and seriousness of the current offence – exert a significantly positive effect on sentence length, as does being sentenced in the city of London.

A comparison of the coefficients between the overall sample and the Black subsample (see columns 5 through 8) demonstrates that, similar to the findings with respect to the imprisonment decision, Black offenders in the two youngest age groups were treated significantly more severely than young offenders overall. It is also notable that, while offence seriousness exerted a significant positive effect in the overall sample, the effect for Blacks is even greater, indicating that Blacks charged with more serious property offences were treated particularly severely by the courts. The disproportional lenience towards Blacks charged in the cities of Hamilton and Windsor that occurred with respect to the imprisonment decision also applies to the sentence-length decision. Finally, it is notable that, while the coefficient for the 1950–61 period was significantly negative in the overall property-offender sample, it is even more strongly negative for Blacks, perhaps indicating that at least some magistrates were becoming cognizant of the existence of racial sentencing disparities, and were beginning to sentence Blacks more leniently.

These analyses of the imprisonment and sentence-length decisions for property offenders provide strong evidence for the disproportionately severe treatment of Blacks and suggest that Black property offenders, particularly those from the two youngest age groups, were significantly more likely to be convicted and, when convicted, were sentenced to longer terms of imprisonment than Whites.

Violent Offences

As was the case with respect to their underrepresentation in the commission of property offences, table 7.4 reveals that Chinese were not commonly charged for the commission of violent offences.[2] Of the entire sample of 1,643 violent offenders, there are only 35 Chinese, slightly more than 2 per cent of the sample. It is also clear that criminal justice system officials were aware of the relative rarity of violent crimes in the Asian community, as is evidenced in the case of James Chong, who was convicted of wounding his roommate, Fong Dong. In this case, the sentencing magistrate commented, 'You tried to lay him out with a hammer and then cut him with a knife. One does not find many men of your race in trouble here' (*Hamilton Spectator*, 9 March 1943).

Notwithstanding the relative rarity of Chinese violent offenders appearing in Ontario courts, a consideration of media and criminal justice officials' descrip-

Table 7.4: Descriptive Data: Violent Offences, 1892–1961 (Means)

Variable	Overall	Blacks	Chinese	Native	White
Black	0.28				
Chinese	0.02				
Native	0.12				
White	0.57				
Imprisonment	0.79	0.80	0.89	0.80	0.79
Sentence length	8.58	10.51	6.89	11.41	7.09
Female	0.09	0.08	0.00	0.08	0.09
Single	0.52	0.48	0.57	0.55	0.53
Age	31.48	31.48	35.09	29.29	31.82
Age 16–24	0.15	0.14	0.11	0.16	0.15
Age 25–34	0.42	0.40	0.29	0.50	0.41
Age 35–44	0.24	0.26	0.34	0.23	0.23
Age 45–54	0.12	0.12	0.17	0.05	0.13
Age 55+	0.08	0.07	0.09	0.06	0.08
No occupation	0.04	0.03	0.09	0.02	0.06
Working class	0.87	0.85	0.77	0.97	0.86
Middle class	0.06	0.03	0.00	0.01	0.08
Upper class	0.00	0.00	0.00	0.00	0.00
Second offence	0.05	0.03	0.00	0.02	0.06
Previous offence	0.35	0.39	0.06	0.54	0.30
Offence seriousness	1.92	2.01	1.83	2.00	1.87
Hamilton	0.22	0.20	0.23	0.27	0.21
Windsor	0.18	0.41	0.11	0.03	0.09
London	0.15	0.11	0.09	0.47	0.11
Ottawa	0.10	0.00	0.03	0.00	0.17
Thunder Bay	0.08	0.01	0.03	0.22	0.09
Toronto	0.28	0.27	0.51	0.01	0.34
1892–1909	0.24	0.30	0.23	0.23	0.21
1910–19	0.12	0.16	0.14	0.10	0.10
1920–29	0.11	0.14	0.09	0.12	0.10
1930–39	0.14	0.14	0.26	0.16	0.13
1940–49	0.17	0.13	0.20	0.16	0.19
1950–61	0.21	0.12	0.09	0.22	0.26
N of cases	1,643	465	35	202	941

tions of other violent crimes involving Asian offenders demonstrates how these also contributed to the stereotypical attitudes towards the Chinese held by members of Canadian society. In 1927, for instance, an individual described by the *Toronto Daily Star* (31 March 1927) as a 'maniac Chinaman' killed an eleven-year-old girl and wounded four men when he went on an 'insane orgy' with a butcher knife. In a description of his crimes, and in portraying Fong Yong as a particularly vicious individual, the *Star* noted that, after seizing the knife from a proprietor of a grocery store, he

proceeded out the door with a slinking little dog trot. He zig-zagged his way up Elizabeth Street muttering 'I get 'em, me kill everybody ... The Chinese went to pass the child and then stopping for just a few seconds, he raised his hand and plunged the knife into her back. As she crumpled on the sidewalk, the enraged Chinese was seen to kick the dying girl in the face.

The *Star* noted that, because of Fong Yong's previous incarceration in the Queen Street Mental Asylum, he was to have been deported, and, in the coverage of the incident, immigration officials and officials from the asylum blamed each other for the fact that Yong's deportation order had not been carried out. J.C. Mitchell, an immigration agent and controller of Chinese immigration for the district, argued, 'if this is the man, it is the asylum which will have to explain how he came to get out. It is not the immigration department.' Mitchell blamed the confusion on 'the common habit of Chinamen changing their names so often.'

Also notable in the media coverage of Fong Yong's case was the attempt by the *Toronto Daily Star* to sensationalize the case and create the image of a violent crime wave in Toronto's Chinese community. Towards the end of the article describing the murder, the *Star* (31 March 1927) notes, 'last night's affray was the second stabbing in Chinese circles within five days. Last Saturday night George Kwong was stabbed to death at 243 Simcoe Street.' Interestingly, however, in a previous article describing the Kwong case (*Toronto Daily Star*, 28 March 1927), it had been suggested that Kwong had committed suicide.

The focus on this alleged wave of violent crime in Toronto's Chinese community in 1927 was also evidenced in the 1927 annual report of the Toronto police, which made reference to the same above-mentioned cases (Toronto, *Annual Report of the Chief Constable*, 1927: 3). 'Tong Yong, a Chinaman, ran about Elizabeth Street armed with a large butcher knife, attacking citizens, overtaking a 12-year old girl ... He stabbed her in the back, killing her almost instantly. In the second case, Go Wing Chow, a Chinaman, is alleged to have stabbed Margaret Mason, and then committed suicide.'

While violent offences committed by Asians and descriptions of such offenders in media sources were relatively rare, table 7.4 demonstrates that 28 per cent of the violent offenders in the sample were Black. In addition, one of the most striking features of the police-court reports of Black offenders was a tendency to portray them as being particularly prone to the commission of the most brutal forms of violence. For instance, in a possession-of-weapons and assault case, the *Hamilton Spectator* (14 November 1910) described the offences committed by James Crawford this way:

Of all the instruments conceived by the human mind for the punishment of the body, that made by the hands of a colored man was one of the most cruel. The material necessary was of the simplest nature – a stocking-leg, a boot lace, two cubic inches of granite with several sharp corners and a piece of wood to make a handle, and lastly, a fiend with the nerve to use it. James Crawford filled the last bill to perfection and in police court this morning got three months in jail for carrying the instrument and will likely get a longer term for using it on the cranium of Phillip Roy. Roy appeared in the witness box with every mark of the Indian rajah.

Similarly, in describing Louis Tolliver, the 'mulatto burglar,' sentenced to seven years imprisonment, the *Toronto Daily Star* (16 March 1898) noted, 'the colored thief, who has several times threatened in the police docks to kill Detective Harrison as soon as he secured freedom, ... was searched and in his pocket was found an iron bar, sharpened at one end and crooked at the other. With that bar Tolliver could have leaned over and killed Harrison, had the latter passed near the pen, as the officers all do during the court's session.' In another case involving an altercation between an allegedly dangerous and violent Black criminal and the police, Chief Constable Draper described Clifford Hynes, 'colored,' who was arrested for attempted break and enter after a violent struggle with the Toronto police. 'Two of the four officers boarded [his] car, and Hynes struck one of the officers in the face with some instrument, causing a nasty wound over the eye. ... [Hynes] was sentenced to 10 years. [He] had a previous bad record' (Toronto, *Annual Report of the Chief Constable*, 1929: 9). The invocation of Blacks' more extensive prior criminal records in order to emphasize their dangerousness was also evidenced in the *London Free Press* (5 January 1940) description of 'William More, alias Albert James, alias John Finnie, alias Thomas More, alias James Finnie ... a 'Negro' [who] had a criminal record so long that police, using a single-spaced typewriter, could not get it all on one sheet of paper.'

The dangerousness and violent nature of Blacks was further emphasized through reference to their large physical size compared with their White victims, as in the case of Arthur Jones, a 'burly colored cook,' who appeared for assaulting William Tasker, 'an old and decrepit man,' who was 'weak and puny looking, while Jones is in the Dempsey class' (*Hamilton Spectator*, 22 February 1922).

Table 7.5 presents the results of a logistic regression of the imprisonment decision for violent offenders. These results suggest that the perception of

Table 7.5: Logistic Regression on Imprisonment Decision: Violent Offences, 1892–1961

Variable	All Offenders		Black Offenders		Comparison	
	Coefficient	Odds ratio	Coefficient	Odds ratio	Diff.	T-ratio
Black	0.35*	1.43				
Chinese	0.63	1.88				
Native	−0.05	0.95				
Female	−0.22	0.81	−0.71	0.49	0.49	0.92
Single	0.73**	2.07	0.77	2.15	−0.04	0.10
Age 16–24	−0.57**	0.56	−0.22	0.80	−0.35	0.67
Age 25–34	−0.01	0.99	−0.21	0.81	0.20	0.44
Age 45–54	−0.03	0.97	−0.75	0.47	0.72	1.38
Age 55+	−0.42	0.66	−0.95	0.39	0.53	0.95
No occupation	−0.03	0.97	0.67	1.95	−0.70	1.03
Working class	0.16	1.17	1.70**	5.47	-1.54	2.91**
Second offence	0.36	1.44	−0.48	0.62	0.84	1.29
Previous offence	0.28*	1.33	0.55	1.74	−0.27	0.63
Offence seriousness	−0.21**	0.81	−0.33	0.72	0.08	0.30
Hamilton	0.00	1.00	−1.32*	0.27	1.32	2.54*
Windsor	−0.91**	0.40	−2.54**	0.08	1.63	3.26**
London	−0.23	0.80	−0.67	0.51	0.44	0.79
1910–19	−0.30	0.74	0.00	1.00	−0.30	0.63
1930–9	0.04	1.05	−0.19	0.83	0.23	0.47
1950–61	−0.73**	0.48	−0.62	0.54	−0.09	0.19
2 Log Likelihood	1,553.9		383.2			
Chi-square	110.7		79.4			
Goodness of Fit	1,597.5		400.8			
N of Cases	1,643		465			

*p < 0.05   **p < 0.01

Blacks as violent promoted in the media may have influenced judicial perceptions of these offenders, as they were significantly more likely to be imprisoned for the commission of violent offences.

The already documented tendency of magistrates to have difficulty attaching credibility to the testimony of Black property offenders also applied to determinations of guilt and decisions on imprisonment with respect to Black violent offenders. For example, Bert Gray, charged with 'pulling a revolver' on another male who had made remarks about his wife, 'swore on a pack of bibles that he didn't have a gun ... But his story drifted high over the magistrate's head' (*Hamilton Spectator*, 20 January 1915). Similarly, Allan Saunders, charged with raping a Black woman, 'maintained his innocence and swore that he had known the woman quite as intimate as her husband for many weeks,' but Magistrate Boyd of Windsor did not believe his story, and sentenced him to two years' imprisonment for rape (*Windsor Evening Record*, 14 October 1908). Joseph Williams, a 'colored' male, was sentenced to fourteen months' imprisonment for 'grabbing a young woman on the street and using bad language.' In passing sentence on Williams, the magistrate informed the accused, 'I have no faith in the alibi you tried to establish' (*Windsor Evening Record*, 23 April 1909).

The devaluation of Blacks' testimony was also revealed in the case of two Black women charged with aggravated assault on 'three sisters recently arrived from Scotland' who asserted that they had committed the crime only after being provoked. In finding these women guilty, the presiding magistrate 'said that he would sooner take the word of the Scotch girls in preference to that of the defendants' (*Hamilton Spectator*, 24 January 1916).

The first two columns of table 7.5 also demonstrate that non-married violent offenders were more likely to be imprisoned, a finding that is related to the fact that many married offenders were involved in domestic assaults in which magistrates often acquitted or invoked suspended sentences or probation. Offenders who had committed a previous offence were significantly more likely to be imprisoned, while offence seriousness exerts a significant negative effect on imprisonment. This counter-intuitive effect for offence seriousness is attributable to the fact that more stringent standards of evidence were imposed in cases involving serious violent offences. While run-of-the-mill assault cases tended to be processed quite quickly, with little concern for the strength of evidence, the same was not true for more serious violent offences such as rape and murder.

Table 7.5 also indicates that violent offenders from the 16–24 age group, those sentenced in the city of Windsor, and those sentenced in the 1950–61 period were less likely to be imprisoned.

Columns 3 and 4 of this table present results for the subsample of Black violent offenders, while columns 5 and 6 compare the differences in coefficients between the overall sample and Blacks. The most important differences here are that Black working-class offenders were more likely to be imprisoned, while Black offenders sentenced in Hamilton and Windsor were less likely to be imprisoned. Similar to the results for property offences, then, it is clear that the most socially disadvantaged Black violent offenders were treated most severely by the courts.

Table 7.4 showed that Black and Native violent offenders received longer sentences than Chinese and Whites – the mean sentence for Native violent offenders was 11.41 months, for Blacks 10.51 months, for Whites 7.09 months, and for Chinese 6.89 months. Table 7.6 presents the results of sentence-length regressions for violent offenders, and the first two columns of this table, which present the results with only the racial variables entered, indicate that Blacks and Natives were sentenced to significantly longer terms of incarceration. However, when other extralegal, legal, and structural variables are entered in the second model, the coefficients for Natives and Blacks, while still positive, are no longer statistically significant. As would be expected in the context of sentencing for violent offences, the legal variable of having committed a prior offence exerts a significant positive effect on sentence length, with offence seriousness exerting the strongest effect. The findings in the second model of the sentence-length equation thus suggest that at least part of the differential severity towards Black and Native offenders revealed in the first model can be explained by the fact that such offenders were more likely than Whites and Asians to be charged with the commission of more serious violent offences. This interpretation is supported through an examination of the mean offence-seriousness scores in table 7.4, which shows that the mean offence seriousness for Blacks was 2.01, and for Natives 2.00, compared with 1.87 for Whites and 1.83 for Chinese.

The sentence-length equations for Black violent offenders presented in columns 5 and 6, and the comparison of the coefficients with those from the overall sample in columns 7 and 8, reveal no substantively important differences between the two samples.

While these results thus suggest that Blacks were not sentenced to significantly longer periods of incarceration for the commission of violent crimes, it is important to realize that inadequacies in the data – particularly the inability to code for the race of the victim – may mask important differences in the treatment of Black violent offenders. The literature reviewed in chapter 2 indicated that disparities in the sentencing of violent offenders may occur, depending on the race of the victim, and a close examination of the qualitative data indicates that Blacks, and to a lesser extent Chinese, were treated particularly harshly when they victimized Whites, and less so when they victimized other Blacks or Asians. In addition to its manifestation in longer sentences for minority-group violent offenders who victimized Whites, magistrates' negative view of interracial crimes also resulted in the disproportional application of corporal punishment[43] to minority-group offenders.

Although the coefficient for Chinese offenders in the sentence-length equations did not reach statistical significance, and cases involving Chinese violent offenders were not commonly heard in the courts during the 1892–1961 period, qualitative data from a few of these cases underlines the importance of considering the race of the victim when examining sentencing decisions.[4] For

Table 7.6: Regression on Sentence Length: Violent Offences, 1892–1961

	All Offenders				Black Offenders		Comparison	
	Block 1		Block 2					
Variable	B	Beta	B	Beta	B	Beta	Diff.	T-ratio
Black	3.42	0.06**	1.29	0.02				
Chinese	-0.20	0.00	0.30	0.00				
Native	4.32	0.06*	2.29	0.03				
Female			-2.43	-0.03	-0.82	-0.01	-1.61	0.96
Single			2.18	0.04	0.56	0.01	1.62	1.31
Age 16–24			-3.57	-0.05	-1.93	-0.03	-1.64	1.04
Age 25–34			-1.38	-0.03	-3.58	-0.07	2.20	1.64
Age 45–54			-1.61	-0.02	0.47	0.01	-2.08	1.32
Age 55+			-2.24	-0.02	-1.78	-0.02	-0.46	0.27
No occupation			6.72	0.06*	-0.39	0.00	7.11	3.32**
Working class			2.30	0.03	2.90	0.04	-0.60	0.38
Second offence			4.46	0.04	7.45	0.05	-2.99	1.58
Previous offence			2.97	0.06*	2.05	0.04	0.92	0.73
Offence seriousness			8.83	0.36**	8.44	0.34**	0.39	0.47
Hamilton			-5.34	-0.09**	-4.38	-0.07	-0.96	0.67
Windsor			3.04	0.05	3.63	0.07	-0.59	0.41
London			1.67	0.02	-0.31	0.00	1.98	1.27
1910–19			-4.29	-0.06*	-4.64	-0.07	0.35	0.24
1930–9			1.88	0.03	-1.60	-0.02	3.48	2.40**
1950–61			-2.14	-0.03	-5.36	-0.07	3.22	2.24**
r2	0.01		0.15		0.14			
Adjusted r2	0.00		0.14		0.11			
Standard error	25.13		23.33		24.78			
F	2.9		14.5		4.3			
N of cases	1,643				465			

*p < 0.05 **p < 0.01

example, Lee Wheel, 'an exponent of the wash tub,' who was charged with assaulting Charley Soo, 'another celestial,' was fined only $10 for the offence. Similarly, Tom Ing, charged with wounding for 'breaking a [Chinese] laundryman's finger with a meat cleaver,' was sentenced to only three months in jail, and was admonished by Crown attorney McCulloch to 'pursue his occupation of chef in the reformatory kitchen' (*Hamilton Spectator*, 29 July 1942). In an attempted murder–suicide case in Toronto, 'Hoy Man stabbed his wife with a meat-knife, inflicting three serious wounds. He then tried to commit suicide by stabbing himself four times with the same knife' (Toronto, *Annual Report of the Chief Constable*, 1932). Although it is important to remain aware of the fact that, in incidents of domestic violence, most offenders, regardless of their race, were treated less severely in this period, it is notable that Hoy Man was sentenced only to one year's imprisonment upon being found guilty of committing the offence.

However, when Chinese offenders victimized Whites, they were treated quite severely.[5] For instance, Peter Lee, 'a 23-year old Chinese who has operated a laundry for some time,' was sentenced to one year in the Ontario reformatory and six lashes on a charge of indecently assaulting a nine-year-old girl, despite the contention of the accused's defence counsel that 'In my memory, I cannot recall in a long time when any one was given lashes on being convicted under the section on which this boy is charged' (*Hamilton Spectator*, 5 March 1937).

A consideration of the race of the victim is also important in explaining the results for Black violent offenders. In Myrdal's (1944: 1344) description of the treatment of Black offenders in United States jurisdictions, he reports on a letter from a 'white lawyer' who wrote: 'I have noted cases between Negro and Negro are handled somewhat differently than cases between Whites and Whites. I mean, a spirit of levity, an expectation of something "comical" appears to exist.' Representative of this tendency to trivialize crimes involving Black offenders and Black victims in Ontario is the following description of a wounding charge involving two Blacks from the city of Windsor (*Evening Record*, 23 February 1912).

William J. Nelson, a colored barber, failed to sharpen his razor to a fineness suitable for the delicate skin of Robert White, another Negro, and after a few words the barber attempted to put White out of the shop. He succeeded, but in doing so he tripped and fell to the ground. White then jumped on him, and pulling a six shooter, threatened to blow his brains out ... White, who is *black as the ace of spades*, claimed that the razor was pulling and made him mad. (emphasis added)

In a case involving the murder of a Black male by 'Simon Dalgon, a one-eyed Negro,' who had shot his victim in the head thirteen times, the accused was acquitted of the crime, apparently due to the fact that 'the two men knew each other' (*Windsor Evening Record*, 30 September 1912). Similarly, in dismissing the case of Fred and Harry Lewis, 'colored,' charged with robbing another Black male, Hamilton Judge Lazier (*Hamilton Spectator*, 1 November 1938) claimed he was 'not going to convict anybody unless I'm sure.' Edward McGowan, a Black male convicted of assault for 'blackening [his victim's] already dark optic' was fined $25, in default of which he would be forced to spend two months in jail (*Hamilton Spectator*, 11 January 1921), considerably less than the average sentence for assault during this period. Leonard Moses, charged with having 'carnal knowledge' of a young Black female, was told by a Hamilton magistrate, 'I will have to do something to impress on you the sanctity of young womanhood,' but was let go on a suspended sentence (*Hamilton Spectator*, 22 February 1949).

In a case which starkly illustrates the differential treatment of Black violent offenders when they victimized other Blacks, and is reflective of the legal system's devaluation of Black life in general, Archibald Coates, 'aged 19, colored,' was charged with committing a 'serious offence' against a fourteen-year-old 'colored girl.' Rather than imprisoning Coates for the commission of this crime, 'there were efforts made to have the offender and the victim marry each other' (*Windsor Evening Record*, 19 April 1910). Given the prevailing social climate and attitudes surrounding interracial mixes during this period, it is difficult to imagine a similar outcome had the offender victimized a White female.

Another case from the city of Windsor in which two Blacks were charged with attempted murder and rape of a Black woman made specific reference to the differential perceptions of Black-on-Black crime. The magistrate hearing the case 'declared that such crimes [rape] were altogether too prevalent throughout the country. He understood the parties in the case were colored, but this made no difference, as they are entitled to the same protection, [and] must suffer the same penalties as other individuals' (*Windsor Evening Record*, 13 October 1908). Interestingly, however, Allan Saunders was sentenced to only two years' imprisonment for this offence (ibid., 14 October 1908). Another rape case involving Arthur Talbot, 'the Negro,' and a White woman heard less than one year later in the same city resulted in a sentence of three years' imprisonment for the accused, despite the jury's strong recommendation of leniency (ibid., 31 March 1909).

Black offenders, particularly those involved in interracial sexual offences, were portrayed by the press as being especially dangerous, and were given disproportionately severe sentences in the courts. Clearly, part of this severe treatment was related to the prevailing mythology surrounding Black sexual prowess and the concerns surrounding miscegenation documented in chapter 4. Although it involves a case from an earlier period, typical of this mythology and negative stereotyping of Blacks is an account of the conviction of Jacob Briggs, a Black male, for the rape of an eight-year-old White girl in Sandwich, Ontario, in 1840. In this case, Briggs's defence counsel relied on the notion of Black males' possession of large sexual organs in arguing for his client's acquittal. 'It would have been impossible for a full-grown man, particularly a Negro, to have entered the body of [the child]' (as quoted in Winks, 1968: 288).

In cases from the 1892–1961 period, Kenneth Scott, a Black male sentenced to three years in the penitentiary for committing an act of gross indecency against a sixteen-year-old (White) boy, was referred to by Windsor Magistrate Brodie as 'a dangerous man and of no use to the community' (*Border Cities Star*, 18 September 1942). Similarly, Fred Johnston ('colored') sentenced to six months in jail for exposing his person and 'making remarks of the foulest nature to a young woman on the Grand Trunk Station,' was described by Magistrate Love as 'one of the most dangerous men in London, a man who, when at large, was a continual menace to citizens' (*London Advertiser*, 27 December 1907).

Interracial sexual crimes were particularly likely to result in more severe sentences for Black offenders.[6] In the case of Joseph Williams, a 'colored man,' charged with assaulting a White woman, a Windsor magistrate, in sentencing the accused to fifteen months in prison, noted, 'your record is a bad one and you are a menace to the women and children of this city' (*Windsor Evening Record*, 23 April 1909).

Even more problematic in the eyes of court reporters and criminal justice system officials were offences involving older Black men and young White girls. Joshua Miller, sixty-five, a 'colored man,' who was 'black as ink and a very large man, weighing at least 185 pounds,' was sentenced to five years in prison for the commission of a 'horrible crime' against a fifteen-year-old girl. This rape resulted in the girl becoming pregnant, and she was 'expected to give birth to a child in the course of a month or two.' In sentencing Miller, Magistrate Vance of Hamilton 'said that the crime [he had been convicted of] was a most despicable one, and that he had *ruined the reputation and life of a child of another race*' (*Hamilton Spectator*, 24 March 1926; emphasis added).

While it did not involve a charge for the commission of a violent crime, the case of James Lawson, 'colored bigamist,' provides further evidence of the negative view Ontario magistrates held towards interracial crimes. Lawson, who was found guilty of 'having gone through a form of marriage with a 13-year old White girl,' was told by Magistrate Grayden of London (*Advertiser*, 16 August 1917), 'the crime you have been convicted of does not alone affect the girl and yourself, but is an offence against society, which strikes at the very foundations of our social system.'

These principles of differential severity in sentencing for interracial violent crimes also applied to more common forms of assault. In the case of Amos Penn, 'colored,' and charged with 'hitting' a White female, Judge Thompson of Hamilton 'imposed lashes and a jail sentence ... for the first time since he has been on the bench' (*Hamilton Spectator*, 15 March 1937). Similarly, although the sentence of one month's incarceration given to Frederick Johnston, 'the burly Negro with the unenviable name as a frightener of women,' was not overly severe, it seems rather disproportional when considered in the context of the nature of his specific offence. The *London Free Press* (22 July 1902) reported that 'the assault merely consisted of an attempt to place his hat over the young woman's head, and the Negro promptly apologized upon being accosted by her escort.' However, conviction and imprisonment were apparently warranted for this offence, due to the fact that Johnston [is] 'an unpleasant man for a lady to meet when in his cups.'

A series of indecent-assault cases heard on the same day in the city of Windsor is perhaps most reflective of the differences in how Black and White sexual offenders were perceived and treated by the courts. Four 'colored' men were sentenced to fifteen years in the penitentiary, with fourteen lashes, for assaulting 'three little White girls, two of them fourteen-years old and the other only twelve years old.' On the same day and in the same court, Frank Huzurak, a White offender, was sentenced to two years in prison, with seven lashes, for assaulting 'two little children under twelve years of age,' apparently because his crime was considered to be 'of a less brutal nature, even though the girls were younger' (*Border Cities Star*, 22 November 1918). In another particularly fascinating case demonstrating the differential treatment of Black and White offenders, 'three white youths and a colored girl were sent down' in a 'shamefully indecent case.' The three boys, reported to be sons of 'respectable parents,' were accused of having 'criminal relations' with a 'little colored girl.' The magistrate attributed blame for this interracial union to the Black girl and in criticizing her moral values, sentenced her to six months' imprisonment while the three boys were given three months each. The magistrate noted that he 'would have sent the girl down for a longer period if it was within his power to do so' (*Windsor Evening Record*, 19 January 1894).

For violent offences, then, when Black offenders victimized Whites, they were treated much more severely by the courts. These interracial crimes were perceived as particularly problematic by court officials, and judges confirmed their disdain for those who crossed racial lines by invoking the full weight of the law, both by imposing corporal punishment on such offenders and by sentencing them to lengthy terms of incarceration. These findings thus provide considerable support for the theoretical arguments presented by Johnson (1941), Hawkins (1987), and Spohn (1994), as they reveal that the reasons for this differential treatment were twofold: (1) that Black offender/White victim crimes represented the greatest threat to the prevailing White structure of authority; and (2) that Black victims and Black life, in general, were devalued in this period of Ontario's history. The differential treatment of Black violent offenders revealed in these analyses provides further evidence of the existence of systemic racism in Ontario's criminal justice system over the period from 1892 to 1961.

8

Summary and Prospects for Change

I can say to you that your race and colour have in no way created prejudice in my mind. You were given a fair trial and I have taken into consideration every representation made on your behalf. (Police Court Magistrate, quoted in *London Advertiser*, 16 August, 1917)

I strongly disagree with those who allege there is systemic discrimination and racism in the court system in Ontario. There will always be anecdotal evidence to this effect, but the hard evidence is exactly to the contrary. My extensive experience is that judges, lawyers, and court personnel treat all people coming into conflict with the law in the same way. (Ontario General Division Judge, quoted in Ontario, *Report of the Commission on Systemic Racism in the Ontario Criminal Justice System*, 1995: 31)

Despite prevailing beliefs that minority groups have generally not been significantly disadvantaged in Canada and that Canada is an egalitarian society, the discussion in the previous chapters illustrates that Asians and Blacks were subjected to considerable discrimination in virtually all spheres of the Canadian social, legal, and criminal justice systems in the period from 1892 to 1961. Racist sentiments were reflected in Canadian immigration laws, and the discourse surrounding these laws, resulted in restrictions on Asian and Black immigration to the country. Negative stereotypes of Asians and Blacks were frequently and prominently displayed in the Canadian popular press, and these stereotypes influenced racial minority groups' access to housing and property, employment, and social services. While the reluctance of Canadian political officials to enact legislation to establish equal rights for Asians and Blacks waned somewhat beginning in the 1940s, informal racist practices were pervasive in several spheres of Canadian social life despite these legal changes, and judicial officials often interpreted legislation to the disadvantage of racial-minority groups.

The experiences of Asians and Blacks in Ontario's criminal justice system was similarly characterized by systemic racism. Canada's initial drug legislation was enacted to control the immigrant Chinese population, and was vigorously enforced against that population in the 1908–30 period. Asian drug offenders were frequently stereotyped in a negative fashion in the popular media, and although Asian drug possessors were not subject to disproportionately harsh treatment at the sentencing stage, Chinese who were believed to be spreading their drug-taking habits to Whites were punished particularly severely. The enforcement of laws against public-order crimes focused disproportionately on Asians and Blacks involved in gambling, prostitution, and other immoral activities, and Blacks were not only more likely to be convicted for the commission of such offences, but, when convicted, were sentenced to longer terms of imprisonment.

The analysis of criminal justice outcomes for property and violent crimes revealed that court officials were reluctant to attach credibility to the testimony of racial-minority-group offenders, which resulted in higher rates of conviction for such offenders. Even more important, it was apparent that differential justice was applied to minority-group offenders on the basis of the race of their victims. While minority-group violent offenders who victimized members of their own group were treated relatively leniently, those who victimized Whites, and thus were more threatening, were treated particularly severely.

In interpreting the reasons for the prevalence and persistence of racism against Asians and Blacks in Canadian society, it is important to stress that no single theory is adequate explanation. While racism was certainly manifested in the individual decisions of influential public officials such as police officers, crown attorneys, and judges, the data suggest that we must question attempts to attribute legal and criminal justice system biases solely to prejudices or racial stereotypes that influence the decisions of such officials. While individual racism was certainly an important component that influenced the disadvantaged position of Asians and Blacks in virtually all aspects of social and economic life and their disproportionately severe treatment in the criminal justice system in the 1892–1961 period, there can be little doubt that institutional and systemic racism as expressed in official policies and legislation, and interpretations of those policies and legislation, was a more important contributor to these disadvantages. At the same time, theories that explain racism solely as the result of reactions of capitalist governments to the perceived economic and political threats posed by minority groups are too simplistic and reductionist. The racism against Asians and Blacks documented in this book was the result of a complex interplay of both individual and social-structural factors.

There is also little doubt that the situation for Asians and Blacks has not improved significantly since the 1960s, despite attempts to deny the existence of racist practices in Canadian social policy and the administration of justice. As chapter 1 documented, the 1990s has witnessed a renewed attention to minority-group overinvolvement in crime, and the popular media have shown an increased tendency to racialize crime and criminal problems in Canadian society.

There is also evidence to suggest that negative attitudes towards racial-minority groups have become further entrenched among Canadians. In eight national surveys conducted between 1994 and 1996, approximately 50 per cent of Canadians agreed that there are already too many immigrants in the country. Furthermore, a 1996 *Maclean's/CBC News* survey found that almost half of the respondents felt that immigrants are responsible for taking jobs away from Canadians, and more than two-thirds thought that immigrants contribute to the country's crime rate (Kaihla, 1996). The vote-conscious federal government has responded by enacting stringent immigration legislation, deporting immigrants who commit crimes and imposing a $975 'head tax' on immigrants.

It is also clear that these negative attitudes towards minority groups have translated into perceptions and personal experiences of discrimination. A 1992 study examining perceived discrimination on the part of minority groups in Toronto (Dion and Kawakami, 1996) noted that 78 per cent of Blacks and 53 per cent of Chinese perceived discrimination against their groups in obtaining work; 46 percent of Blacks and 33 per cent of Chinese respondents perceived discrimination against their groups in wage rates. Furthermore, 41 per cent of Blacks and 22 per cent of Chinese claimed to have experienced personal discrimination in attempting to find work.

These perceptions of discrimination also extend to minority groups' dealings with the criminal justice system. Wortley (1996), reporting on data from a survey conducted for the Commission on Systemic Racism in the Ontario Criminal Justice System, documents widespread perceptions of police and judicial discrimination on the part of minority groups, in particular Blacks, in the city of Toronto. Seventy-six per cent of Blacks in this survey expressed the belief that the police treat Black people differently from Whites, and 60 per cent believed judges do the same. Such perceptions of discrimination on the part of Blacks are apparently based on their experience with the criminal justice system, as 43 per cent of Blacks reported being stopped by the police in the previous two years, while one-third reported being stopped on two or more occasions (see also Foster, 1996).

It is also important to note that perceptions of bias against minority groups in the criminal justice system are not unique to those who are directly experiencing it. Fifty-two per cent of the lawyers with greater than 40 per cent minority clientele interviewed by the Commission on Systemic Racism (Ontario, 1995) felt that Black and other racial-minority people are not treated the same as White people. In fact, the commission report provides several examples of Black lawyers who were misidentified as accused persons or interpreters when appearing in court. In addition, 33 per cent of provincial division judges appointed since 1989 perceive differential treatment of White and racial-minority people in the system (Ontario, 1995).

While sceptics might (and often do) dismiss such findings as mere perceptions that have no validity, the commission provided more objective evidence regarding the possible existence of racism in the criminal justice system. Relying on correctional admissions figures, the commission noted that, from 1986/7 to 1992/3, the number of Blacks admitted to Ontario prisons increased by 204 per cent, while the number of Whites admitted increased by 23 per cent. As Roberts and Doob (1996) point out, these numbers translate to a prison admission rate per 100,000 of 705 for Whites, compared with 3,686 for Blacks. When the data for males are analysed separately, the Black admission rate rises to 6,796 per 100,000 population, compared with 1,326 for Whites. These statistics leave little doubt that there has been increased attention to Black offenders in Ontario's criminal justice system.

Similar to the situation in the United States (Irwin and Austin, 1997; Mosher, 1997; Tonry, 1995), it appears as though one of the most important factors contributing to this increased incarceration of Blacks in Ontario is a disproportionate enforcement focus on Black drug users. As the Commission on Systemic Racism (Ontario, 1995: 69) noted, Black admissions to prisons in the Metropolitan Toronto area for drug trafficking and drug importing increased by 'several thousand per cent' between 1986 and 1993. These increases appear to be the result of 'the intensive policing of low income areas in which Black people live ... One of the effects of the war on drugs, intended or not, has been the increase in the imprisonment of Black people.' Just as drug laws were used in the past to control minority populations in both the United States in Canada, so are they being used now.

The reactions of the popular media and certain criminal justice system officials to the findings of the Ontario commission are notable for their scepticism, and for their tendency to deny the existence of a problem. Although initial media reports summarizing the commission's findings attributed validity and importance to the results and recommendations (Makin, 1996), a subsequent *Globe and Mail* editorial (18 January 1996) asserted that the commission's research was not objective, and implied that the entire effort was a waste of money and time.

Racism is about looking at the world through a distorting lens, the better to see what you want to see, the better to avoid a confrontation with unpleasant surprises. This self-reinforcing and parochial world view is unfortunately often shared by investigations of racism. So it was with Stephen Lewis's 30-day inquiry into the 1992 Yonge Street 'riot,' and so it is with the task force he recommended and its $5-million, two-years in the making Report.

However, in its own misleading and selective interpretation of the report (Doob, 1996; Roberts, 1996), the *Globe* essentially trivialized and dismissed the commission's claims of the existence of systemic racism, arguing that, 'The Commission on Systemic Racism in the Ontario Criminal Justice System appears to have performed the unexpected feat of proving that a convicted black man is no more likely to be sent to prison than a white man. Surprise indeed ... and this report, despite its best efforts, gives us no reason to believe that the overrepresentation of blacks in prison is more than marginally related to racism.' As Doob (1996) noted in his response to the *Globe*'s editorial, 'The cause of improving the operation and fairness of the criminal justice system for all of us is not furthered by selective and deceptive reporting of the Commission's findings.'

While the *Globe*'s response to the commission's report is somewhat disturbing, it is perhaps even more notable that most other mainstream media outlets have chosen to virtually ignore the findings, and that individuals holding influential positions within the Ontario criminal justice system, like some of those in the media, are essentially in a state of denial regarding the existence of racism in the system. One crown attorney interviewed by the commission stated, 'You are creating racism by falsely accusing people of being racist. Racial minorities should receive training in Canadianism. You are creating expectations that people who come to Canada have a right to their own piece of their old country in Canada. This creates and perpetuates racism' (Ontario, 1995: 22). A General Divisional Court judge similarly denied the existence of racism in the system, noting, 'I anticipate that the Commission, driven by the force of political correctness, will find that racism is rampant in the justice system ... A conclusion that will not be based on hard evidence but ... on anecdote and unsubstantiated complaint. Failing all else, the Commission will find invisible racism, visible only to the commissioners' (ibid.: 1995: 222). Such comments can only serve to exacerbate the existing problems, for, as the commission's report aptly noted, one significant impediment to removing the barriers between the criminal justice system and 'racialized communities' is the frequency with which minority perceptions of bias are dismissed as insignificant, wrong, or held by only a small unrepresentative minority of the community.

The commission advanced several seemingly reasonable recommendations to begin to address the problem of systemic racism in Ontario's criminal justice system. Among other recommendations, the commission called for anti-racism training for criminal justice personnel, increased employment of racial-minority groups in the administration of justice, and increased participation of racial-minority groups in the development of justice policies. In addition, the commission recommended a modification of courtroom practices that contribute to the appearance of racial injustice, restraint in the use of prison sentences, action plans to secure equality in law-enforcement practices, the preparation of guidelines for the exercise of police discretion to stop and question people, and an enhancement of the complaints system to promote systemic monitoring of police practices.

But the prospects for implementation of any of these specific proposals, let alone policies to ameliorate the decaying social conditions that some minority-group members experience, seem far less than promising under the Ontario Conservative government of Mike Harris. In fact, it seems more probable that the situation will deteriorate even further. In addition to instituting major cuts to welfare programs in the province, which will undoubtedly have a negative impact on already economically disadvantaged minority groups, the Harris government has repealed the provincial employment equity legislation that required private firms to implement hiring targets for women and minorities. Furthermore, the Harris government has announced major cuts to the province's legal aid plan (Tyler, 1997) and proposed reducing the powers of civilian review boards to monitor the activities of police, thus providing police chiefs with increased power to dismiss complaints (Scrivener, 1997). It thus appears unlikely that any of the commission's recommendations will be implemented in the foreseeable future, and the problem of the overrepresentation of minority groups in the criminal justice system will increase.

While the unwillingness of governments to recognize the existence of systemic racism and their reluctance to implement policies to ameliorate these problems are certainly disturbing, another important and related issue that needs to be addressed is the tendency towards the racialization of crime and 'demonization' (Foster, 1996: 11) of minority groups in the Canadian media. As was documented in chapter 1 of this book, in recent years the media has devoted a great deal of attention to criminal acts committed by members of minority groups, frequently presenting unsubstantiated and often distorted statistics on the extent of the minority-crime problem. Such biased portrayals can lead to more general problems of racism, owing to the fact that the general public derive their images of racial-minority groups and structure their behaviour towards such groups largely on the basis of information they are exposed to in the media (Bennett, 1980).

An initial step towards countering this problem of media distortion, although certainly a controversial one, would be to begin collecting criminal justice system statistics on the basis of race. Currently, the Canadian criminal justice system collects racial data only for the homicide survey and in correctional statistics (Roberts, 1994). While concerns that such statistics may be misused by those in power to assert that racial-minority groups are somehow inherently prone to crime should not be ignored, this is by no means an inevitable outcome of collecting such statistics. It is equally possible that such statistics could be employed to refute these often distorted media and 'official' claims, and to determine if, and at what stage(s), bias is occurring in the system, especially if such studies were used in combination with self-report and victimization studies. As the discussion of sentencing practices in chapters 6 and 7 of this book demonstrated, intelligent use of such statistics can be of assistance in identifying the locus and extent of racial discrimination in the system.

The use of race-based criminal justice statistics to influence progressive criminal justice policy changes is not without precedent, both in the United States and Canada. For example, the revelations of bias in several of the American sentencing studies reviewed in chapter 2 of this book were influential in generating sentencing-guideline statutes in several states. And while these guidelines have by no means eliminated racial, gender, and social-class disparities in sentencing in the United States (Miethe and Moore, 1985; Moore and Miethe, 1986), they do appear to be a step in the right direction (Dixon, 1995).

In a more specific example of the ability of race-based statistics to influence policy, a study from the state of Minnesota provided statistical documentation of racial bias in the arrest and sentencing of crack- and powder-cocaine users. The study demonstrated that 100 per cent of those arrested under a crack-cocaine statute that mandated a forty eight-month sentence of imprisonment for those possessing three grams or more were Black, while those sentenced under the powder-cocaine statute (66 per cent of whom were White) received only a twelve-month sentence for possession of 10 grams of powder-cocaine (Blumstein, 1993). Based on this evidence, the court found that the legislative distinction was racially discriminatory in its impact, and declared the statute unconstitutional. Similarly, as Hurst (1993) points out, there is some Canadian precedent for the positive use of such statistics. 'Since Ottawa, with the full approval of Aboriginals, began keeping separate track of their crime rates seven years ago, natives have finally been given a bigger role in the justice system.'

This is not to deny the existence of certain practical considerations regarding the collection of such statistics. Given the fact that many Canadians are of mixed ancestry and given differences in opinion regarding what constitutes a race, Roberts (1994: 179) asserts that 'a major reason not to collect racial statistics is simply that they cannot be gathered with any reasonable degree of reliability or validity.' However, it seems reasonable to suggest that such difficulties regarding coding can be overcome through consultation with experts in the field. The information such statistics can provide, and the potential for this information to be used to counteract distorted media protrayals of the minority-crime problem and thereby exert a more positive influence on public attitudes towards minority groups, would appear to be worth the effort. As Gabor (1994: 157) points out, 'statistics, if people choose to consult them, can actually reveal a lower level of involvement in crime by minorities than impressions they may otherwise gain through media sensationalism, word-of-mouth, and personal experience.'

Conclusion

Denying the existence of systemic racism is a disservice to both the minority groups directly affected by it and the larger Canadian society. Until Canadians in general, and legislators and criminal justice system officials in particular, acknowledge that this problem exists, there is little likelihood that progressive policies to combat systemic racism will be enacted. As was noted in a recent Ontario Court of Appeal decision,

Racism ... is a part of our community's psyche. A significant segment of our community holds overtly racist views. A much larger segment subconsciously operates on the basis of negative racial stereotypes. Furthermore, our institutions, including the criminal justice system, reflect and perpetuate those negative stereotypes. These elements combine to infect our society as a whole with the evil or racism. (*R* v *Parks* 1993)

As Foster (1996: 52) notes, and has been documented in this book, the perception of Canada as a non-racist country appears to be 'for foreign consumption only.' Racism, while perhaps not as open as in the United States, is certainly as pervasive in Canada.

The discussion and analysis in this book have provided a background for understanding the kinds of distrust, scepticism, anxiety, and hostility that prevail among representatives of racial- and ethnic-minority groups in contemporary Canadian society. In short, the lengthy history of discriminatory treatment of Asians and Blacks documented here has left a legacy which contemporary legal and criminal justice system institutions in Canada must confront in their dealings with members of these groups.

Postscript

In early 1997, two White males, one the grandson of a former New Democratic Party cabinet minister, the other the son of a professor of social work at the University of Regina, were sentenced to six years each for killing a Native woman (Pamela George) in Saskatchewan (Roberts, 1997). Steven Kummerfield, one of the assailants, when asked by a friend what he had done on the night this woman was murdered, replied, 'Not much. We drove around, got drunk and killed this chick.' Although these two males had been charged with first-degree murder, the jury convicted them of manslaughter, and they will be eligible for parole in approximately forty months. Justice Ted Malone of the Saskatchewan Court of Queen's Bench described the killing as 'cowardly and despicable,' but told jurors that it would be 'dangerous' to convict the young men of murder, because the Native woman 'was indeed a prostitute.'

Also in early 1997, York Region police officer Robert Wiche was charged with manslaughter for the killing of a sixteen-year-old Black male in 1996 (Levy, 1997). Interestingly, Wiche experienced no disciplinary consequences for his actions, and was not suspended pending his trial, remaining on active duty as an investigator. While it is perhaps notable that Wiche was charged at all, York Region police chief Bryan Cousineau expressed support for his officer, suggesting, 'We take the position that our officer was acting lawfully and within his authority when he used his firearm.' As Clayton Ruby, lawyer for the mother of the slain black male, argued, 'I would have expected that a responsible chief of police would not in any way attempt to influence the outcome of this case by prejudging ... What confidence can ordinary citizens approach this police force with, knowing that on a matter of this seriousness they prejudge the case without waiting to hear the evidence and without waiting to hear the trial?'

As the contrast of the criminal justice system's handling of the Pamela George and Wiche cases starkly illustrates, there continue to exist two standards of justice in this country. There seems to be little room for optimism that this situation will soon change.

Data-Analysis Methods

1 Dependent Variables

a Decision to Convict/Imprison

Sentencing researchers (Peterson and Hagan, 1984; Wheeler, Weisburd, and Bode, 1982) have suggested that sentencing should be viewed as a two-stage process, involving, first, the decision whether to imprison an offender, and, second, if imprisonment is selected, a decision about the length of sentence. There is strong evidence to suggest that decisions about the type and duration of punishment are conceptually and empirically distinct phenomena (Myers and Talarico, 1987; Spohn, Gruhl, and Welch, 1981–2; Wheeler, Weisburd and Bode, 1982) and thus should be modelled separately. Thus the analyses that appear in chapters 6 and 7 code the decision to imprison an offender as one, and non-custodial outcomes as zero. It is important to note that this general category of non-custodial outcomes represents a number of separate dispositions, including the dismissal of charges, the withdrawal of charges, acquittals, suspended sentences, and terms of probation. It is also important to note that, in several of the cases analysed, particularly those involving relatively minor offences, individuals were sentenced to fines, with the option of imprisonment if they were unable to pay the fine. Although it is impossible to determine consistently from the records whether individuals so sentenced were able to pay their fines and thereby avoid incarceration, it is apparent from the limited data available that only a small proportion of offenders successfully paid their fines. Thus, for the purposes of analysis, only cases where the disposition was a fine without the option of imprisonment were treated as non-custodial decisions.

The first stage of the analyses in chapters 6 and 7 thus deal with the binary decision of whether individual offenders were sentenced to imprisonment, a decision which should not be statistically modelled using ordinary least-squares regression. While estimates derived from regression analysis are robust against violations of certain statistical assumptions, other assumptions are crucial, and their violation will lead to quite unreasonable coefficient estimates (Hanushek and Jackson, 1977). One particular example of such a problem is the case where the dependent variable is a qualitative measure rather than a continuous, interval measure. Having such binary observations creates two problems – one related to the nature of the error term implicit in each observation, and the other related to the functional form of the model. Because the observed values of the dependent variable are dichotomous, there are only two possible values for error terms for any value of the independent variable. Thus, ordinary least-squares estimates of the linear probability model provide inaccurate measurements of the true probability function in these circumstances. In such a case, regression estimates may underestimate the magnitude of the effects of independent variables, making it necessary to employ alternative models in the analysis of binary data.

Given the potential statistical problems associated with using ordinary least-squares regression to analyse binary data, in the analyses presented I estimate logit parameters by the method of maximum-likelihood estimation (Aldrich and Nelson, 1984; Amemiya, 1981; Chambers and Cox, 1967; Hanushek and Jackson, 1977). The conceptual difference between ordinary least-squares regression and maximum-likelihood estimation is that the former is concerned with identifying parameter estimates that yield the smallest sum of squared errors in the fit between the model and the data, while maximum-likelihood estimation is concerned with deriving parameter estimates that imply the highest probability of having obtained the observed sample Y (Aldrich and Nelson, 1984).

In the analyses of the imprisonment decision that appear in chapters 6 and 7, I present maximum-likelihood logistic regression coefficients and odds ratios for the independent variables. Odds ratios have intuitive appeal in understanding the effects of independent variables on the imprisonment decision, as an odds ratio of 1.0 indicates that the odds of receiving or not receiving a prison sentence are roughly equal. An odds ratio of greater than 1.0 indicates that the odds of receiving a sentence of imprisonment are increased, while an odds ratio of less than 1.0 suggests that the odds are decreased (see Boritch, 1992).

b Sentence Length

The second decision modelled is the length of sentence imposed by judges on offenders. As mentioned above, in several criminal cases identified in the sample, offenders were sentenced to a fine only, and a certain amount of prison time in default of the fine. In several other cases, however, offenders were sentenced to time in prison plus a fine, and a certain amount of prison time in default of the fine. A separate analysis of a sample of such cases that were traced to provincial jail records indicates that a high percentage of offenders were unable to pay these fines and were thus forced to serve the additional prison time. Thus, the dependent variable 'sentence length' adds the number of months of sentence in default of the fine to the number of months of imprisonment sentenced.

It is also important to note that, from the mid-1920s to the mid-1940s, several magistrates had a tendency to give offenders indeterminate sentences of, for instance, six months to two years less a day. In such cases, the longer sentence · was treated as the dependent variable, as data on the actual amount of time served by individual offenders was not attainable for the majority of cases. Furthermore, the concern in the analyses is with the potential severity of the sentence imposed by magistrates, rather than the actual amount of time served by offenders.

2 Independent Variables

One of the most serious problems in conducting analyses of criminal justice outcomes is related to the manner in which different variables included in the analyses are measured. If the variables included in outcome models are inaccurately measured, the results of the analysis will be distorted, and hence interpretations of the effects of individual variables will be suspect. The nature of this distortion will vary, depending on whether the error in measurement is random or is positively or negatively correlated with the observed value of the dependent variable being analysed (Klepper, Nagin, and Tierney, 1983).

Several studies have attempted to unravel the effects of what are known as 'legal' and 'extralegal' variables on sentencing outcomes. The distinction frequently made in studies of sentencing has been that variables such as offence seriousness and prior record are legal, or 'legitimized' (Hagan and Bumiller, 1983) variables that should legitimately influence an offender's sentence, while variables such as race, sex, age, and socio-economic status are extralegal, or 'non-legitimized' factors that should not be taken into account by sentencing judges. As the literature review in chapter 2 noted, several studies that have uncovered racial effects on sentencing have not included adequate controls for the impact of legal variables.

As Hagan and Bumiller (1983) point out, however, there are conceptual difficulties in distinguishing between these two types of variables. On the one hand, what are referred to as legal variables may vary across time and social space; for instance, statutory rankings of offence seriousness are often diverse in different jurisdictions and time periods. Furthermore, what is considered a legal variable at one stage of the decision-making process in the criminal justice system may not be so considered at another stage. For example, while ties to the community may be considered relevant for bail decisions, they may not be legitimately relevant with respect to the determination of sentence length. And what may be considered a legitimate variable at the sentencing stage, for instance, offence seriousness, may be the product of discrimination at earlier stages of the criminal justice system. In a similar fashion, the use of prior record as a legal variable may actually compound the discretion exercised in previous adjudications.

In addition to the conceptual difficulties associated with extralegal and legal variables, there are also specific measurement problems to consider. Some variables, such as sex and race, are likely to be measured quite accurately. However, other variables, such as the seriousness of the offence and the prior record of the offender are less likely to be accurately measured. This is primarily attributable to the fact that sentencing studies are often reliant on available data, which are typically in the form of documents that omit, or at best provide incomplete accounts of, important information. These measurement issues must be kept in mind in the discussion of the independent variables below.

Although the impact of race on criminal justice outcomes is the primary focus of the analyses in chapters 6 and 7, a number of other independent variables are included in the analyses in order to control for their effects. Following the conventional classifications in the literature, I categorize the independent variables into extralegal and legal factors.

a Extralegal Variables

Hagan and Bumiller (1983) point out that there are several conceptual difficulties in delineating legal from extralegal variables. Most relevant to the analyses conducted in this book is their suggestion that 'conceptions of what constitutes justice change' (Hagan and Bumiller, 1983: 6) – in other words, extralegal and legal factors are historically specific.

i Race

The jail records from all six jurisdictions included information on the race of the offender. Two racial groups are of primary concern for the outcome analyses: Chinese and Blacks. Although not a primary focus of the discussions, I also include a variable identifying Native offenders. For Chinese offenders, information on race was derived from two separate entries in the jail records – the first listing 'Country of Birth,' and the second listing 'Colour.' Chinese offenders were referred to in the 'Colour' column of these records as 'Yellow.'

In a similar fashion, variables indicating 'Black' (identified in in the records as 'Coloured' or 'Black') and 'Native' (referred to as 'Red') were constituted from information in the 'Colour' column. In the analyses dummy variables for each of these racial minority groups will be included.

ii Gender and Marital Status

The literature on criminal justice outcomes points to the importance of considering gender when modelling sentencing decisions (Daly, 1987a, 1987b; Green, 1961; Kratcoski, 1974; Kruttschnitt, 1984; Nagel, 1969; Nagel, Cardascia, and Ross, 1982; Nagel and Hagan, 1983; Singer, 1973; Temin, 1973; Terry, 1967). Given the general findings from the sentencing literature, it is predicted that female offenders will generally be treated less severely than males; however, this may not be the case across all offence types and in all jurisdictions. Thus, a dummy variable for females is included in the analyses in order to examine the specific effects of gender, and also to address possible interactions between gender, offence type, and, most important, racial variables.

Some sentencing studies have also indicated that individuals who are less attached to traditional personal relationships, as measured by their marital status, are treated more severely by the courts (Daly, 1987a, 1987b; Kruttschnitt, 1982; Kruttschnitt and Green, 1984; Kruttschnitt and McCarthy, 1985; Nagel, Cardascia, and Ross, 1982). Thus, a dummy variable for 'single' is included in the analyses, both to address the independent effects of marital status and to examine its possible interaction with other variables.

iii Age

Most analyses of sentencing treat age as a continuous variable, asserting that it has a linear effect on length of sentence. These studies generally indicate that the chances of going to prison increase with age (Boland and Wilson, 1978; Petersilia, Greenwood, and Lavin, 1977; Peterson and Braiker, 1980), and that older defendants, all things being equal, are sentenced to longer prison terms. Although the recording of the age variable in the jail records would have allowed for the coding of this variable as continuous, it is categorized into five groups (16–24, 25–34, 35–44, 45–54, 55 and over), with four of these entered into the regression equations and the 35–44 age group serving as the reference category. This strategy is followed because age may not be related to court outcomes in a linear fashion. It is also possible that, owing to changes in sentencing philosophies over time, in some periods and for some offences, younger offenders would be treated more leniently and, in other times and for other offences, more severely.

iv Occupation

Some research on criminal justice outcomes has indicated that racial disparities in sentencing, rather than reflecting criminal justice system bias against members of minority groups, is instead attributable to a more general bias against individuals from lower social-class groups. In order to separate the effects of race and social class, then, I include dummy variables for occupational categories in the equations.

Similar to the treatment of age, much of the sentencing literature that has utilized occupation as an indicator of socio-economic status has assumed that its effects on sentencing outcomes will be linear. Typically, the argument is that offenders from the lower social classes receive harsher treatment from criminal justice system officials at the sentencing stage. However, given the historical context of this study, linearity in the effects of occupation is not assumed. The analyses thus include dummy variables for occupation, categorizing offenders into 'no occupation,' and 'working-class,' 'middle-class,' and 'upper-class,' occupations (for a detailed description of the coding of these variables, see Appendix B. Owing to the fact that there was an insufficient number of individuals in upper-class occupations across all offence groups, dummy variables for only the categories of 'no occupation' and 'working-class occupations' are included in the analyses, with middle-class occupations, serving as the reference category.

b Legal Variables

i Presence of Second Offence

A dummy variable identifying offenders who were currently charged with more than one offence is included in the analyses, with the prediction that offenders charged with more than one offence would be treated particularly harshly by sentencing magistrates.

ii Previous Offence

Several studies have pointed out that the impact of prior record on sentencing decisions can differ according to how this variable is measured (Farrell and Swigert, 1978; Welch, Gruhl, and Spohn, 1984). The analyses will include a variable that takes into account the prior record of the accused, which will be coded as a dummy variable, separating offenders who had previously committed an offence from those who had not.

iii Seriousness of Offence

Hagan and Bumiller (1983) note that a variety of approaches have been employed in measuring the seriousness of offence and that the manner in which this variable is operationalized will have an impact on the results obtained. One approach to measuring seriousness involves the Sellin and Wolfgang (1964) seriousness scale, which rates offences based on several aspects of the crime and its victim. Another approach asks judges to indicate how serious they perceive a particular offence to be (Hogarth, 1971). Other researchers have utilized survey responses from the general public regarding the type and length of sentence they would apply for particular offences as a measure of seriousness (Blumstein and Cohen, 1980). Given the historical context of the data examined in these analyses and changes in the statutory maximum penalties for various offences over time, I utilize the maximum sentence allowed by law for a particular offences as the measure of seriousness (Hagan, Nagel, and Albonetti, 1980), relying on successive Canadian criminal codes to categorize the various offences on a 5-point scale (see Appendix B).

c Structural Variables

i City

The literature reviewed in chapter 2 documented the effects of spatial variables on court outcomes. Although the jurisdictions to be examined in the analyses cannot be dichotomized into rural and urban, it is clear that there were substantial differences in the size of the six cities, in the amount of criminal activity each experienced, and in the racial composition of each. Thus, in recognition that spatial context may be important in determining sentence outcomes, dummy variables for the cities of Hamilton, London, and Windsor were created and entered into the equations, treating Toronto as the reference category. Dummy variables for the cities of Ottawa and Thunder Bay were not included. In the case of Ottawa, this decision is based on inconsistencies in the coding of the race variable. In the case of Thunder Bay, the dummy variable is excluded because of the limited number of cases across offence categories.

ii Decade of Sentence

Owing to the fact that the analyses cover a seventy-year period, it is necessary to control for possible changes in sentence severity or leniency over time. Thus, dummy variables for the 1910–19, 1930–9, and 1950–1961 periods are entered into the equations.

3 Analysis Strategies

Table A.1 presents descriptive data for the entire sample of more than 23,000 criminal offences. This table indicates that approximately 12 per cent of offenders in the overall sample are Black, 6 per cent are Chinese, and 68 per cent are White. The table also demonstrates that there were differences in the treatment of offenders according to their racial characteristics. At the aggregate level, Blacks were more likely to be imprisoned for the commission of criminal offences than Whites or Chinese, with 88 per cent of Blacks, compared with 85 per cent of Chinese and 84 per cent of Whites, being subject to imprisonment. The disproportionally severe treatment of Blacks is also revealed in the mean-sentence-length figures. The mean sentence length for Blacks was 6.40 months, for Whites 4.32 months, and for Chinese 3.01 months.

Table A.1 also indicates that approximately 22 per cent of the sample consists of drug offences, 51 per cent were public-order crimes, 19 per cent were property crimes, and 7 per cent were violent crimes (for details on the coding of offences into these four categories, see Appendix B). In recognition of the fact that diverse principles and philosophies may have been applied in determining criminal justice outcomes for these different categories of offences, the quantitative analyses deal with these four categories of crime separately.

In chapter 6, I first present a logistic-regression analysis of the decision to imprison all drug offenders, followed by separate analyses for Chinese offenders, and statistical comparisons of the results from the overall sample with the Chinese subsample. These comparisons are conducted in order to ascertain whether certain independent variables assumed differential importance in the sentencing of minority-group offenders compared with others. I then conduct analyses of sentence length for all drug offenders and Chinese drug offenders separately, once again comparing the results of the two analyses. In the second section of chapter 6, I present analyses of the imprisonment decision for public-order offenders, followed by analyses of sentence length, for the overall sample, and then separately for Blacks. A similar strategy is followed in chapter 7, where separate analyses are conducted for property and violent offences.

For the sentence-length regressions, the race variables are entered by themselves in the first model, and are followed by the inclusion of the other extralegal, legal, and structural variables. By conducting the analyses in this manner, it is possible to examine the relative contributions of racial variables

Table A.1: Descriptive Data: All Offences (Means)

Variable	Overall	Blacks	Chinese	Native	White
Black	0.12				
Chinese	0.06				
Native	0.08				
White	0.68				
Drug	0.22	0.03	0.79	0.00	0.17
Public order	0.51	0.49	0.14	0.71	0.57
Property	0.19	0.30	0.05	0.18	0.21
Violent	0.07	0.17	0.02	0.11	0.06
Imprisonment	0.85	0.88	0.85	0.91	0.84
Sentence length	4.85	6.40	3.01	3.70	4.32
Female	0.20	0.19	0.01	0.22	0.19
Single	0.54	0.53	0.30	0.58	0.60
Age	34.74	32.32	37.70	33.07	35.44
Age 16–24	0.12	0.17	0.05	0.14	0.12
Age 25–34	0.33	0.36	0.31	0.38	0.30
Age 35–44	0.26	0.24	0.33	0.24	0.26
Age 45–54	0.17	0.13	0.19	0.13	0.18
Age 55+	0.13	0.10	0.11	0.11	0.14
No occupation	0.08	0.07	0.02	0.05	0.09
Working class	0.75	0.81	0.61	0.94	0.78
Middle class	0.08	0.03	0.01	0.01	0.11
Upper class	0.01	0.00	0.02	0.00	0.01
Second offence	0.06	0.03	0.02	0.03	0.06
Previous offence	0.39	0.38	0.04	0.58	0.43
Offence seriousness	0.91	1.09	0.93	0.83	0.88
Hamilton	0.16	0.17	0.06	0.34	0.16
Windsor	0.09	0.26	0.07	0.03	0.07
London	0.12	0.13	0.05	0.40	0.11
Ottawa	0.09	0.00	0.01	0.00	0.13
Thunder Bay	0.10	0.03	0.03	0.23	0.10
Toronto	0.46	0.41	0.79	0.00	0.45
1892–1909	0.11	0.23	0.04	0.12	0.10
1910–19	0.12	0.17	0.35	0.10	0.10
1920–9	0.16	0.19	0.44	0.11	0.14
1930–9	0.14	0.16	0.11	0.15	0.15
1940–9	0.20	0.14	0.04	0.20	0.23
1950–61	0.28	0.12	0.01	0.32	0.28
N of cases	23,005	2,806	1,402	1,855	15,755

separately, and to discuss how, for instance, the effects of racial variables are mediated by legal variables such as prior record and seriousness of offence.

Coding Classifications

Occupation

Middle-Class Occupations

Auctioneer	Disc Jockey	Photographer
Actor	Draughtsman	Police Officer
Agent	Engineer	Professional
Air Force	Entertainer	Real Estate
Artist	Florist	Reception
Attendant	Fruit Seller	Reporter
Bailiff	Funeral Operator	Restaurant Owner
Bookkeeper	Furrier	Sales Clerk
Buyer	Gentleman	Salesman
Cartoonist	Government	Secretary
Cashier	Grocer	Shipper
Chemist	Hockey Player	Stenographer
Clerk	Hostess	Stockbroker
Collector	Hotel Keeper	Storekeeper
Commercial	Inspector	Supervisor
Concessioner	Interpreter	Surveyor
Conductor	Jeweller	Tailor
Contractor	Journalist	Teacher
Copywriter	Mailman	Technician
Dealer	Manager	Telegrapher
Decorator	Model	Tourist Business
Dental Mechanic	Musician	Typist
Depositor	Nurse	Undertaker
Designer	Operator	Writer
Detective	Orderly	X-Ray Technician

Unemployed

Beggar	No Occupation	Student
Dope Fiend	Prostitute	Traveller
Housewife	Retired	

Upper-Class Occupations

Architect	Druggist	Minister
Banker	Economist	Optician
Barrister	Lawyer	Physician
Businessman	Manufacturer	Psychologist
Dentist	Merchant	Veterinarian

Working-Class Occupations

Acid Maker	Carter	Factory Worker
Ammunition	Charwoman	Farmer
Assembler	Chauffeur	Farm Help
Baker	Checker	Finisher
Barber	Chipper	Fire Builder
Bartender	Chocolate Maker	Fireman
Basket Maker	Cigar Maker	Fisherman
Bell Boy	Cleaner	Fitter
Blacksmith	Cloth Cutter	Foreman
Block Maker	Coalman	Furnace Man
Body Builder	Compositor	Gardener
Boilermaker	Construction	Gilder
Bookbar	Cook	Glass Blower
Bookbinder	Cooper	Grain Trimmer
Boxer	Coremaker	Grill Worker
Box Maker	Corn Doctor	Groom
Bricklayer	Cosmetics	Hairdresser
Broom Maker	Cowboy	Harness Maker
Buffer	Crane Operator	Hatter
Bulldozer	Dairy Man	Horseman
Bushman	Die Caster	Housekeeper
Butcher	Dishwasher	Huckster
Butter Maker	Domestic	Hunter
Cap Maker	Driller	Insulator
Caretaker	Egg Grader	Iron Worker
Carpet Layer	Electrician	Labourer
Carpenter	Engraver	Landscaper

Lather	Presser	Stonecutter
Laundry	Press Hand	Stovemount
Leather Worker	Printer	Switchman
Lithographer	Projectionist	Taxi Driver
Liveryman	Prospector	Teamster
Lunch Counter	Radio Op	Textile Worker
Machinist	Railroad Worker	Tinsmith
Map Maker	Rigger	Tire Builder
Marble Cutter	Rivetter	Tobacconist
Mason	Roller	Toolmaker
Masseuse	Roofer	Tractor Operator
Mattress Maker	Rubberworker	Trainer
Mechanic	Sailor	Trapper
Messenger	Sail Maker	Trimmer
Milkman	Sawyer	Truck Driver
Millwright	Seaman	Television Repair
Miner	Seamstress	Typesetter
Moulder	Seed Burner	Upholsterer
Newsboy	Servant	Usher
Oiler	Service Station	Vulcanizer
Packer	Ship Builder	Wagon Maker
Painter	Shoemaker	Waiter
Paperhanger	Shoe Shine	Washwoman
Paper Maker	Silk Dresser	Watchman
Peddlar	Soldier	Watch Maker
Piano Maker	Sorter	Welder
Pipefitter	Spinner	Weighman
Plasterer	Spotter	Winder
Plater	Spring Maker	Windowcleaner
Plumber	Steamfitter	Wireman
Polisher	Steelwork	Weaver
Porter	Steeplejack	
Poultry	Stoker	

Offence Categories

Domestic Offences

Abandon Child	Attempt Abortion
Abduction	Bigamy
Assault Wife	Breach Child Welfare Act

Breach Deserted Wives Act
Breach Unmarried Parents Act
Conceal Childbirth
Corrupt Children

Desertion
Incest
Neglect Children
Non-Support

Drug Offences
Administer Drugs
Carrying Drugs
Dope Fiend
Found in Opium Den
Have Opium Pipe

Possess Drugs
Sell Drugs
Smoke Opium
Trafficking

Miscellaneous Offences
Aid Escape
Assist Escape
Blackmailing
Breach Air Force Act
Breach Bankruptcy Act
Breach Defence of Canada Act
Breach Dental Act
Breach Female Refuge Act
Breach Game and Fish Act
Breach Health Act
Breach Master/Servant Act
Breach Medical Act
Breach National Regulations
Breach Official Secrets Act
Breach Post Office Act
Breach Power Act
Breach Radio Act
Breach Rubber Control Act
Contempt Court (debt)

Criminal Negligence
Debt to Pay
Default Debt
Distress Warrant
Enemy
Escape Custody
Fail to Appear
Habitual Criminal
Illegally Practise Medicine
Neglect to Obey Order
Prisoner of War
Refuse to Pay Board
Refuse to Pay Wages
Show Cause
Suspicion
Unspecified
Witness

Property Offences (Figures in square brackets indicate offence-seriousness score)

Accessory	[1.0]	Breach Maintenance Act	[1.0]
Arson	[3.0]	Breach Metal Sales Act	[1.0]
Breach Excise Act	[1.0]	Breach Securities Act	[1.0]
Breach Income Tax Act	[1.0]	Breach Unemployment Insurance Act	[1.0]
Breach Inland Control	[1.0]	Breach and Enter	[2.5]
Breach Inland Revenue	[1.0]	Burglary	[2.5]

Conspiracy	[2.0]	Joyriding	[1.5]
Conversion	[1.0]	Larceny	[1.0]
Counterfeit Money	[1.5]	Possess Stolen Property	[1.0]
Embezzlement	[2.0]	Possess Forgery Instrument	[1.0]
Extortion	[2.0]	Receive Stolen Property	[1.0]
False Pretenses	[1.5]	Retain Stolen Property	[1.0]
Falsification	[1.5]	Robbery	[2.5]
Forgery	[1.5]	Shopbreaking	[2.5]
Fraud	[1.5]	Theft	[1.0]
Fraudulent Debt	[1.0]	Theft Aubomobile	[1.5]
Have Explosives	[2.0]	Utter Forged Document	[1.5]
Housebreaking	[2.5]	Wilful Damage	[1.0]
Housebreaking Instrument	[1.5]		

Public-Order Offences

Abusive Language	[.6]	Desert Army	[.5]
Alcohol Habitué	[.7]	Disorderly Conduct	[.7]
Begging	[.7]	Disturb Peace	[.5]
Breach By-law	[.1]	Drunk	[.4]
Breach Drug Act	[1.0]	Drunk and Disorderly	[.5]
Breach Highway Traffic Act	[.3]	Drunk Driving	[.7]
Breach Hotels Act	[.1]	False Fire Alarm	[.7]
Breach Immigration Act	[.1]	Frequent Disorderly House	[.7]
Breach Indian Act	[.3]	Fighting	[.8]
Breach Lord's Day Act	[.4]	Gambling	[.7]
Breach Lotteries Act	[.4]	Grave Misconduct	[1.0]
Breach Military Act	[.5]	Have Drugs	[1.0]
Breach Probation	[.5]	Have Liquor	[.4]
Breach Railway Act	[.7]	Have Opium Pipe	[.7]
Breach Recognizance	[.5]	AWOL	[.5]
Breach Temperance/Liquor Act	[.5]	Idle, Disorderly	[.7]
Breach Traffic Act	[.3]	Illegally Wear Uniform	[.5]
Breach Venereal Disease	[.8]	Immorality	[.8]
Breach War Services Act	[.5]	Impersonating	[.8]
Bribery	[.8]	Incorrigible	[.8]
Carry Firearms	[1.0]	Indecent Act	[1.0]
Cause Disturbance	[.7]	Indecent Exposure	[1.0]
Contr. Juv. Delinquency	[1.0]	Indecent Language	[.7]
Cruelty to Animals	[.2]	Indecent Pictures	[1.0]
Dangerous Driving	[.5]	Insane	[.7]

Keep Cockpit	[.9]	Refuse to Work	[.7]
Keep Bawdy-House	[1.0]	Resist Police	[.6]
Keep Disorderly House	[.9]	Sedition	[1.0]
Kill & Slay (animal)	[.2]	Sell Drugs	[1.5]
Live Avails Prostitution	[1.0]	Sell Liquor	[.6]
Loitering	[.7]	Sell Liquor to Indian	[.5]
Mail Drugs	[1.0]	Treason	[5.0]
Mischief	[.7]	Trespass	[.5]
Obscene Pictures	[1.0]	Truancy	[.6]
Obstruct Police	[.6]	Unlawful Association	[1.0]
Procuring	[1.0]	Vagrancy	[.7]
Prostitution	[1.0]	Window Peeping	[.7]

Violent Offences

Aggravated Assault	[3.0]	Intimidation	[1.0]
Armed Robbery	[4.0]	Manslaughter	[3.0]
Assault	[1.0]	Motor Manslaughter	[1.5]
Assault Bodily Harm	[2.0]	Murder	[5.0]
Assault Police	[1.5]	Permit Sex Girl < 18	[3.5]
Attempt Disfigure	[2.0]	Obstruction on Rail Track	[2.0]
Attempt Murder	[3.0]	Rape	[4.0]
Attempt Rape	[3.0]	Seduction	[2.0]
Attempt Suicide	[2.0]	Sex Offence	[2.0]
Buggery	[3.0]	Shoot With Intent	[2.5]
Carnal Knowledge	[3.0]	Threaten Violence	[1.0]
Discharge Firearm	[1.5]	Unlawful Sex Intercourse	[4.0]
Grievous Bodily Harm	[3.0]	Wounding	[2.0]
Gross Indecency	[2.5]		
Indecent Assault	[2.0]		

Notes

1: Introduction

1 As later chapters of this book demonstrate, the racialization of crime has been prevalent in Canadian print media throughout the 1900s.

2 Later in 1994, the Reform Party obtained RCMP figures showing that one out of six refugee claimants had been charged with or convicted of a crime subsequent to their arrival in Canada (Greenspon and Sallot, 1994). Although Immigration department officials and refugee advocates disputed the statistics, the Reform Party asserted that the criminal behaviour of refugees necessitated restrictions on immigration.

3 Henry (1994) also notes that Trinidadians share the view that Jamaicans are troublesome.

4 Henry, Hastings, and Freer (1996: 472) provide evidence that such media portrayals may influence the general public's perceptions of minority crime, noting that 'the racialization of crime, and even more specifically, the criminalization of Jamaicans, is a pervasive belief which goes far beyond the borders of Metropolitan Toronto.'

5 More recently, there have been allegations in the media that Native youth are also forming criminal gangs in Western Canadian cities. In an article appearing in *Maclean's* magazine, titled 'Young and Dangerous' and subtitled 'Native Gangs Terrorize Winnipeg,' Eisler (1997) notes 'assaults, armed robbery, drive-by shootings, prostitution and murder are all part of the gang-related violence that is making parts of north-central Winnipeg seem more like the streets of Los Angeles.'

6 Anti-Asian sentiment has been particularly prominent on Canada's west coast and, in addition to the Asian-crime issue, has focused on Asians' demand for English-as-a-second-language programs and the building of 'monster homes.' For example, in 1994, the leader of the provincial Reform Party in British Columbia claimed that 'We have a problem right now with immigration. For example, in the Richmond area there is a very heavy influx of Asians. It's a drain on our resources. A lot of the peo-

ple can't speak English. In British Columbia we should be looking for the kind of immigrants we want to have in this province' (Hunter, 1994). Similar xenophobic attitudes were expressed by Doug Collins, a Vancouver journalist, who asserted that 'Vancouver is becoming a suburb of Asia; Toronto, once the queen city of English Canada, has become the tower of babel, with every race except ours bawling for special rights and receiving them. Montreal is a target for the enlightened folk of Haiti. And the politicians wouldn't care if voodooism became the leading religion' (Collins, 1991; as cited in Henry et al., 1995: 242–3). As Henry et al. (1995) note, ironically, Collins was presented with an award that honours Canadians who have made a significant contribution to their fellow citizens, community, or country.

7 Further evidence of Ringma's racist attitudes was provided in 1995, when he claimed that he could see nothing wrong with a shop owner firing a Black employee, if customers objected to the presence of the employee (Foster, 1996).

8 Although Foster (1996: 215) notes that Constable Carl Sokolowski was convicted of shooting Jonathan Howell in 1991, the presiding judge in the case noted that the humiliation Sokolowski experienced from being tried for the crime was sufficient punishment and granted him an absolute discharge.

9 Although it is important to treat these statistics with some caution because of possible problems in the coding of racial variables (see Hill, 1960), they are instructive in the sense that they identify offenders who were sentenced to more than two years' incarceration, and thus had been deemed by the courts to be relatively serious offenders.

2: Theoretical Perspectives and Methological Approaches

1 Although it has been noted by some commentators (Friedrichs, 1980; Hinch, 1987) that Quinney's career has been marked by a number of shifts in theoretical perspective, I treat him here as representative of the instrumentalist Marxist school of thought with respect to law formation.

2 Weaver's (1995) assertion that there was a disproportional focus on racial-minority groups in the enforcement of morals offences is supported in chapter 6 of this book. However, his claim that magistrates convicted very few of those arrested and levied light fines in such cases is not supported on the basis of the data presented in chapter 6.

3 Although this study was criticized on the grounds that Hood failed to statistically control for additional 'legitimate factors that may have accounted for racial discrimination' (Halevy, 1995), Hood (1995) noted that it was not possible to 'explain away' the racial differences in the use of custody and other penalties by the characteristics of the cases.

4 The sampling strategy involved different sampling ratios for the individual cities,

proportional to the size of the city (for example, every 150th case was sampled from Toronto's jail records, and every 50th from Hamilton's), and an oversampling of minority-group and female offenders. Jail records from the city of Ottawa did not contain consistent information on the race of offenders; hence racial-minority-group offenders are underrepresented for that city. In addition, the coding of race in the Toronto (Don) jail records was not complete for the entire period under consideration. Minority-group offenders from Toronto were identified by reference to their country of birth and religion, with records being cross-checked with City of Toronto police records and provincial jail records, which were more consistent in their coding of race. After 1954, it is not possible to obtain race-of-offender information from the Toronto jail records.

5 The records were arranged chronologically by the date of arrest, thereby reducing the possibility of bias on the offence-type variable.

6 Police-court reports from newspapers were collected for the entire period for the cities of Toronto (using the *Toronto Daily Star* and *Globe*), Ottawa (the *Ottawa Citizen* and *Ottawa Journal*), Thunder Bay (the *Fort William Daily Times Journal* and *Port Arthur News Chronicle*), London (the *London Free Press* and *London Advertiser*), Hamilton (the *Hamilton Spectator*), and Windsor (the *Evening Record* and *Border Cities Star*).

7 Evidence that crime news was consumed quite voraciously by the public is provided in Clark (1898: 33). Discussing a special edition of the *Toronto Telegram* which was published after the execution of an offender in 1892, Clark notes that the 'enormous total' of 47,000 newspapers were sold, all of them in the city of Toronto.

3: Asians: Imigration and Restrictive Legislation

1 Nichol was also the editor of the *Vancouver Province* newspaper.

2 Friedman (1993) notes that a 1876 'queue ordinance' in the city of San Francisco required that the hair of every male prisoner in the county jail be cut to within one inch of his scalp. He argues that the intent of this law was to inflict shame on Chinese prisoners.

3 The 1902 legislation imposed a head tax of $500 on all Chinese immigrants, with the exception of members of the diplomatic corps, returning children born in Canada, servants of British subjects, and merchants with their families. Importantly, these taxes did not apply to European immigrants, and Nelson (1921a) reports that, from 1886 to 1919, the Canadian government collected more than $20 million from the head tax on Asian immigrants.

4 Ward (1978) notes that, in 1901, almost 11 per cent of the population of British Columbia was of Asian origin, a figure that remained relatively stable into the 1910s.

5 There was certainly no consensus among the anti-immigration advocates of this

period regarding the number of Asians resident in Canada, and it is apparent that some authors exaggerated the proportions of Asians in order to justify their arguments for restrictions on Asian immigration. For instance, Nelson (1921a), referring to the same 1921 census figures as Hope and Earle (1933), claimed that one person in every eight in British Columbia was Oriental.

6 Although the issue of East Asian immigration and crime is not the focus of this book, it is notable that, as part of the more general xenophobic attitudes in Canadian society, anti-Hindu sentiments were also prevalent, especially in the province of British Columbia. Nelson (1921a) notes that the 'Hindu invasion reached its most acute stage in July and August of 1914, when the *Komogata Maru* brought a shipload of them to Vancouver where they were refused landing.' In response, the federal government enacted section 98 of the Immigration Act, the 'continuous journey' clause, which stipulated that any immigrants who had come to Canada other than by continuous journey from countries of which they were citizens or natives, and on through tickets purchased in that country, would be excluded. This provision temporarily ended immigration to Canada from the country of India.

7 Friedman (1993) notes how local ordinances in San Francisco also had the effect of restricting Chinese business. In the early 1900s in San Francisco, it was unlawful to conduct a laundry business without the consent of the Board of Supervisors, except in a building constructed of either brick or stone. The problem for Asians was that almost all of their laundries were in wooden buildings. Friedman indicates that, if a Caucasian owned the building, the supervisors would give their approval, but if a Chinese proprietor was involved, 'the answer was invariably no.'

4: Blacks: Immigration and Restrictive Legislation

1 For discussions of the situation in Canada's eastern provinces, which had large numbers of Black colonists, see Walker, 1980, and Winks, 1971.

2 For instance, Black resident Miffin Winstar Gibbs was elected to Victoria's town council, and eventually became chairman of the city's finance committee in the 1850s (Winks, 1971).

3 This is not to suggest that challenges to such racist ideology did not appear in the media. For instance, Reinhart (1927–8: 254) while noting that Blacks had 'thick lips, broad noses, and kinky hair,' questioned the purported biological inferiority of Blacks. He suggested that 'with the 'characteristic kinky hair and absence of body hair, in these traits the white man is more apelike than the Negro.' Reinhardt also disputed the evidence from army and other intelligence tests that had indicated that Blacks were inferior in intelligence, noting that Blacks in the northern United States far surpassed those in the southern states on such measures, and in fact had higher intelligence scores than Whites in many southern states.

4 The year 1904 represents the first for which figures on Black immigration were provided by the Canadian government.

5 The member of Parliament apparently arrived at the figure of 17,000 through reference to the total number of Blacks in Canada as reported in the 1901 census.

6 Interestingly, evidence indicates that the immigration advertisements sent to the United States by the Canadian government emphasized the fact that Canada had mild winters (Troper, 1972).

7 *The Canadian Negro* was published weekly in Toronto from June 1953 until December 1956 (Winks, 1971).

8 In the 1950s, controversy also surrounded the immigration of women from the Caribbean who filled positions as domestic servants for middle-class Canadians on a contract basis. A quota of 2,000 women per year was established, and the women were initially granted entry to Canada on a migrant-labour basis, with their stay in the country being contingent on their remaining in domestic employment for one year after their arrival. While these women were recruited to fill a genuine demand for domestic labour, it appears that Caribbean women were admitted to Canada through a process of racialization. Satzewich (1991) asserts that incorporating these women as migrant labourers was more desirable to the extent that the costs of reproduction of labour power were to be borne in the Caribbean rather than in Canada. However, while government officials wanted Canada's middle class to have access to these women's labour, they also consistently expressed concern over the possibility that Caribbean women might form families, give birth to Canadian-born offspring, and thus form a growing resident Black population. This concern was rooted in racist and sexist stereotypes regarding the allegedly sexually promiscuous nature of Black women. Canadian government officials thus feared the growth of such a population, which might lead to race-relations problems in the country.

9 Although Blacks certainly experienced difficulty in securing access to employment, it is perhaps notable that a Black served as the executioner in the city of Hamilton in the late 1820s, and as a police matron in the same city in the 1890s. Weaver (1995: 180) reports that the Hamilton Police Commission clashed with the local chapter of the Woman's Christian Temperance Union over the hiring of a Black woman for the police-matron position, with the commission defending her (Mrs Lewis) in the following manner: 'Mrs Lewis may not be highly cultured, and it is true her complexion is dark, but she is a good, kind woman.'

10 Hill (1960: 133) reports on a National Employment Service study which found that Black women were not hired as switchboard operators because they could not pronounce the 'w' and 'r' distinctly.

11 This newspaper was founded in London in 1923 by James F. Jenkins, and was the official voice for the Canadian League for the Advancement of Coloured People (Winks, 1971).

12 Such discriminatory practices were not formally addressed in legislation until the early 1950s. For instance, a city of Toronto by-law, passed in June 1950, prevented proprietors in such places of business as barber shops, ladies' hairdressing establishments, and swimming pools from discriminating against any person on the basis of race, creed, or colour. A similar piece of legislation passed in the city of Windsor in 1950 made it clear that a license was responsible for refusals of '[his] employee[s] to serve or admit any person who bona fide seeks to purchase goods or the services provided by the licensee' (Saalheimer, 1952: 9).

13 Cox (1959) asserts that, in the United States, a White man/Black woman encounter was seen as the White blood enriching the Black, whereas the White woman/Black man dyad was believed to cause a debasing of the White blood.

14 Although one newspaper asserted that the Toronto Klan had a membership of 8,000, Sher (1983) suggests that a more realistic estimate was in the neighbourhood of 1,000 members.

15 Robin Winks's (1971) description of this case asserts that the Negro involved was actually an Indian. I was unable to uncover any evidence to corroborate his view.

5: Criminal Courts and the Racialization of Crime in Ontario

1 In 1903, the Hamilton police court hired its first translator, an appointment that Weaver (1995) asserts was testimony to the ethnic aspect of that city's early 1900s industrial boom. Weaver also notes that foreign translators acquired an influential position in the Hamilton courts, serving not only in their official role, but also as interpreters of cultural differences for the court, and for complainants and defendants.

2 Some commentators, however, were critical of the manner in which Denison dispensed justice in his court. Clark (1898), in questioning Denison's sentencing of a young male to five years in the penitentiary and fifteen lashes for the commission of a sexual offence, asserted, 'Colonel Denison is generally right, but the case in point is proof that he is not above trifling away a prisoner's liberty and ruining his life in order that he may get through the day's work before 11 a.m.' Similarly, Popple (1927), writing in the *Canadian Bar Review*, expressed concern about the potential discriminatory impact of the rapid disposition of cases in police courts.

3 This practice was not restricted to Chinese offenders, but applied to newspaper descriptions of offenders from several ethnic-minority groups. For example, the *Globe* (10 June 1908) prefaced its description of an offender charged with obstructing a thoroughfare with the headline, 'Not His Name that Did It,' and went on to suggest, 'Some argument was caused in the police court yesterday when B. Progohontchky was called on a charge of obstructing Montrose Avenue. Many questioned as to whether the gentleman had left his name lying around, but it transpired that it

was merely a pushcart that he had obstructed the street with.' In an aggravated-assault case, the *Hamilton Spectator* (11 July 1906) referred to 'John Cropquinskie, the pronunciation of which almost prostrated the Sergeant Major.' Similarly, reporting on a police raid of a gambling den in Toronto (*Toronto Daily Star*, 7 May 1917), the reporter noted, 'Four Italians and nine Austrians with names so unpronounceable that the court's pronunciation sounded like a bad attack of bronchitis, paid $5 and costs for gambling.'

4 This practice was of course not restricted to Asian and Black offenders. In a 1915 case involving an Italian offender who was hanged for murder in the Northern Ontario city of Port Arthur, '[Palma] dropped out of sight and the hangman, with a sort of forced smile, stepped down to the ground with the remark "there's one dago less"' (*Port Arthur News Chronicle*, 30 June, 1915).

5 Popular stereotypes of this period associated Blacks with 'flashy dress': 'The Negro is very fond of dress. He may go in rags during the week, but on Sunday he will dress like a prince if he can afford it' (Delesser, 1900: 120).

6 Stereotyping of other ethnic-minority offenders was similarly accomplished in this fashion. For example, Sam Sonsonia and Tonia Speenzza, 'Italian banana pedlars,' charged with 'not keeping on the move with their push carts ... wailed pathetically "howa con we mova when we makka change?"' (*London Free Press*, 13 August, 1902).

6: Drug and Public-Order Crimes

1 The formation of drug laws on the basis of race has not been restricted to North America. In 1911, for example, the White South African government outlawed marijuana in an effort to control the growing radicalization of Blacks in that country. 'Dagga' was blamed for causing Blacks to rebel against White power. In fact, South Africa led the early international campaign to ban hemp, and drug prohibitionists from that country had a direct influence on political leaders and legislators in the American South (Lusane, 1991). Similarly, in The Netherlands, Chinese offenders were singled out for prosecution under opium laws in the 1920s. DeKort (1994) notes that Asians represented an easily distinguishable and isolated group for the Dutch police to focus on in their enforcement of drug legislation.

2 Prior to 1908, the opium business was legal in Canada. Neither the federal nor the provincial governments were interested in criminalizing the industry, primarily because it served as a lucrative source of revenue. In 1906, for example, the value of crude and powdered opium imports amounted to approximately $321,000; duty on this amount was nearly $47,500. In addition, the annual licence fee on an opium firm in Victoria, British Columbia, was $500 in the late 1800s (Lai, 1988).

3 Murphy also made a number of public appearances across the country to promote her

views. In 1922, she delivered a widely advertised address in Toronto's Allen Theatre entitled 'Drug Menace to Anglo-Saxon Race' (*Toronto Daily Star*, 21 October, 1922).

4 The qualitative data did reveal some isolated incidents where narcotics arrests were the result of citizen complaints. For instance, the *Toronto Daily Star* (23 August 1923) reported that the police 'were approached by a woman who offered to take them to a man selling drugs.' However, the bulk of the arrests in the data set appear to be the result of police-initiated activity.

5 In his submission to the court before the sentencing of his Chinese client, defence counsel Eric Armour noted, 'We can't be too trusting of these foreign agents because what they are after is their share of the fine' (*Toronto Daily Star*, 11 April 1913).

6 Similar practices apparently occurred in Chinatowns in the United States, where many of the opium dens 'boasted thick oaken doors, studded with bolts, and with sentries posted in warning' (Light, 1974: 372).

7 For a detailed discussion of the methodological strategies employed and variables used in these analyses, see Appendix One.

8 For an interpretation of the reduced likelihood of imprisonment for female drug offenders, see Mosher 1992.

9 In one Toronto case (*Toronto Daily Star*, 28 February 1921) involving five Chinese drug offenders, 'two young Chinamen' pleaded not guilty 'and because their faces were so much fresher than those of the confessed addicts, Magistrate Jones took their plea and dismissed the charge.' While this report of Magistrate Jones's actions should not necessarily be taken literally, there was a perception on the part of those reporting on court activities that decisions were often made on an ad hoc basis. As Craven (1983: 274) suggests, 'Whatever limits [the case law] might have attached to the magistrate's decision to dismiss a case, it is evident that personalistic and indeed paternalistic considerations were deeply embedded in magisterial practice.'

10 The selective nature of police activity towards the enforcement of gambling legislation in the early 1900s has also been revealed in American jurisdictions. For example, describing the situation in San Francisco, Coolidge (1929) notes: 'For years, while the Chinese gambling dens were periodically raided by the police, there were many places where poker and other games were openly played by white men in which far larger sums of money were lost, and in several of the principal saloons, pools were sold on the races and prize fights. San Francisco is of all places the one where gambling can least appropriately be called an "Oriental" vice, since every form of it has flourished among the white population under the sufferance of municipal authority.'

11 Liquor offences included public drunkenness, violations of the Ontario Temperance Act, selling liquor without a permit, etc. Disorderly-house offences included keeping a disorderly or bawdy-house, or house of ill-fame, and frequenting, being an inmate of, or being found in a disorderly or bawdy-house or house of ill-fame.

12 The fact that fifteen out of the twenty variables in the equation for all public-order offences have significant effects on the imprisonment decision is at least in part attributable to the large sample size.

13 It is important to note that such practices occurred in Toronto, although apparently not as frequently. In the vagrancy case of William Oliver ('colored'), the accused 'doffed his hat to the court upon a charge of vagrancy. He was given 24 hours by his worship to shake the dust of the city from his shoes. Judging by the expedition with which he left the court, Oliver was going to make it in considerably less than 24 hours; a jump from the court dock to the door was the matter of a second, and with the ring of the amused laughter of the court curiosity seekers in his ears, he disappeared' (*Toronto Daily Star*, 9 September, 1927).

14 The tendency to devalue evidence presented by individuals from minority groups also applied to Chinese. For example, N.W.T. Drake, testifying before the 1885 Royal Commission on Chinese Immigration, asserted that 'The Chinese are utterly unacquainted with truth, and it is a universal comment on their evidence that you cannot believe anything they say. They shelter themselves under their ignorance of the English language so that no cross-examination can reach them, and it is generally believed that the interpreters guide the evidence' (Canada, Royal Commission on Chinese Immigration, 1885). Interestingly, in the state of California, the Supreme Court formally prevented Chinese (and Native peoples) from testifying in cases involving Whites in the early 1900s (Smedley, 1993).

7: Property and Violent Crimes

1 Hayner (1937–8) also reports on police records from the city of Seattle for the 1900–4 period, which showed 1,676 arrests of Japanese females, with all but 4 of these being for commercialized prostitution or keeping a disorderly house. In the same period, there were only 406 arrests of Japanese males, including 147 for keeping a disorderly house.

2 Although violent crime was apparently not common in Asian-Canadian communities, Gilmour (1949) reports that certain practices in Vancouver may have led the general public to believe otherwise. One individual who ran a tourist bureau in that city's Chinatown in the 1930s hired jobless Chinese to 'run yelling through the crowd, holding rubber daggers dripping with ketchup as he and his entourage approached.' These excursions were 'conducted with the full knowledge and consent of Chinese leaders in the community.'

3 Although a detailed analysis is not presented here, whipping became a common sanction for violent offences in the 1910s and 1920s, and was applied in particular to minority-group offenders. As the following excerpt from a Woman's Christian Temperance Union report (1913: 113) on the merits of whipping as a sanction for wife

assaults indicates, the use of this punishment was justified on the basis of retribution, and its specific and general deterrent effects. 'Since wife beaters have been whipped in Toronto, the crime has decreased to one quarter of the former number of offenders, and while it was formerly a common occurrence for men to be brought to court again and again, since this punishment has been inflicted, not one has repeated the offense. Evidently, they do not like their own medicine, and have escaped taking a second dose. We therefore are still of the opinion that what has proved efficient in the one case doubtless will in the other, and womanhood will be better protected.'

In an Ontario Supreme Court decision (*Rex* v *DeYoung, Liddiard, and Darling*, 1927) involving an appeal by three offenders in a rape case who were sentenced to be whipped, the Court indicated its support for the deterrent aspects of this sanction. 'Canada is but sparsely settled in many places where women are often alone or insufficiently protected from men [of the tendencies of the respondents], and a severer deterrent than previously existed was manifestly thought to be necessary.'

4 Although cases of Whites victimizing members of minority groups were relatively rare, it is apparent from the qualitative data that such criminals were treated less severely by the courts. In the case of John Sova, who murdered Chin Tang, 'a Chinese who operated a laundry,' the accused was sentenced to only seven years' imprisonment (Toronto, *Annual Report of the Chief Constable*, 1945).

5 In a notable exception to the general rule of disproportional severity for those convicted of interracial crimes, one Chinese male was sentenced to one years' imprisonment and his accomplice to three months' imprisonment for the killing of a White man in the Northern Ontario city of Fort William. However, the *Daily Times Journal* (21 April 1910) was not convinced of the accuseds' contention that they had acted in self-defence, and commented on the lenience accorded these offenders. 'Some people say that they cannot understand why two Chinamen should have to serve a total of 15 months for hitting a white man on the head and inflicting a wound which caused death, when a white man who killed another white man convicted of perjury goes up for five years.'

6 It is notable, however, that in some cases where White females were seemingly complicit in these interracial unions, sentences were somewhat less severe. For instance, Lulu Robinson, a 'white Detroit woman,' and William Bedford, 'colored,' headlined by the *Windsor Evening Record* (21 December 1895) as a 'Foul Pair,' were charged with 'bestial conduct.' The newspaper noted that the evidence in this case was 'unfit for publication,' and reported that Bedford was sent to the Central Prison for three months, and the woman to Sandwich jail for two months.

References

Abel, E. 1980. *Marijuana: The First Twelve Thousand Years.* New York: Premium

Adamson, J.E. 1933. 'Judicial Sentences.' *Canadian Bar Review* 11: 681–6

Alberta. 1991. *Report of the Task Force on the Criminal Justice System and Its Impact on the Indian and Metis People of Alberta.* Edmonton

Aldrich, J., and F. Nelson. 1984. *Linear Probability, Logit and Probit Models.* Beverly Hills: Sage

Althusser, L. 1971. *Lenin and Philosophy and Other Essays.* London: New Left

Amemiya, T. 1981. 'Qualitative Response Models: A Survey.' *Journal of Econometric Literature* 19: 1483–1536

Amiel, B. 1992. 'Racism: An Excuse for Riots and Theft.' *Maclean's,* 18 May

Anderson, A.B., and J.S. Frideres, 1981. *Ethnicity in Canada: Theoretical Perspectives.* Toronto: Butterworths

Anderson, K. 1991. *Vancouver's Chinatown.* Montreal: McGill–Queen's University Press

Angus, H.F. 1931. 'The Legal Status in British Columbia of Residents of the Oriental Race and Their Descendants.' *Canadian Bar Review* 9: 1–12

Angus, W. 1967. 'Judicial Selection in Canada – The Historical Perspective.' *Canadian Legal Studies* 1: 220–51

Appleby, T. 1991. 'Fighting the Criminal Mosaic: Would Ethnic Data Help?' *Globe and Mail,* 5 October

– 1992a. 'Officer's Kick at Suspect Captured by Camera.' *Globe and Mail,* 24 February

– 1992b. 'Embattled Police Seek Solutions.' *Globe and Mail,* 9 May

– 1992c. 'Island Crime Wave Spills Over.' *Globe and Mail,* 10 July

– 1992d. 'The Twisted Arm of the Law.' *Globe and Mail,* 12 July

– 1992e. 'Identifying the Problem.' *Globe and Mail,* July 13

Archambault, J. 1938. *Report of the Royal Commission to Investigate the Penal System of Canada.* Ottawa: King's Printer

Austin, T. 1981. 'The Influence of Court Location on Type of Criminal Sentence: The Urban-Rural Factor.' *Journal of Criminal Justice* 9: 305–16

Backhouse, C. 1985. 'Nineteenth-Century Canadian Prostitution Law: Reflection of a Discriminatory Society.' *Social History* 18: 387–423

Balbus, I. 1977. 'Commodity Form and Legal Form: An Essay on the Relative Autonomy of the Law.' *Law and Society Review* 7: 571–88

Baird, K.A. 1958. 'Race Prejudice.' *The Dalhousie Review* 38: 281–94

Barber, J. 1994. 'Case Raises Questions No Citizen Should Ignore.' *Globe and Mail*, 18 February

Beach, W. 1932. *Oriental Crime in California*. New York: AMS

Becker, Howard. 1963. *Outsiders: Studies in the Sociology of Deviance*. New York: Free Press

Bedford, Judy. 1981. 'Prostitution in Calgary: 1905–1914.' *Alberta History* 29: 1–15

Beirne, P. 1979. 'Empiricism and the Critique of Marxism on Law and Crime.' *Social Problems* 26: 373–85

Bellett, G., and M. Young. 1992. 'Probe Starts Into Beating of Suspect.' *Vancouver Sun*, 12 February

Bennett, L. 1980. *Public Opinion in American Politics*. New York: Harcourt Brace Jovanovich

Berrill, N.J. 1956. 'The Myth of White Supremacy.' *Saturday Night*, 27 October

Bernstein, I., W. Kelly, and P. Doyle. 1977. 'Societal Reaction to Deviants: The Case of Criminal Defendants.' *American Sociological Review* 42: 743–55

Berridge, V., and G. Edwards. 1987. *Opium and the People: Opiate Use in Nineteenth-Century England*. New Haven: Yale University Press

Bertley, L.W. 1977. *Canada and Its People of African Descent*. Pierrefonds, PQ,: Bilongo

Bienvenue, R., and J. Goldstein. 1985. *Ethnicity and Ethnic Relations in Canada*. Toronto: Butterworths

Blalock, H. 1967. *Towards a Theory of Minority Group Relations*. New York: Capricorn

Blumstein, A. 1993. 'Making Rationality Relevant.' *Criminology* 31: 1–16

Blumstein, A., and J. Cohen. 1980. 'Sentencing of Convicted Offenders: An Analysis of the Public's View.' *Law and Society Review* 14: 223–61

Boland, B., and J. Wilson. 1978. 'Age, Crime, and Punishment.' *Public Interest* 22: 51

Bonger, W. 1943. *Race and Crime*. Montclair, NJ: Patterson Smith

Bonnie, R., and C. Whitebread. 1974. *The Marijuana Conviction*. Virginia: Charlottesville University Press

Border Cities Star (Windsor) 1892–1961

Boritch, H. 1985. 'The Making of Toronto the Good: The Organization of Policing and Production of Arrests, 1859 to 1955.' Unpublished PhD Dissertation, University of Toronto

– 1992. 'Gender and Criminal Court Outcomes: An Historical Analysis.' *Criminology*
30: 293–325

Boyd, Neil. 1984. 'The Origins of Canadian Narcotics Legislation.' *Dalhousie Law
Journal* 8: 102–36

– 1986. *The Social Dimensions of Law.* Scarborough: Prentice-Hall

Brecher, E. 1972. *Licit and Illicit Drugs.* Boston: Little, Brown

Breton, R. 1964. 'Institutional Completeness of Ethnic Communities and the Personal
Relations of Immigrants.' *American Journal of Sociology* 70: 193–205

Bridges, G., and M. Myers. 1994. 'Problems and Prospects in the Study of Inequality,
Crime and Social Control.' In *Inequality, Crime and Social Control.* ed. G. Bridges
and M. Myers, 3–18. Boulder: Westview Press

British Colonist (Victoria). 1859, 1960

British Columbia. 1880–2. Sessional Papers

Brockman, J., and D. Chunn, eds. 1993. *Investigating Gender Bias.* Toronto: Thompson
Educational

Bryant, I. 1935. 'News Items about Negroes in White Urban and Rural Newspapers.'
Journal of Negro Education 4: 169–78

Bullock, H. 1961. 'Significance of the Racial Factor in the Length of Prison Sentences.'
Journal of Criminal Law Criminology and Police Science 52: 411–17

Burke, P., and A. Turk. 1975. 'Factors Affecting Postarrest Dispositions: A Model for
Analysis.' *Social Problems* 22: 313–32

Burtch, B. 1992. *The Sociology of Law.* Toronto: Harcourt Brace Jovanovich

Byron, W. 1919. 'The Menace of the Alien.' Maclean's 32 (October), 6

Calkins, A. 1871. *Opium and the Opium Appetite.* Philadelphia: Lippincott

Canada. 1882–1961a. *House of Commons Debates.* Ottawa: Queen's Printer

– 1882–1961b. *Statutes of Canada.* Ottawa: King's Printer

– 1885. *Royal Commission on Chinese Immigration.* Ottawa: King's Printer

– 1902. *Royal Commission on Chinese and Japanese Immigration.* Ottawa: King's
Printer

– 1904. *The Chineses Immigration Act.* Ottawa: King's Printer

– 1908. *Report on the Need for the Suppression of the Opium Traffic in Canada.*
Ottawa: Queen's Printer

– 1911. Census of Canada

– 1911. *Royal Commission Appointed to Investigate Alleged Chinese Fraud and Opium
Smuggling on the Pacific Coast.* Sessional Papers. Ottawa: King's Printer

– 1921–55. *Department of Pensions and National Health Annual Report* Ottawa:
Queen's Printer

– 1922–38. *Annual Report of the RCMP.* Ottawa: Queen's Printer

Canadian Bar Association. 1916. *Canadian Bar Association Journal*

– 1956. 'Inequalities in the Criminal Law.' *Canadian Bar Review* 34, 265–80

Canadian Forum. 1925. 'The Color Problem.' August, 336
– 1943. 'Editorial,' 23 (October), 164–5
Canadian Law Times. 1904
Canadian Law Times and Review. 1908. 'Immigration and Nation-Building,' 28: 130–1
Canadian Unionist. 1954 'Toronto NCA Protests Discrimination against Negroes,' May, 181
Carrigan, O. 1991. *Crime and Punishment in Canada – A History.* Toronto: McClelland and Stewart
Chambers, E.A., and D.R. Cox. 1967. 'Discrimination between Alternative Binary Response Models.' *Biometrica* 54: 573–8
Chambliss, W. 1974. 'The State, the Law, and the Definition of Behavior as Criminal or Delinquent.' In *Handbook of Criminology*, ed. D. Glaser, 7–43. Indianapolis: Bobbs-Merrill
Chambliss, W., and R.B. Seidman. 1971. *Law, Order and Power.* Reading, MA: Addison Wesley
Chapman, P. 1995. 'Enter the Dragon,' Vancouver Province, 23 July
Chapman, T. 1979. 'The Anti-Drug Crusade in Western Canada, 1885–1925.' In *Law and Society in Canadian Historical Perspective*, ed. D. Bercuson and L. Knafla, 89–116. Calgary: University of Calgary Press
Chicago Commission on Race Relations. 1922. *The Negro in Chicago: A Study of Race Relations and a Race Riot.* Chicago: University of Chicago Press
Christie v York Corporation. 1940. *Dominion Law Reports* 1: 81
Clairmont, D., and D. Magill. 1987. *Africville: The Life and Death of a Canadian Black Community.* Toronto: Canadian Scholars
Claridge, T. 1996. 'Gayle Gets Second Sentence of Life for Attempted Murder.' *Globe and Mail*, 3 Februrary
Clark, C.S. 1898. *Of Toronto the Good.* Montreal: Toronto Publishing
Clark, S.D. 1962. *The Developing Canadian Community.* Toronto: University of Toronto Press
Clarke, A. 1963. 'A Black Man Talks about Race Prejudice in Toronto.' *Maclean's*, 20 April, 5
– 1992. *Police Violence and Black Youth.* Toronto: HarperCollins
Clarke, S., and G. Koch. 1976. 'The Influence of Income and Other Factors on Whether Criminal Defendants Go to Prison.' *Law and Society Review* 11: 57–92
Clayton, O. 1983. 'A Reconsideration of the Effects of Race on Criminal Sentencing.' *Criminal Justice Review* 8: 15–20
Colbourn, G. 1993. 'Strip-Search of Woman Has Toronto Stunned.' *Vancouver Sun*, 7 October

Coleman, J. 1986. 'Social Theory, Social Research, and a Theory of Action.' *American Journal of Sociology* 91: 1309–20

Comack, A.E. 1985. 'The Origins of Canadian Drug Legislation – Labelling Versus Class Analysis.' In *The New Criminologies in Canada*, ed. T. Fleming, 65–86. Toronto: Oxford University Press

Cook, S. 1969. 'Canadian Narcotics Legislation, 1908–23: A Conflict Model Interpretation.' *Canadian Review of Sociology and Anthropology* 6: 36–46

Coolidge, M.R. 1929. *Chinese Immigration.* New York: Henry Holt

Corelli, R. 1994. 'Murder Next Door.' *Maclean's,* 18 April, 14–15

Cox, O.C. 1959. *Caste, Class and Race.* New York: Monthly Review

Craven, Paul. 1983. 'Law and Ideology: The Toronto Police Court, 1850–1880.' In *Essays in the History of Canadian Law*, ed. D. Flaherty, 248–307. Toronto: University of Toronto Press

Crowe, I. and J. Cove. 1984. 'Ethnic Minorities and the Courts.' *Criminal Law Review* 28: 413–17

Cuff, J.H. 1994. 'Southern Justice, Canadian Style.' *Globe and Mail,* 18 October

Curry, J.N. 1906. 'Reorganize the Crown Attorney's Office.' *Saturday Night,* 1 September, 6–7

Daly , K. 1987a. 'Discrimination in the Criminal Courts: Family, Gender, and the Problem of Equal Treatment.' *Social Forces* 66: 152–75

– 1987b. 'Structure and Practice of Familial-Based Justice in a Criminal Court.' *Law and Society Review* 21: 267–90

Dannefer, D., and R. Schutt. 1982. 'Race and Juvenile Justice Processing in Court and Police Agencies.' *American Journal of Sociology* 87: 1113–32

Davis, M., and J. Krauter. 1971. *The Other Canadians: Profiles of Six Minorities.* Toronto: Methuen

Dawn of Tomorrow. 1934. 'Hotel London Discharges Colored Help and Replaces Them with White Ex- Service Men.' June

– 1945. 'Canadian Citizens.' May

– 1946. 'Fight Race Hatred in Ontario.' 18 December

Delesser, H.G. 1900. 'The West Indian Negro of Today.' *Canadian Magazine* 15, 115–21

DeKort, M. 1994. 'A Short History of Drugs in the Netherlands.' In *Between Prohibition and Legalization: The Dutch Experiment in Drug Policy*, ed. E. Leuw and I.H. Marshall, 3–22. New York: Kugler

Denison, G.T. 1920. *Recollections of a Police Magistrate.* Toronto: Carswell

DiManno, R. 1993. 'Hostile Reaction to Police Board Official Is Unfair.' *Toronto Star,* 6 September

Dion, K., and K. Kawakami. 1996. 'Ethnicity and Perceived Discrimination in Toronto:

Another Look at the Personal/Group Discrimination Discrepancy.' *Canadian Journal of Behavioral Science* 28: 203–13

Ditton, J. 1979. *Controlology: Beyond the New Criminology*. London: Macmillan

Dixon, J. 1995. 'The Organizational Context of Criminal Sentencing.' *American Journal of Sociology* 100: 1157–98

Doob, A. 1996. 'Racism in the Criminal Justice System.' *Globe and Mail*, 20 January

Driedger, L. 1989. *The Ethnic Factor*. Toronto: McGraw-Hill Ryerson

Durkheim, Emile. 1938. *The Rules of the Sociological Method*. New York: Free Press

Duster, T. 1970. *The Legislation of Morality*. New York: Free Press

Edmonds, W.L. 1929. 'The Colored Race in Canada.' *Saturday Night* 44: (20 July), 4

Eisler, D. 1997. 'Young and Dangerous.' *Maclean's*, 3 February, 24–5

Elliott, J., and A. Fleras. 1992. *Unequal Relations*. Scarborough: Prentice-Hall

Ericson, R. 1981. *Making Crime: A Study of Detective Work*. Toronto: Butterworths

– 1982. *Reproducing Order*. Toronto: University of Toronto Press

Ericson, R., and P. Baranek. 1982. *The Ordering of Justice*. Toronto: University of Toronto Press

Essex Real Estate Co. Ltd. v *Holmes*. 1930. *Ontario Weekly Notes* 39: 111

Farnsworth, C. 1995. 'Black in Quebec: Escaping the Streets.' *New York Times*, 13 October

Farrell, R., and V. Swigert. 1978. 'Prior Offense as a Self-Fulfilling Prophecy.' *Law and Society Review* 12: 437–53

Feeley, M. 1979. *The Process Is the Punishment: Handling Cases in a Lower Criminal Court*. New York: Russell Sage Foundation

Fennell, T. 1992. 'Drawing the Battle Lines.' *Maclean's*, 16 November, 18–21

Fingard, J. 1984. 'Jailbirds in Mid-Victorian Halifax.' In *Law in Colonial Society: The Nova Scotia Experience*, ed. P. Waite, S. Oxner, and T. Barnes, 81–90. Toronto: Carswell

Fisher, L. 1995. 'The Brutal Truth – Violent Gangs Instil Fear in Once-Staid Ottawa.' *Maclean's*, 13 November, 66

Fisher, M. 1911. 'The Negro Problem in the Canadian West.' *Saturday Night*, 15 April, 2

Forcese, D. 1992. *Policing Canadian Society*. Scarborough: Prentice-Hall

Fort William Daily Times Journal. 1892–1961

Foster, C. 1996. *A Place Called Heaven: The Meaning of Being Black in Canada*. Toronto: HarperCollins

Frankfurter, F. 1922. 'Newspapers and Criminal Justice.' In *Criminal Justice in Cleveland*, ed. R. Pound and F. Frankfurter, 515–55. Montclair, NJ: Patterson Smith

Franklin v *Evans*. 1924. *Ontario Law Reports* 55: 349

Friedman, L. 1993. *Crime and Punishment in American History*. New York: Basic

Friedrichs, D. 1980. 'Radical Criminology in the United States: An Interpretive Understanding.' In *Radical Criminology: The Coming Crises*, ed. J. Inciaridi, 35–60. Beverly Hills: Sage

Gabor, T. 1994. 'The Suppression of Crime Statistics on Race and Ethnicity: The Price of Political Correctness.' *Canadian Journal of Criminology* 36: 153–63

Garcia, J.L.A. 1996. 'The Heart of Racism.' *Journal of Social Philosophy* 27: 5–45

Garfinkel, H. 1949. 'Research Note on Inter- , and Intra-racial Homicides.' *Social Forces* 27: 369–81

Gibson, J. 1978. 'Race as a Determinant of Criminal Sentences: A Methodological Critique and a Case Study.' *Law and Society Review* 12: 455–78

Giffen, P.J., S. Endicott, and S. Lambert. 1991. *Panic and Indifference: The Politics of Canada's Drug Laws*. Ottawa: Canadian Centre on Substance Abuse

Gilmour, C. 1949. 'What, No Opium Dens?' *Maclean's*, 15 January 1949: 16

Gist, J. 1932. 'The Negro in the Daily Press.' *Social Forces* 10: 405–11

Globe (Toronto). 1892–1961

Globe and Mail (Toronto). 1994a. 'Manning Defends MP's Move.' 15 March
– 1994b. 'Study Backs Immigrants.' 14 July
– 1995. 'One Dead, Five Injured, in Bar Fight.' 11 December
– 1996a. 'Murder Verdict in Constable's Slaying.' 12 January
– 1996b. 'Unanswered Questions on Race and Crime' 18 January

Goff, C., and C. Reasons. 1978. *Corporate Crime in Canada: A Critical Analysis of Anti-Combines Legislation*. Scarborough: Prentice-Hall

Goldstein, J. 1960. 'Police Discretion Not to Invoke the Criminal Process,' *Yale Law Journal* 69: 543–94

Gomme, I. 1993. *The Shadow Line: Deviance and Crime in Canada*. Toronto: Harcourt Brace Jovanovich

Gramsci, A. 1971. *Selections from the Prison Notebooks*. London: Lawrence and Wishart

Grange, M. 1995. 'Toronto Shooting Leaves One Dead, Two Hurt.' *Globe and Mail*, 18 December

Green, E. 1961. *Judicial Attitudes in Sentencing*. London: Macmillan
– 1964. 'Inter- and Intra-Racial Crime Relative to Sentencing.' *Journal of Criminal Law, Criminology and Police Science* 55: 348–58

Green, M. 1979. 'A History of Canadian Narcotics Legislation.' *University of Toronto Faculty of Law Review* 49: 42–79

Greenberg, D. 1981. 'Instrumental and Structural Theories of Law.' In *Crime and Capitalism: Readings in Marxist Criminology*, ed. D. Greenberg, 190–208. Mountain View, CA: Mayfield

Greenspon, E., and J. Sallott. 1994. 'Reform Releases Refugee Crime Data.' *Globe and Mail*, 5 November

Griffiths, C.T., and S.N. Verdun-Jones. 1994. *Canadian Criminal Justice*. Markham: Butterworths

Grow, S. 1974. 'The Blacks of Amber Valley: Negro Pioneering in Northern Alberta.'
    Canadian Ethnic Studies 6: 17–38
Hackler, J. 1994. *Crime and Canadian Public Policy*. Scarborough: Prentice-Hall
Hagan, J. 1977. 'Criminal Justice in Rural and Urban Communities: A Study of the
    Bureaucratization of Justice.' *Social Forces* 55: 597–612
– 1980. 'The Legislation of Crime and Delinquency: A Review of Theory, Research,
    and Method.' *Law and Society Review* 14: 603–28
– 1991. *The Disreputable Pleasures: Crime and Deviance in Canada*. Toronto:
    McGraw-Hill Ryerson
Hagan, J., and K. Bumiller. 1983. 'Making Sense of Sentencing: A Review and Critique
    of Sentencing Research.' In *Research on Sentencing: The Search for Reform*, vol. 2,
    ed. A. Blumstein, J. Cohen, S. Martin, and M. Tonry, 1–54. Washington, D.C.:
    National Academy
Hagan, J., and J. Leon. 1977. 'Rediscovering Delinquency: Social History, Political Ide-
    ology and the Sociology of Law.' *American Sociological Review* 42: 587–98
Hagan, J., I. Nagel, and C. Albonetti. 1980. 'The Differential Sentencing of White-
    Collar Offenders in Ten Federal District Courts.' *American Sociological Review* 45:
    802–20
Hagan, J., and M. Zatz. 1985. 'The Social Organization of Criminal Justice Processing:
    An Event History Analysis.' *Social Science Research* 14: 103–25
Halevy, T. 1995. 'Racial Discrimination in Sentencing? A Study with Dubious Conclu-
    sions.' *Criminal Law Review* 267–71.
Hall, J., and H. Stancu. 1994. 'Four Sought after Woman Dies in Crash Robbery.'
    Toronto Star, 7 April
Hall, Stuart, and Phil Scraton. 1986. 'Law, Class, and Control.' In *Crime and Society*,
    ed. M. Fitzgerald, G. McLennan, and J. Pawson, 460–97. London: Routledge and
    Kegan Paul
Hall, S., S. Crutcher, T. Jefferson, J. Clarke, and B. Roberts. 1978. *Policing the Crisis*.
    New York: Holmes and Meier
Haller, M. 1976. 'Historical Roots of Police Behavior, Chicago, 1890–1925.' *Law and
    Society Review* 10: 308–23
Hamilton. 1908–61. Jail Records
– 1911. *Annual Police Report*
Hamilton Spectator. 1892–1961
Hanushek, E., and J. Jackson. 1977. *Statistical Methods for Social Scientists*. New York:
    Academic
Harkness, R. 1963. *J.E. Atkinson of the* Star. Toronto: University of Toronto Press
Harris, F. 1932. *The Presentation of Crime in Newspapers*. Hanover: Sociological Press
Hartnagel, T. 1992. 'Correlates of Criminal Behavior.' In *Criminology: A Canadian
    Perspective*, ed. R. Linden, 91–126. Toronto: Harcourt Brace Jovanovich

Hatt, K. 1994. 'Reservations about Race and Crime Statistics.' *Canadian Journal of Criminology* 36: 164–5

Hawkins, D.F. 1987. 'Beyond Anomalies: Rethinking the Conflict Perspective on Race and Criminal Punishment' *Social Forces* 65: 719–45

– 1995. *Ethnicity, Race and Crime*. Albany: State University of New York Press

Hayner, N.S. 1937–8. 'Social Factors in Oriental Crime.' *American Journal of Sociology* 43: 909–19

Helmer, J. 1975. *Drugs and Minority Oppression*. New York: Seabury

Henry, F. 1994. *The Caribbean Diaspora in Toronto: Learning to Live with Racism*. Toronto: University of Toronto Press

Henry, F., P. Hastings, and B. Freer. 1996. 'Perceptions of Race and Crime in Ontario: Empirical Evidence from Toronto and the Durham Region.' *Canadian Journal of Criminology* 38: 469–76

Henry, F., C. Tator, W. Mattis, and T. Rees. 1995. *The Colour of Democracy: Racism in Canadian Society*. Toronto: Harcourt Brace Jovanovich

Hess, H. 1995. 'Police Say Slain Man Had Criminal Links.' *Globe and Mail*, 19 December

Hewitt, R. 1947. 'Racial Prejudice.' *Trades and Labor Congress Journal* 26: 15

Hill, D. 1960. 'Negroes in Toronto: A Sociological Study of a Minority Group.' PhD dissertation. University of Toronto

– 1979. 'Blacks In Canada: A Forgotten History.' *Toronto Star*, 17 February

Hinch, R. 1983 'Marxist Criminology in the 1970s: Clarifying the Clutter.' *Crime and Social Justice* 19: 65–74

– 1992 'Conflict and Marxist Theories.' In *Criminology: A Canadian Perspective*, ed. R. Linden, 267–91. Toronto: Harcourt Brace Jovanovich

Hogarth, J. 1971. *Sentencing as a Human Process*. Toronto: University of Toronto Press

Homel, G. 1981. 'Denison's Law: Criminal Justice and the Police Court in Toronto, 1877–1921.' *Ontario History* 73: 171–85

Hood, R. 1962. *Sentencing in Magistrate's Courts*. London: Stevens and Sons

– 1992. *Race and Sentencing*. Oxford: The Clarendon Press

– 1995. 'Race and Sentencing: A Reply.' *Criminal Law Review* 272–9.

Hope, C.E., and W.K. Earle. 1933. 'The Oriental Threat.' *Maclean's* 46 (1 May), 12

Hopkins, A. 1975. 'On the Sociology of Criminal Law,' *Social Problems* 22: 608–19

Hopkins, E. 1931. *Our Lawless Police*. New York: Viking

Hudson, B. 1989. 'Discrimination and Disparity: The Influence of Race on Sentencing.' *New Community* 16: 23–34

Hudson, J., and J. Roberts, eds. 1993. *Evaluating Justice*. Toronto: Thompson Educational

Hudson, J., J. Hornick, and B. Burrows, eds. 1988. *Justice and the Young Offender in Canada*. Toronto: Wall and Thompson

Hunter, J. 1994. 'Anger Follows BC Reform Party Leader's Stand on Asians.' *Vancouver Sun*, 28 September

Hurst, L. 1993. 'Coloring Crime Stats by Race.' *Toronto Star*, 27 November

Ignatieff, M. 1983. 'Social Histories of Punishment.' In *Legality, Ideology and the State*, ed. D. Sugarman, 38–67. London: Academic

Irwin, J. 1985. *The Jail: Managing the Underclass in American Society*. Berkeley: University of California Press

Irwin, J., and J. Austin. 1997. *It's about Time: America's Imprisonment Binge*. Belmont, CA: Wadsworth

Jackson, M., and C.T. Griffiths. 1991. *Canadian Criminology: Perspectives on Crime and Criminality*. Toronto: Harcourt Brace Jovanovich

Jessop, B. 1982. *The Capitalist State*. Oxford: Martin Robertson

Johnson, E. 1957. 'Selective Factors in Capital Punishment.' *Social Forces* 36: 165–9

Johnson, G. 1941. 'The Negro and Crime.' *The Annals of the American Academy of Political and Social Science* 271: 93–104

Johnston, J.P. 1994. 'Academic Approaches to Race-Crime Statistics Do Not Justify Their Collection.' *Canadian Journal of Criminology* 36: 166–74

Johnston, L. 1921. 'The Case of the Oriental in B.C.' *Canadian Magazine* 57, 315–18

Journal of Criminal Law, Criminology and Police Science. 1910–11. 'Discrimination against Negro Criminals in Arkansas.' 1: 947–8

Kaihla, P. 1996. 'Canada's Changing Face.' *Maclean's*, 30 December, 38–9

Katz, S. 1949. 'Jim Crowe Lives in Dresden.' *Maclean's* 62 (1 November), 8

Kavanaugh, M. 1928. *The Criminal and His Allies*. Indianapolis: Bobbs-Merrill

Kelly, H. 1976. 'Comparison of Defense Strategy and Race as Influences on Differential Sentencing.' *Criminology* 14: 241–9

Kitsuse, I., and A. Cicourel. 1963. 'A Note on the Uses of Official Statistics.' *Social Problems* 11: 131–9

Kleck, G. 1981. 'Racial Discrimination in Criminal Sentencing: A Critical Evaluation of Evidence with Additional Evidence on the Death Penalty.' *American Sociological Review* 46: 783–805

Klepper, S., D. Nagin, and L.J. Tierney. 1983. 'Discrimination in the Criminal Justice System: A Critical Appraisal of the Literature.' In *Research on Sentencing: The Search for Reform*, vol.2, ed. A. Blumstein, J. Cohen, S. Martin, and M. Tonry, 55–128. Washington, DC: National Academy

Kobayashi, A. 1990. 'Racism and the Law.' *Urban Geography* 11: 447–73

Kratcoski, P. 1974. 'Differential Treatment of Delinquent Boys and Girls in a Juvenile Court.' *Child Welfare* 53: 16–22

Kruttschnitt, C. 1984. 'Sex and Criminal Court ispositions: The Unresolved Controversy.' *Research in Crime and Delinquency* 21: 213–32

Kruttschnitt, C., and D. Green. 1984. 'The Sex- Sanctioning Issue: Is It History?' *American Sociological Review* 49: 541–51

Kruttschnitt, C., and D. McCarthy. 1985. 'Familial Social Control and Pretrial Sanctions: Does Sex Really Matter?' *Journal of Criminal Law and Criminology* 76: 151–75

LaFree, G. 1980. 'The Effect of Sexual Stratification by Race on Official Reactions to Rape.' *American Sociological Review* 45: 842–54

Lai, D. 1988. *Chinatowns: Towns within Cities in Canada*. Vancouver: University of British Columbia Press

Landon, F. 1925. 'Amherstburg, Terminus of the Underground Railroad.' *Journal of Negro History* 1: 1–9

Lee, R.M. 1994. 'One Bad Apple in Toronto Costs the West Millions in Investment.' *Globe and Mail*, 5 November

Lemert, E. 1951. *Social Pathology*. New York: McGraw-Hill

Lemert, E., and J. Rosberg. 1948. *The Administration of Justice to Minority Groups in L.A. County*. Berkeley: University of California Press

Lempert, R. 1990. 'Docket Data and "Local Knowledge": Studying the Court and Society Link Over Time.' *Law and Society Review* 24: 321–32

Levin, M. 1972. 'Urban Politics and Judicial Behaviour,' *Journal of Legal Studies* 1: 220–1

– 1977. *Urban Politics and the Criminal Courts*. Chicago: University of Chicago Press

Levitt, C., and W. Shaffir. 1987. *The Riot at Christie Pits*. Toronto: Lester and Orpen Dennys

Li, P. 1988. *The Chinese in Canada*. Toronto: Oxford University Press

Light, I. 1974. 'From Vice District to Tourist Attraction: The Moral Career of American Chinatowns.' *Pacific Historical Review* 43: 367–94

Linden, R., ed. 1992. *Criminology: A Canadian Perspective*. Toronto: Harcourt Brace Jovanovich

Lindesmith, A. 1967. *The Addict and the Law*. New York: Vintage

Liska, A., ed. 1992. *Social Threat and Social Control*. Albany: State University of New York Press

Lizotte, A. 1978. 'Extra-Legal Factors in Chicago's Criminal Courts: Testing the Conflict Model of Criminal Justice.' *Social Problems* 25: 564–80

Loew's Montreal Theatre v *Reynold*. 1919. *Quebec K.B.* 30: 459

London. 1908–61. Jail Records

London Advertiser. 1892–1930

London Free Press. 1892–1961

Lukas, E. 1945. 'Questions and Answers.' *Journal of Criminal Law, Criminology and Police Science* 35: 272–4

Lusane, C. 1991. *Pipe Dream Blues*. Boston: South End

MacFarlane, B.A. 1979. *Drug Offences in Canada*. Toronto: Canada Law Book

Maclean's. 1956. 'Let's Face Our Own Color Problem First.' 12 May, 1

– 1992. 'Frustration in Blue.' 16 November, 21–2

MacLennan, D. 1943. 'Racial Discrimination in Canada.' *Canadian Forum* 23: 164–5

Mahood, V. 1950. 'Toward Better Race Relations.' *Food for Thought* 10: 24–5

Makin, K. 1994. 'Questions Surround Laws Case.' *Globe and Mail*, 2 April

– 1996. 'Black Imprisonment Trends Shocking, Says Racism Report.' *Globe and Mail*, 16 January

Manitoba. 1991. *Report of the Aboriginal Justice Inquiry of Manitoba*. Winnipeg: Queen's Printer

Mann, C. 1993. *Unequal Justice: A Question of Color*. Bloomington: Indiana University Press

Mascoll, P. 1994. 'Cafe Killers Linked to Another Robbery,' *Toronto Star*, 8 April

Matza, D. 1967. *Becoming Deviant*. Englewood Cliffs, NJ: Prentice-Hall

McConville, M., and J. Baldwin. 1982. 'The Influence of Race on Sentencing in England.' *Criminal Law Review* 26: 147–55

McGeachy, J.B. 1931. 'The Race Wrangle.' *Maclean's* 44, 15 April, 34

McInnes, C. 1994. 'Narcotic-Trade Stigma Burden on Innocent.' *Globe and Mail*, 22 November

McKenzie, R. 1940. 'Race Prejudice and the Negro.' *The Dalhouise Review* 20: 197–205

McRuer, J.C. 1949. 'Sentences.' *Canadian Bar Review* 27: 1001–19

Middleton, G. 1992. 'Enter the Dragons.' *Vancouver Province*, 1 March

Miethe, T., and C. Moore. 1985. 'Socioeconomic Disparities under Determinant Sentencing Systems: A Comparison of the Preguideline and Postguideline Practices in Minnesota.' *Criminology* 23: 337–63

Miliband, R. 1972. 'Reply to Poulantzas.' In *Ideology in Social Sciences: Readings in Critical Social Theory*, ed. R. Blackburn. New York: Pantheon

Milner, J.B. 1947. 'Civil Liberties.' *Canadian Bar Review* 25: 915–24

Mitchell, G. 1923. 'Canada – Saviour of the Nordic Race.' *Canadian Magazine* 61, 138–40

Monkkonen, E. 1995. 'Racial Factors in New York City Homicides, 1800–1874.' In *Ethnicity, Race and Crime*, ed. D. Hawkins, 99–120. Albany: State University of New York Press

Moore, C., and T. Miethe. 1986. 'Regulated and Unregulated Sentencing Decisions: An Analysis of First-Year Practices under Minnesota's Felony Sentencing Guidelines.' *Law and Society Review* 20: 253–77

Moore, J.W., R. Garcia, L. Cerda, and F. Valencia. 1978. *Homeboys: Gangs, Drugs and Prisons in the Barrios of Los Angeles*. Philadelphia: Temple University Press

Moses, E. 1947. 'Differentials in Crime Rates between Negroes and Whites, Based on Comparisons of Four Socioeconomically Equated Areas.' *American Sociological Review* 12: 411–20

Mosher, C. 1992. 'The Legal Response to Narcotic Drugs in Five Ontario Cities – 1908–61.' PhD dissertation, University of Toronto

– 1995. *Crime and Colour, Cops and Courts – Systemic Racism in the Ontario Criminal Justice System in Social and Historical Context – 1892–1961*. Report for the Commission on Systemic Racism in Ontario's Criminal Justice System

– 1996. 'Minorities and Misdemeanours: The Treatment of Black Public Order Offenders in Ontario's Criminal Justice System – 1892–1930.' *Canadian Journal of Criminology* 38: 413–38

– 1997. 'The Social Production of Drug Crime: City-Level Variation in Possession and Trafficking Offenses in the United States – 1989.' Unpublished paper

Mosher, C., and J. Hagan. 1994. 'Constituting Class and Crime in Upper Canada: The Sentencing of Narcotics Offenders, circa 1908–1953.' *Social Forces* 72: 613–41

Moton, R. 1929. *What the Negro Thinks*. Garden City, NY: Doubleday, Doran

Multiculturalism and Citizenship Canada. 1989. *Eliminating Racial Discrimination in Canada*. Ottawa: Supply and Services Canada

Murphy, Edgar. 1909. *Problems of the Present South*. New York: Macmillan

Murphy, E. 1922a. *The Black Candle*. Toronto: Thomas Allen

– 1922b. 'Joy Shots That Lead to Hell.' *Maclean's*, 15 June

– 1922c. 'Curbing Illicit Vendors of Drugs.' *Maclean's*, 5 July, 18–19

Murray, G. 1987. 'Cocaine Use in the Era of Social Reform: The Natural History of a Social Problem in Canada, 1880–1911.' *Canadian Journal of Law and Society* 2: 29–43

Musto, D. 1987. *The American Disease*. New Haven, CT: Yale University Press

Myers, M. 1989. 'Symbolic Policy and the Sentencing of Drug Offenders.' *Law and Society Review* 23: 295–315

Myers, M., and S. Talarico. 1986. 'The Social Contexts of Racial Discrimination in Sentencing.' *Social Problems* 33: 236–51

– 1987. *The Social Contexts of Criminal Sentencing*. New York: Springer Verlag

Myrdal, G. 1944. *An American Dilemma*. New York: Harper and Brothers

Nagel, I., J. Cardascia, and C. Ross. 1982. 'Sex Differences in the Criminal Processing of Defendants.' In *Women and the Law: A Social-Historical Perspective*, ed. D.K. Weisberg, 259–82. Cambridge, MA: Schenkman

Nagel, I., and J. Hagan. 1983. 'Gender and Crime: Offense Patterns and Criminal Court Sanctions.' In *Crime and Justice: Annual Review of Research*, vol. 4, ed. M. Tonry and N. Morris, 91–144. Chicago: University of Chicago Press

Nagel, S. 1969. *The Legal Process from a Behavioral Perspective*. Homewood, Il: The Dorsey Press

Negro Yearbook. 1931–2. Alabama: Tuskegee Institute

Nelson, J. 1921a. 'Will Canada Go Yellow?' *Maclean's*, 34, 15 October, 15

– 1921b. 'Will Canada Go Yellow?' *Maclean's* 34 1 November, 11

– 1922. 'Shall We Bar the Yellow Race?' *Maclean's* 35, 15 May, 13

Nichol, W.C. 1900. 'The Chinaman in the Household.' *Canadian Magazine* 15, 113–14

Noble and Wolf v *Alley et al.* 1951. *Canada Law Reports* 29: 64

Nova Scotia. 1989. *Provincial Royal Commission on the Donald Marshall Jr. Prosecution.* Halifax

O'Halloran, C.H. 1945. 'Punishment of Criminal Offenders.' *Canadian Bar Review* 23: 555–63

Ontario. 1951. 'An Act to Promote Fair Employment Practices in Ontario.' *Statutes of Ontario*

– 1995. *Report of the Commission on Systemic Racism in the Ontario Criminal Justice System.* Toronto

Ontario Ministry of Citizenship. 1991. *Ontario: A Diverse and Changing Society: A Report on Selected Demographic Changes.* Toronto: Queen's Printer for Ontario

Ottawa. 1892–1961. Jail Records

Ottawa Citizen. 1892–1961

Ottawa Journal. 1892–1961

Partington, D. 1965. 'The Incidence of the Death Penalty for Rape in Virginia.' *Washington and Lee Law Review* 22: 43–75

Patton, M. 1990. *Qualitative Evaluation and Research Methods.* London: Sage

Pestle, P. 1925. 'The Colour Problem.' *Canadian Forum* 5: 336–7

Petersilia, J., P. Greenwood, and M. Lavin. 1977. *Criminal Careers of Habitual Felons.* Santa Monica, CA: Rand

Peterson, M., and H. Braiker. 1980. *Doing Crime: A Survey of California Prison Inmates.* Santa Monica, CA: Rand

Peterson, R., and J. Hagan. 1984. 'Changing Conceptions of Race: Towards an Account of Anomalous Findings of Sentencing Research.' *American Sociological Review* 49: 56–70

Petgrave, M. 1944. 'Must Overcome Race Prejudice.' *The Dawn of Tomorrow*, September

Picard, A. 1991. 'Fears on Both Sides, Police Shootings Show' *Globe and Mail*, 8 November

– 1992. 'Just the Usual Story, Except ...' *Globe and Mail*, 24 April

Platt, A. 1974. 'The Triumph of Benevolence: The Origins of the Juvenile Justice System in the United States.' In *Criminal Justice in America*, ed. R. Quinney 356–89. Boston: Little, Brown

Poirier, P. 1992. 'Cry for Help Has Been Heard.' *Globe and Mail*, 8 May

Pope, C. 1975. *Sentencing of California Felony Offenders.* Washington, DC: U.S. Department of Justice

Popple, A. 1921. 'Police Court Systems.' *Canadian Law Times* 41: 32
– 1927. 'The Police Court.' *Canadian Law Times* 47: 33
Port Arthur News Chronicle. 1892–1961
Porter, J. 1965. *The Vertical Mosaic.* Toronto: University of Toronto Press
Potter, H. 1964. 'Negroes in Canada.' In *Social Problems: A Canadian Profile*, ed. R.
    Laskin, 139–47. Toronto: McGraw-Hill
Poulantzas, N. 1973. *Political Power and Social Classes.* London: Verso
Pound, R. 1930. *Criminal Justice in America.* New York: Henry Holt
– 1942. *Social Control through Law.* New Haven, CT: Yale University Press
Pound, R., and F. Frankfurter. 1922. *Criminal Justice in Cleveland.* Montclair, NJ:
    Patterson Smith
Pruitt, C., and J. Wilson. 1983. 'A Longitudinal Study of the Effect of Race on Sentenc-
    ing.' *Law and Society Review* 17: 613–35
Quinney, R. 1970. *The Social Reality of Crime.* Boston: Little, Brown
– 1974. *Critique of the Legal Order.* Boston: Little, Brown
Quong Wing v *the King.* 1914. *Supreme Court Reports* 49: 441
R v *Gilroy and Patrick.* 1949. *Canadian Criminal Cases* 95: 250
R v *Parks.* 1993. *Canadian Criminal Cases* 84: 368
R v *Shewchuck.* 1948. *Canadian Criminal Cases* 92: 157
Re Byers and *Morris.* 1931. *Ontario Weekly Notes* 40: 572
Re Drummond Wren. 1945. *Ontario Reports*, 778
Re McDougall and Waddell. 1945. *Ontario Weekly Notes*, 272
Reasons, C. 1976. 'Images of Crime and the Criminal: The Dope Fiend Mythology.'
    Journal of Research in Crime and Delinquency 13: 133–42
Regina ex rel. Nutland v *McKay.* 1956. *Canadian Criminal Cases* 115: 104
Regina v *Emerson.* 1955. *Canadian Criminal Cases* 113: 69
Regina v *Jones.* 1956. *Ontario Weekly Notes*, 396
Regina v *McKay.* 1955. *Canadian Criminal Cases* 113: 56
Reiner, R. 1989. 'Race and Criminal Justice.' *New Community* 16: 5–21
Reinhart, J. 1927–8. 'The Negro: Is He a Biological Inferior?' *American Journal of Soci-
    ology* 33: 248–61
Reitz, J. 1980. *The Survival of Ethnic Groups.* Toronto: McGraw-Hill Ryerson
Reitz, J., and R. Breton. 1994. *The Illusion of Difference.* Toronto: C.D. Howe
    Institute
Renner, K.E., and A.H. Warner. 1981. 'The Standard of Social Justice Applied to an
    Evaluation of Criminal Cases before the Halifax Courts.' *Windsor Yearbook of Access
    to Justice.* Windsor: University of Windsor
Reynolds, C.N. 1934–5. 'The Chinese Tongs.' *American Journal of Sociology* 40:
    612–23
Rex v *Brown.* 1908. *Ontario Law Reports* 17: 197

Rex v *DeYoung, Liddiard, and Darling.* 1927. *Ontario Law Reports* 40: 155

Rex v *Louie Chong.* 1914. *Ontario Law Reports* 32: 66

Rex v *Phillips.* 1930. *Ontario Weekly Notes* 38: 323

Rex v *Sam Sing.* 1910. *Ontario Law Reports* 22: 613

Rex v *Wing.* 1913. *Ontario Law Reports* 29: 553

Rex v *Wong and Seto.* 1950. *Ontario Weekly Notes* 1950: 24

Rex v *Yok Yuen.* 1929. *Ontario Weekly Notes* 37: 257

Riddell, W.R. 1919. 'The Slave in Upper Canada.' *Journal of Negro History* 4: 372–95

Roberts, D. 1997. 'Natives Scorn Killers Sentences.' *Toronto Star*, 31 January

Roberts, J. 1994. 'Crime and Race Statistics: Toward a Canadian Solution.' *Canadian Journal of Criminology* 36: 175–85

Roberts, J., and T. Doob. 1996. 'Race, Ethnicity, and Criminal Justice in Canada.' In *Race, Ethnicity and Criminal Justice*, ed. N. Morris. New York: Oxford University Press

Rogers v *Clarence Hotel Co. Ltd.* 1940. *Dominion Law Reports* 3: 583

Root, W.T. 1927. *A Psychological and Educational Survey of 1,916 Prisoners in the Western Penitentiary of Pennsylvania.* Pittsburgh: n.p.

Roy, P. 1989. *A White Man's Province.* Vancouver: University of British Columbia Press

Ryan, S. 1965 'The Adult Court.' In *Crime and Its Treatment in Canada*, ed. W.T. McGrath, 136–206. Toronto: Methuen

Saalheimer, M. 1949. 'Laws Also Educate.' *Food for Thought* 10: 39–43

– 1952. 'Group Discrimination and Canadian Law,' *Food for Thought* 13: 6–9

Sacco, V. 1992. *Deviance: Conformity and Control in Canadian Society.* Scarborough: Prentice-Hall

Sampson, R. 1986. 'Effects of Socioeconomic Context on Official Reaction to Juvenile Delinquency.' *American Sociological Review* 51: 876–85

Samuelson, L. 1985. 'New Parallels between the Marxist and Non-Marxist Theories of Law and State.' In *The New Criminologies in Canada*, ed. T. Flemming, 270–84. Toronto: Oxford University Press

Sapir, E. 1925. 'Are the Nordics a Superior Race?' *Canadian Forum* 5: 265–6

Sarick, L. 1993. 'Minority Teenagers Accuse Police of Unfair Treatment.' *Globe and Mail*, 3 November

– 1994. 'Deportation Crackdown Unveiled.' *Globe and Mail*, 8 July

Saturday Night. 1888. 'The Colored Population of Toronto.' 9 June, 1

– 1892. 'Chinese Immigration.' 5 (8 October), 2

– 1905. 'The Chinese in Toronto.' 23 December, 11

– 1906. 'Editorial.' 27 October, 1

– 1925. 'Girls, Be Careful Who You Marry.' 15 August, 1

– 1936. 'The Color Ban.' 1 August, 3

Satzewich, V. 1991. 'Social Stratification: Class and Racial Inequality.' In *Social Issues and Contradictions in Canadian Society*, ed. S. Bolaria, 91–107. Toronto: Harcourt Brace Jovanovich

Sawer, G. 1965. *Law in Society*. Oxford: The Clarendon Press

Schissel, B. 1993. *Social Dimensions of Canadian Youth Justice*. Toronto: Oxford University Press

Scrivener, L. 1997. 'Rally Slams Police Review Law.' *Toronto Star*, 2 February

Sellin, T. 1928. 'The Negro Criminal: A Statistical Note.' *Annals of the American Academy of Political and Social Science* 139: 52–64

– 1935. 'Race Prejudice in the Administration of Justice.' *American Journal of Sociology* 41: 212–17

Sellin, T., and M. Wolfgang. 1964. *The Measurement of Delinquency*. New York: Wiley

Shaw, C. 1924. 'Canada's Oriental Problem.' *Canadian Magazine*, October, 334–8

Shepard, R. 1991. 'Plain Racism: The Reaction against Oklahoma Black Immigration to the Canadian Plains.' In *Racism in Canada*, ed. O. McKague, 11–31. Saskatoon: Fifth House

Sher, J. 1983. *White Hoods: Canada's Ku Klux Klan*. Vancouver: New Star

Sifton, C. 1922. 'The Immigrants Canada Wants.' *Maclean's* 35 (1 April 1), 16

Silverman, R., and M. Nielsen. 1992. *Aboriginal Peoples and the Canadian Criminal Justice System*. Toronto: Butterworths

Simpson, G. 1936. *The Negro in the Philadelphia Press*. Philadelphia: University of Pennsylvania Press

Singer, L. 1973. 'Women and the Correctional Process.' *American Criminal Law Review* 11: 295–308

Sissons, P.L. 1979. *The Hispanic Experiences of Criminal Justice*. New York: Fordham University Hispanic Research Centre

Skocpol, T. 1984. 'Sociology's Historical Imagination.' In *Vision and Method in Historical Sociology*, ed. T. Skocpol, 1–21. Cambridge: Cambridge University Press

Skolnick, J. 1975. *Justice without Trial: Law Enforcement in a Democratic Society*. New York: John Wiley and Sons

Smandych, R. 1985. 'Marxism and the Creation of Law: Re-Examining the Origins of Canadian Anti-Combines Legislation, 1890–1910.' In *The New Criminologies in Canada*, ed. T. FLeming, 87–99. Toronto: Oxford University Press

Smart, R. 1983. *Forbidden Highs*. Toronto: Addiction Research Foundation

Smedley, A. 1993. *Race in North America*. Boulder: Westview

Solomon, R., and T. Madison. 1976–7. 'The Evolution of Non-Medical Opiate Use in Canada: Part I – 1870–1929.' *Drug Forum* 5: 237–65

Spector, M., and J. Kitsuse. 1977. *Constructing Social Problems*. Menlo Park, CA: Benjamin Cummings

Spitzer, S. 1983. 'Marxist Perspectives and the Sociology of Law.' *Annual Review of Sociology* 9: 103–24

Spohn, C. 1994. 'Crime and the Social Control of Blacks: Offender/Victim Race and the Sentencing of Violent Offenders.' In *Inequality, Crime and Social Control*, ed. G. Bridges and M. Myers, 249–68. Boulder: Westview

Spohn, C., J. Gruhl, and S. Welch. 1981–82. 'The Effect of Race on Sentencing: A Re-Examination of an Unsettled Question.' *Law and Society Review* 16: 71–88

Staebler, E. 1956. 'Would You Change the Life of These People?' *Maclean's*, 12 May, 30

Stall, B. 1995. 'Cops Will Be Red-Faced.' *Vancouver Province* 23 April, 1995

Steiner, J.F., and R.M. Brown. 1927. *The North Carolina Chain Gang*. Chapel Hill: University of North Carolina Press

Stevens, H. 1911–12. 'Oriental Immigration,' *Canadian Club of Toronto Addresses* 9: 138–46

Surrette, R. 1992. *Media, Crime, and Criminal Justice*. Pacific Grove, CA: Brooks/Cole

Sutherland, H. 1941. 'The Shing Wah Daily News Reflects the Life of Toronto's Chinese Community.' *Saturday Night* 57 (20 September), 4

Tannenbaum, F. 1938. *Crime and the Community*. Boston: Ginn

Taylor, I., P. Walton, and J. Young. 1973. *The New Criminology*. London: Routledge and Kegan Paul

Temin, C. 1973. 'Discriminatory Sentencing of Women Offenders: The Argument for ERA in a Nutshell.' *American Criminal Law Review* 11: 355–72

Terry, C., and M. Pellens. 1970. *The Opium Problem*. Montclair, NJ: Patterson Smith

Terry, R. 1967. 'Discrimination in the Handling of Juvenile Offenders by Social Control Agencies.' *Journal of Research in Crime and Delinquency* 4: 218–30

The Canadian Negro. 1953–6

Thompson, R. 1989. *Toronto's Chinatown*. New York: AMS

Thomson, C.A. 1979. *Blacks in Deep Snow: Black Pioneers in Canada*. Don Mills, ON: J.M. Dent and Sons

Thorsell, W. 1995. 'Let the Facts Speak for Themselves.' *Globe and Mail*, 18 February

Thunder Bay. 1892–1961. Jail Records

Tittle, C. 1994. 'The Theoretical Bases for Inequality in Formal Social Control.' In *Inequality, Crime and Social Control*, ed. G. Bridges and M. Myers, 21–52. Boulder: Westview

Tolmie, J.R. 1929. 'The Orientals in British Columbia.' Bachelor of History thesis, University of British Columbia

Tolnay, S., and E. Beck. 1992. 'Toward a Threat Model of Southern Lynchings.' In *Social Threat and Social Control*, ed. A. Liska, 33–52. Albany: State University of New York Press

Tonry, M. 1995. *Malign Neglect: Race, Crime and Punishment in America*. New York: Oxford University Press

Toronto. 1892–1961. Jail Records

– 1908–29. *Minutes of the Board of Police Commissioners*

– 1908–56 *Annual Report of the Chief Constable*

Toronto Daily Star. 1892–1961

Toronto Mail and Empire. 1892–1961

Toronto Telegram. 1892–1961

Trasov, C. 1962. 'The History of the Opium and Narcotic Drug Legislation in Canada.' *Criminal Law Quarterly* 4: 274–90

Troper, H. 1972. 'The Creek Negroes of Oklahoma and Canadian Immigration, 1909–11.' *Canadian Historical Review* 53: 272–89

Tulloch, H. 1975. *Black Canadians*. Toronto: NC Press

Turk, A. 1969. *Criminality and the Legal Order*. Chicago: Rand McNally

Tyler, T. 1997. 'Duty Lawyer Access May Face Means Test.' *Toronto Star*, 23 February

Unnever, J. 1982. 'Direct and Organizational Discrimination in the Sentencing of Drug Offenders.' *Social Problems* 30: 212–25

Unnever, J., C. Frazier, and J. Henretta. 1980. 'Race Differences in Criminal Sentencing.' *Sociological Quarterly* 21: 197–207

Valpy, M. 1994. 'Presumption of Innocence, Anyone?' *Globe and Mail*, 12 July

Vancouver Sun. 1992. 'Singling Out Offender's Race Called Dodge for Discrimination.' 22 October

– 1995a. 'Poor Police Judgement.' 20 April

– 1995b. 'Letter to the Editor.' 12 May

Vincent, C. 1994. *Police Officer*. Ottawa: Carleton University Press

Vincent, I. 1995. 'Violent Home Invasions on the Rise in Cities.' *Globe and Mail*, 5 December

Vold, G. 1958. *Theoretical Criminology*. New York: Oxford University Press

Walker, J. 1980. *A History of Blacks in Canada*. Ottawa: Minister of Supply and Services

Walker, M. 1983. 'The Court Disposal of Young Males, By Race, in London in 1983.' *British Journal of Criminology* 28: 441–60

Walkom, T. 1992. 'Blaming Hooliganism Seems a Little Too Easy.' *Toronto Star*, 6 May

Ward, P. 1978. *White Canada Forever*. Montreal: McGill–Queen's University Press

Weaver, J. 1995. *Crimes, Constables, and Courts*. Montreal: McGill–Queen's University Press

Weber, M. 1949. *The Methodology of the Social Sciences*. Trans. by E. Shils and H. Finch. New York: Free Press

Weber, R.E. 1971. 'Riot in Victoria, 1860.' *Journal of Negro History* 56: 141–8

Welch, S., J. Gruhl, and C. Spohn. 1984. 'Sentencing: The Influence of Alternative Measures of Prior Record.' *Criminology* 22: 215–27

Wheeler, S., D. Weisburd, and N. Bode. 1982. 'Sentencing the White-Collar Offender: Rhetoric and Reality.' *American Sociological Review* 47: 641–59

Wilkes, J. 1992. 'Shootings by Police "Troubling," Rae States.' *Toronto Star*, 4 May

Williams, J. 1985. 'Redefining Institutional Racism.' *Ethnic and Racial Studies* 8: 323–47

Willmott, W.E. 1970. 'Approaches to the Study of the Chinese in British Columbia.' *BC Studies* 4: 42–63

Wilson-Smith, A. 1994. 'Debating the Numbers.' *Maclean's*, 7 November, 22

Windsor. 1892–1961. Jail Records

Windsor Evening Record. 1892–1930

Winks, R. 1968. 'The Canadian Negro: A Historical Assessment.' *Journal of Negro History* 53: 283–300

– 1969. 'The Canadian Negro: A Historical Assessment – Part II: The Problem of Identity.' *Journal of Negro History* 55: 1–18

– 1971. *The Blacks in Canada: A History.* Montreal: McGill–Queen's University Press

Wodson, H. 1917. *The Whirlpool: Scenes from the Toronto Police Court.* Toronto: Coles

Wolfgang, M., and M. Riedel. 1973. 'Race, Judicial Discretion, and the Death Penalty.' *The Annals of the American Academy of Political and Social Science* 407: 119–33

Woman's Christian Temperance Union. 1913. *Annual Report of the WCTU*

Wood, C. 1989. 'Police under Fire.' *Maclean's*, 9 January

Woodsworth, C.J. 1941. *Canada and the Orient: A Study in International Relations.* Toronto: Macmillan

Woollacot, A.P. 1930. 'Canadian-Born Orientals.' *Canadian Forum* 11: 52–4

Work, M.N. 1913. 'Negro Criminality in the South.' *Annals of the American Academy of Political and Social Science* 49: 74–80

Wortley, S. 1996. 'Justice for All? Race and Perceptions of Bias in the Ontario Criminal Justice System.' *Canadian Journal of Criminology* 38: 439–67

Yerbury, C., and C.T. Griffiths. 1991. 'Minorities, Crime, and the Law.' In *Canadian Criminology*, ed. M. Jackson and C.T. Griffiths, 315–46. Toronto: Harcourt Brace Jovanovich

Zatz, M. 1984. 'Race, Ethnicity and Determinate Sentencing: A New Dimension to an Old Controversy.' *Criminology* 22: 147–71

Index

Abel, E., 39
accommodations, access to, 98
Adamson, J.E., 135
age, 209; influence on sentencing, 137
Alberta, task force on the criminal justice system, 43
Albonetti, C., 211
Aldrich, J., 206
Althusser, L., 37
Amemiya, T., 206
Amiel, B., 21
Anderson, A.B., 24, 73, 93
Anderson, K., 24
Angus, H.F., 73
Angus, W., 123
Appleby, T, 7–9, 16, 19, 20, 21
Archambault, J., 136
army, Blacks in, 100
Asians: and gangs, 12–13; home invasions, 13–14; overrepresentation of in crime statistics, 12
Asiatic Exclusion League, 66, 69
assimilation, and the Chinese, 69–70, 79
Austin, J., 199

Backhouse, C., 43
Baird, K.A., 116

Balbus, I., 37
Baldwin, J., 42, 45
Baranek, P., 22, 23, 51
Barber, J., 18, 19
Baylis, T., killing of, 9–11
Beach, W., 176
Beck, E., 36, 88
Becker, H., 35, 39
Bedford, J., 43
Beirne, P., 37
Bellet, G., 16
Bennett, L., 201
Bernstein, I., 41, 53
Berridge, V., 140
Berrill, N.J., 116
Bertley, L.W., 91, 92
Bienvenue, R., 24
biological theories of race differences, 47, 64–5, 111, 115–16, 224
Blacks: devaluation of testimony of, 172–3, 179–80, 186–8; negative images of in media, 87; overrepresentation of in criminal justice system, 4, 6, 9, 25–7, 199; physical characteristics of, 131; purported weakness of intellect of, 134; ridiculing of, 132–3; in schools, 84–5, 116; in Victoria,

British Columbia, 86; in Western Canada, 90–2; *see also* Ontario, Fair Employment Practices Act, immigration, interracial mixing; restrictive land covenants; slavery, United States
Blalock, H., 36
Blumstein, A., 139, 202, 211
Bode, N., 205
Boland, B., 209
Bonger, W., 47
Bonnie, R., 39
Boritch, H., 77, 206
Boyd, N., 34, 39, 40, 139, 141
Braiker, H., 209
Brecher, E., 140
Breton, R., 24
Bridges, M., 32
British Columbia: Asian crime in, 12–13; sessional papers, 67
Brockman, J., 23
Brown, R.M., 49
Bryant, I., 124
Bullock, H., 41
Bumiller, K., 41, 42, 53, 207, 208, 211
Burke, P., 41
Burtch, B., 23, 24
Byron, W., 64–5

Calkins, A., 140
Canada: Census of Canada, 26; criminal code, 112, Department of Health reports, 159; Department of Multiculturalism and Citizenship, 3; House of Commons Debates, 67, 91, 92, 99–100, 143, 144, 145; *Report on the Need for Suppression of the Opium Traffic in Canada*, 141; Royal Commission on Chinese Immigration, 66, 229; Statutes of Canada, 94, 142, 143, 144, 149

Canadian Bar Association, 123, 136
Canadian criminology; lack of attention to race in, 22–5
Canadian Law Times and Review, 70, 123
Canadian Negro, The, 94, 103, 108, 109, 111, 117
Cardascia, J., 209
Carrigan, O., 12, 23
Chambers, E.A., 206
Chambliss, W., 35, 36, 38, 42
Chapman, P., 13
Chapman, T., 39, 139, 145
Chicago Commission on Race Relations, 51, 52, 124, 125
Chinese: bribery cases involving, 78–9; eastward migration of 71–2; employment of White females by, 74–6; and franchise, 67–8; name pronunciation, 127–8, 226–7; purported moral inferiority of, 65, 129; and restrictive legislation, 68–9, 73–7; tongs, 166–7; wages, 66; *see also* Asiatic Exclusion League; deportation; gambling; head taxes; immigration; interracial mixing; language discrimination; Lord's Day Act; narcotics
Chunn, D., 23
Cicourel, A., 35
Clairmont, D., 24
Claridge, T., 10
Clark, C.S., 223, 226
Clark, S.D., 24
Clarke, A., 21, 115
Clarke, S., 41
Clayton, O., 58
Cohen, J., 211
Colbourn, G., 17
Coleman, J., 59
Comack, E., 39, 66, 67, 69, 139
Commission on Systemic Racism,

(Ontario), 4, 19, 25–6, 29, 42, 43, 45, 196; reactions to, 199, 200
conflict theory, 34–41, 42; and narcotics legislation, 143
Cook, S., 39, 143
Coolidge, M.R., 158, 228
Corelli, R., 9
corporal punishment, 189, 229–30
courts: Denison, 121–3, 226; in Hamilton, 121, 123, 130, 226; in Toronto, 120–3, 130; in United States, 120; in Windsor, 130
Cove, J., 45
Cox, D.R., 206
Cox, O.C., 226
Craven, P., 61, 121, 228
crime statistics, and race, 7, 12, 43, 202–3
Crowe, I., 45
Cuff, J.H., 18
cultural racism, 29
Curry, J.N., 122

Daly, K., 209
Dawn of Tomorrow, The, 108
DeKort, M., 227
Delesser, H.G., 87, 227
Denison, G., 121, 131–2; views on Blacks, 131–2; see also courts
deportation, 10, 144–5; informal, 164, 229
DiManno, R., 19
Dion, K., 198
Ditton, J., 35
Dixon, J., 202
Doob, A., 199, 200
Doyle, P., 41, 53
Dresden, discrimination towards Blacks in, 109–11
Driedger, L., 24
Durkheim, E., 33
Duster, T., 141

Earle, W.K., 63, 70, 71, 224
East Asians, 224
Edmonds, W.L., 87
education of Blacks, 101
Edwards, G., 140
Eisler, D., 221
Elliott, J., 24
employment, of Blacks, 99–103, 225; of Chinese, 66, 69, 74, 127
Endicott, S., 67, 139, 142
Ericson, R., 22, 23, 51
extra-legal variables, 207–10

Fair Accommodation Practices Act, 107, 108–9, 111
Fair Employment Practices Act, 102
Farnsworth, C., 16, 17
Farrell, R., 210
Feeley, M., 56, 120
female offenders, public-order offences, 173
Fennell, T., 19, 20
Fingard, J., 43
Fisher, L., 3
Fisher, M., 90
Fleras, A., 24
Forcese, D., 19, 20, 23, 24
Foster, C., 10–11, 198, 201, 203, 222
Frankfurter, F., 120, 125
Frazier, C., 41
Freer, B., 221
Frideres, J., 24, 73, 93
Friedman, L., 54, 119, 120, 223
Friedrichs, D., 222
functionalist approach to law, 33–4

Gabor, T., 43, 203
gambling, and Blacks, 129, 160–1, 170–1; and Chinese, 126, 166–70
gangs: Asian, 12–13; Native, 221

Garcia, J.L.A., 28
Garfinkel, H., 41, 54
gender and sentencing decisions, 209
Gibson, J., 41
Giffen, J., 67, 139, 142
Gilmour, C., 80, 229
Gist, J., 125
Goff, C., 39
Goldstein, J., 24, 51
Gomme, I., 23, 24
Gramsci, A., 38
Grange, M., 14
Green, D., 209
Green, E., 41, 209
Green, M., 40, 69, 139, 140, 141, 142
Greenberg, D., 37
Greenspon, E., 221
Greenwood, P., 209
Griffiths, C.T., 22, 23, 43
group-conflict theory, 35
Grow, S., 93
Gruhl, J., 41, 205, 210

Hackler, J., 23
Hagan, J., 23, 33, 38, 39, 41, 42, 51, 52,
    57, 58, 62, 120, 151, 157, 160, 205,
    207, 208, 209, 211
Halevy, M., 45, 222
Hall, S., 33, 38
Haller, M., 119
Hamilton, annual police report, 167,
    168
Hanushek, E., 206
Harkness, R., 90
Harris, F., 61
Hartnagel, T., 22
Hastings, P., 221
hate groups, 4
Hatt, K., 43
Hawkins, D., 42, 47, 55, 195

Hayner, N.S., 167, 176, 177, 229
head taxes, 67–9, 91
hegemony, Gramsci's concept of, 38
Helmer, J., 39
Henretta, J., 41
Henry, F., 3, 5, 6, 17, 25, 28, 29, 68, 83,
    100, 138, 221, 222
Hess, H., 14
Hewitt, R., 89
Hill, D., 43, 84, 89, 94–5, 96, 98, 100,
    102, 103, 115, 222, 225
Hinch, R., 36, 37, 222
historical sociology, 59
Hogarth, J., 211
Homel, G., 120, 121, 122
Hood, R., 42, 46, 56, 222
Hope, C.E., 63, 70, 71, 224
Hopkins, A., 34
Hopkins, E., 51
Hudson, B., 42, 46
Hudson, J., 23
Hunter, J., 222
Hurst, L., 12, 202

Ignatieff, M., 32
immigration, and Blacks, 83–4, 89–95,
    225; and Chinese, 64–73, 142; and
    crime, 11; restrictions on, 4, 5, 10
imprisonment decisions: drug offenders,
    152–3; public-order offenders, 162–4;
    property offenders, 178–81; violent
    offenders, 186–8
individual racism, 28
individualized justice, 135, 136–7
institutional racism, 28–9
Insurance Act, 108
interracial mixing, and Blacks, 84, 92, 98,
    112–15, 192–4, 226, 230; and Chinese,
    74, 77–80
Irwin, J., 52, 199

Jackson, J., 206
Jackson, M., 22, 23
jail records, 60
Jamaicans: and crime, 7–9, 11, 221
Japanese, and crime, 229; immigration, 70, 71
Jessop, B., 38
Jews, discrimination against, 107
Joint Labour Committee for Human Rights, 109, 110
Johnson, E., 41
Johnson, G., 41, 48, 50, 52, 54, 195
Johnston, L., 166
Johnston, J.P., 43
juries, Blacks serving on, 85

Kaihla, P., 198
Katz, S., 109
Kavanaugh, M., 48
Kawakami, K., 198
Kelly, H., 41
Kelly, W., 41, 53
King, Mackenzie, and immigration, 69; and narcotics legislation, 39, 141–2
Kitsuse, J., 34, 35
Kleck, G., 41, 42, 56–7, 160
Klepper, S., 207
Kobayashi, A., 29, 68–9
Koch, G., 41
Kratcoski, P., 209
Kruttschnitt, K., 209
Ku Klux Klan, 112–14, 226

labelling theory, 34–5
LaFree, G., 55
Lai, D., 24, 77, 227
Lambert, S., 67, 139, 142
Landon, F., 84, 85
language discrimination, and Blacks 133–4; and Asians, 128

Lavin, M., 209
Lee, R.M., 4, 11
legal variables, 207
Leimonis, G., killing of, 9, 14
Lemert, E., 34, 35, 41
Lempert, R., 61
Leon, J., 121
Levin, M., 41, 56
Levitt, C., 90
Levy, K., 204
Lew, C., 15
Li, P., 24, 63, 71–2, 74, 75, 76, 77, 81
Light, I., 228
Linden, R., 22
Lindesmith, A., 39
liquor offences, 228
Lizotte, A., 41
logistic regression, 206
Lombroso, C., 47
Lord's Day Act, 74
Lukas, E., 52, 54, 125
Lusane, C., 227

MacFarlane, B.A., 141
MacLennan, D., 100–1, 102
Madison, T., 39, 66, 139, 145, 146
Magill, D., 24
Makin, K., 19, 199
Manitoba, Aboriginal Justice Inquiry, 43
Mann, C., 5, 28, 117, 128
Manning, P., 6
marital status, 209
Marxist theories of law; instrumentalist, 35–7; structuralist, 37–8
Mascoll, P., 9
Matza, D., 180
McCarthy, D., 209
McConville, M., 42, 45
McInnes, C., 13
McKenzie, R., 89, 98

McRuer, J.C., 135–6,
medical professionals, and drug crime,
     155–6
Middleton, G., 12
Miethe, T., 202
Miliband, R., 36
Milner, J.B., 107
Monkkonen, E., 28
Moore, C., 202
Moore, J.W., 41
Moses, E., 47
Mosher, C., 43, 74, 151, 152, 157, 199,
     228
Moton, R., 54
Murphy, Edgar, 48
Murphy, Emily, 64–5, 145, 159; and nar-
     cotics legislation, 145, 159, 227–8
Murray, G., 141
Musto, D., 39, 139
Myers, M., 32, 42, 57, 58, 159, 160, 205
Myrdal, G., 48, 52, 53–4, 124, 191

Nagel, I., 209, 211
Nagin, D., 207
narcotics: and Blacks, 40, 145, 146–7,
     151; and Chinese, 12, 13, 40 65,
     126–7, 146–51; enforcement, 142,
     146–51, 228; legislation (Canada),
     39–40, 139–44; legislation (United
     States), 39, 40, 139, 199; offences,
     218; trafficking, 159–60
National Unity Association, 109, 110
Negro Yearbook, 48–9
Nelson, F., 206
Nelson, J., 71, 75, 79, 176, 223, 224
Nichol, W.C., 65
Nielsen, M., 22
Nova Scotia: Blacks in, 117–18; Donald
     Marshall Inquiry, 42, 43, 44
occupations, 210, 215–17

O'Halloran, C.H., 137
Ontario statutes, 102, 107–8, 109
Opium Act, 141–2
Ottawa, Black crime in, 11–12

Partington, D., 55
Patton, M., 61
Pellins, M., 140
Pestle, P., 111
Petersilia, J., 209
Peterson, M., 209
Peterson, R., 42, 57, 160, 205
Petgrave, M., 96
Picard, A., 16, 17
Platt, A., 38
Poirier, P., 17
police bias, 5, 14; historical, 43–4, 51–2;
     in Montreal, 16; in Toronto, 17–19; in
     United States, 52; in Vancouver, 15–16
police use of deadly force, in Montreal
     16–17; in Toronto, 19–20
Pope, C., 58
Popple, A., 123, 226
Porter, J., 24
Poulantzas, N., 37
Pound, R., 34, 120
previous offence, 210
property offences, Chinese, 158, 176–8,
     218–19
prostitution, 162, 228; and Blacks, 129,
     138, 171–4
Pruitt, C., 57–8
public-order offences, 219

qualitative data sources, 61–2
Quinney, R., 35, 41, 42

race, measurement of, 208–9
Racial Discrimination Act, 107
racialization of crime, 5, 221; Blacks,

7–12; Chinese, 12–14, 126–9; in
United States 124–5
Reasons, C., 39
Reform Party, 6, 221, 222
Reidel, M., 55
Reiner, R., 42, 52
Reinhart, J., 224
Reitz, J., 24
Renner, K.E., 44
restaurants, denial of service to Blacks,
105, 110–11
restrictive land covenants, 96–8
Reynolds, C.N., 167
Riddell, W.R., 83
Roberts, D., 204
Roberts, J., 23, 43, 199, 200, 202, 203
Root, W.T., 47
Rosberg, J., 41
Ross, C., 209
Roy, P., 66, 67, 68, 69, 71, 72
Royal Canadian Mounted Police, enforce-
ment of drug legislation, 146–7

Saalheimer, M., 98, 103, 108, 226
Sacco, V., 23
Sallott, J., 221
Sarick, L., 10, 18
Sampson, R., 52
Samuelson, L., 38
Satzewich, V., 225
Sawer, G., 34
Schissel, B., 23, 24, 43
Scraton, P., 33
Scrivener, L., 201
second offence, 210
Sellin, T., 41, 49, 50, 51, 53, 56, 124, 211
sentence length, 206–7; drug offenders,
153–60; property offenders, 181–3;
public-order offenders, 164–6; violent
offenders, 189–95

sentencing, disparities, 41, 135; social/
temporal context of, 56–8; studies of in
Britain, 45–6; —, in Canada, 42–5;
—, historical, 47–50; —, in United
States, 41–2
seriousness of offence, 211
services: barbers, 108, 109, 226; hotels,
104, 108; lack of access to, 103–11;
restaurants, 105, 110–11; taverns, 105,
106; theatres, 86, 104, 106
Shaffir, W., 90
Shaw, C., 74
Shepard, R., 91, 93
Sher, J., 4, 87, 226
Seidman, R.B., 35, 42
Sifton, C., 64
Silverman, R., 22
Simpson, G., 124
Singer, L., 209
Sissons, P.L., 41
Skocpol, T., 59
Skolnick, J., 51, 148
slavery, in Canada, 83
Smandych, R., 39
Smart, R., 142
Smedley, A., 88, 229
snow-removal by-law, 74
social-structural factors and minority
crime, 47–8
Solomon, R., 39, 66, 139, 145, 146
Spector, M., 34
Spitzer, S., 37
Spohn, C., 41, 55, 57, 195, 205, 210
Staebler, E., 117
Stall, B., 15
Steiner, J.F., 49
Stevens, H.H., 69–70, 79
Surrette, R., 61
Sutherland, E., 47
Sutherland, H., 80

Swigert, V., 210
systemic racism, 4, 29

Talarico, S., 42, 58, 159, 160, 205
Tannenbaum, F., 35
Taylor, I., 36
Temin, C., 209
Terry, C., 140
Terry, R., 209
Thompson, C.A., 93
Thompson, R., 71, 73, 76, 166
threat hypothesis, 36
Tierney, L.J., 207
Tittle, C., 36
Tolmie, J.R., 69
Tolnay, S., 36, 88
Tonry, M., 199
Toronto: *Annual Report of the Chief Con-
    stable*, 3, 74, 77, 122, 148, 158, 167,
    168, 169, 185, 186; Board of Educa-
    tion, 116–17; *Minutes of the Board of
    Police Commissioners*, 76, 77, 157,
    167, 171
Trasov, C., 39, 139
Troper, H., 89, 92, 93, 225
Turk, A., 35, 36, 41
Tyler, T., 201

Unnever, J., 41
United States, influence on Canadian per-
    ceptions of Blacks, 87–9, 92, 93, 95

vagrancy legislation, 38
Valpy, M., 11
Verdun-Jones, S., 22, 23, 43
victim–offender relationships, 53–5,
    189–95, 230
violent offences, 220; and Blacks, 1,
    7–10, 185–6; and Chinese, 12–14,
    183–5, 229
Vincent, C., 23

Vincent, I, 13
Vold, G., 35

Walker, J., 24, 84, 85, 87, 91, 96, 99, 100,
    224
Walker, M., 42, 45–6
Walkom, T., 21
Walton, P., 36
Ward, P., 65, 69, 223
Warner, A.H., 44
Weaver, J., 44, 76, 123, 222, 225, 226
Weber, M., 59
Weber, R.E., 86
Weisburd, D., 205
Welch, J., 41, 205, 210
Wheeler, S., 205
Whitebread, C., 39
White paternalism, 58, 157–9
Wilkes, J., 25
Williams, J., 29
Willmott, W.E., 65–6
Wilson, J.Q., 57–8, 209
Winks, R., 24, 42, 82, 85, 86, 87, 88, 90,
    91, 95, 99, 103, 104, 108, 109, 112,
    118, 193, 224, 225, 226
Wodson, H., 122
Wolfgang, M., 55, 211
Woman's Christian Temperance Union,
    229–30
Woollacott, A.P., 177
Wood, C., 17, 19, 20
Woodsworth, C.J., 65
Work, M., 49
Wortley, S., 198

Yerbury, C., 22
Young, J., 36
Young, M., 16

Zatz, M., 41, 51